Willa Cather's Southern Connections

Willa Cather's Southern Connections

New Essays on Cather and the South

EDITED BY ANN ROMINES

University Press of Virginia

Charlottesville and London

The University Press of Virginia
© 2000 by the Rector and Visitors of the University of Virginia
All rights reserved
Printed in the United States of America
First published in 2000

Frontispiece: Robinson-Cather quilt. Courtesy of Kit Robinson.
Photo by Lauri Bridgeforth, Full Frame Photography, Inc.

DESIGNED BY LAURY A. EGAN

∞ The paper used in this publication meets the minimum requirements of
the American National Standard for Information Sciences—Permanence
of Paper for Printed Library Materials, ANSI Z39.48-1984.

Library of Congress Cataloging-in-Publication Data

Willa Cather's southern connections : new essays on Cather and the
South / edited by Ann Romines.
        p.   cm.
    "This book began in 1997 with the seventh in the ongoing series of
International Willa Cather Seminars, held for the first time in Cather's
birthplace, Frederick County, Virginia . . . a selection of the best of those
papers has become this book"—Acknowledgements.
    Includes bibliographical references and index.
    ISBN 0-8139-1957-6 (alk. paper)—ISBN 0-8139-1960-6 (pbk. : alk.
paper)
        1. Cather, Willa, 1873–1947—Knowledge—Southern   States—
Congresses.   2. Women and literature—Southern   States—History—
20th century—Congresses.   3. Southern States —In literature—Congresses.   I. Romines, Ann, 1942– II. Willa Cather International Seminar
(7th : 1997 : Frederick County (Va.))

PS3505.A87 Z9355 2000
813'.52—dc21   00-025943

Contents

Acknowledgments

This book began in 1997 with the seventh in the ongoing series of International Willa Cather Seminars, held for the first time in Cather's birthplace, Frederick County, Virginia. As program director of that seminar, I watched with growing excitement as more than a hundred papers and presentations emerged, a vivid and stimulating demonstration of how much there was (and is) to say about Willa Cather and the South. A selection of the best of those papers has become this book. Thus, my first thanks are to the many persons who helped to make the 1997 seminar happen. My codirector, John Jacobs of Shenandoah University, was responsible for all of the site arrangements that introduced visiting scholars and readers to Cather's Virginia; he also produced the seminar's title, "Willa Cather's Southern Connections," which became the title of this book. Other important program assistance in Frederick County came from Cynthia Cather Burton of the *Winchester Star*, who is a member of the extended Cather family that remained in Virginia, and from Susan and David Parry, the hospitable owners of Willa Cather's childhood home, Willow Shade.

The seminar program was facilitated by the support of several sponsors: the Willa Cather Pioneer Memorial and Educational Foundation, the Columbian School of Arts and Sciences and Department of English at The George Washington University, and the Humanities Council of Washington, D.C. I am especially grateful to three supportive colleagues at The George Washington University: Edward Caress, Acting Dean of the Columbian School of Arts and Sciences; Christopher Sten, Chair of the Department of English; and Jerilyn Zulli, who served as my able and indispensable seminar assistant. Additional thanks go to Constance Kibler, the English department office manager, and to Lucinda Kilby, the English department secretary, who generously spent hours helping me get the book manuscript properly formatted. And thanks go to Dean Lester Lefton of the Columbian School of Arts and Sciences for support for illustrations, to Carol Sigelman, Associate Dean for Research, for support funds for the index, and to Satarupa Sengupta for assistance with compiling the index. I am grateful to Kit Robinson of Winchester, owner of the splendid Robinson-Cather quilt, who generously permitted us to photograph her heirloom for the cover and frontispiece of this book, and to Susie Williams, expert on Frederick County quilts, and the Frederick County Historical Society for helping me to research the quilt's history. And, as always, I must thank my sister, Marilyn F. Romines, who has patiently spent entirely too many hours (many of them in a closed car!) listening to me talk about "Willa Cather's Southern Connections"—first the seminar, then the book.

From the first moment the idea for this book emerged, I thought that the University Press of Virginia would be the ideal home for it. Fortunately, Nancy Essig, Director of the Press, agreed, and she has become an astute and enthusiastic advocate for this project. Her administrative assistant, Mary MacNeill, has also provided invaluable assistance, keeping track of eighteen far-flung authors who are scattered from the Netherlands to the Pacific Ocean. Colleen Romick has been a helpful copy editor, and Ellen Satrom, Managing Editor of the Press, has shepherded the book through production.

Most of all, I am grateful to the scholars who have contributed their carefully revised work to this book. Through their energy, attention, insights, and care, they make a strong and suggestive case for the importance of Willa Cather's southern connections.

A Note on the Robinson-Cather Quilt

When Willa Cather was born in Back Creek Valley, Virginia, in 1873, she joined a community of women and girls with a tradition of fine quilting. Two surviving quilts made by her great-aunt Sidney Cather Gore in 1849 and 1854 show the meticulous needlework and elegant design that Cather's kinswomen could produce; the Gore quilts are the work of "an accomplished artist, even by the high standards of Southern needlework" (*Oklahoma Heritage Quilts* 17–18).

An even more striking example of the varied work and skills of local quilters is the Robinson-Cather quilt, which was made by a community of Back Creek Valley needlewomen in the 1850s and is featured on the book's cover and frontispiece. This quilt, which has never before been photographed, was brought to the 1887 Seventh International Willa Cather Seminar in Winchester by Kit Robinson, whose husband, James Kenneth Robinson, was a Robinson-Cather descendant. It is an album quilt, each block inscribed or stamped with the name of its maker or a member of her family. All thirty-six blocks are different, five in classic pieced patterns and the rest meticulously appliquéd, some showing a high degree of skill and invention. Naive, fantastic, or realistic flowers and leaves alternate with stars, pinwheels, and intricate lacy cutouts. The prevailing colors are bright reds, greens, and yellows, showing the influence of the new aniline dyes that became widely available in the 1850s. The quilt resembles another well-known Frederick County quilt from the 1850s, the Hollingsworth quilt, which has the same number of blocks in the same formation, a similar quilting pattern, and some similar pattern blocks, especially the distinctive lacy cutouts. (Another similar cutout block serves as a centerpiece for one of Sidney Cather Gore's quilts.) Robinson names appear on both quilts, suggesting that some of the same women may have worked on—or at least seen—both quilts (see Description of Property).

The names that remain legible on the Robinson-Cather quilt sketch a portrait of a tightly woven local community. Several are Cathers: Elizabeth and her daughter Susan G., and two others with indecipherable first names. Another is Hannah Eleanor Robinson, who was born a Cather and whose marriage linked the two families. At least five names are Robinsons. Others are Jacksons, Fentons, Rogerses, Joneses. According to the 1850 census, all these families lived in adjacent dwellings in Back Creek Valley. In the Gainesboro cemetery, where Willa Cather's great-great grandfather and great-grandparents are buried, the same names recur again, forming intricate figures of kinship, friendship, and affiliation.

Willa Cather inherited the quilting tradition of the women who collaborated on the Robinson-Cather quilt. Like many nineteenth-century American girls, she was set to piecing quilts at an early age; in the epilogue to *Sapphira and the Slave Girl*, she recalled that, at the age of five, she was "allowed to sit" with her grandmother and the former slave "Aunt Till" in the kitchen, sewing her patchwork and listening while they talked (287). The stories she heard, remembered for a lifetime, became the stuff of Cather's last novel, and quilting and storytelling were intertwined in the child's memory. Cather's companion Edith Lewis wrote that Cather remembered selecting the calico for her childhood quilt patches with great care and that "Willa Cather took great pride in making these quilts. She did the piecing, and the old women quilted them with lamb's-wool from the lambs on the place [Cather's father raised sheep]" (Lewis 11–12).

The "old women" who quilted Willa Cather's childhood efforts at patchwork may well have been some of the same local women who made the Robinson-Cather quilt some twenty-five years earlier. In 1940, Cather returned again to their southern community in *Sapphira and the Slave Girl*, which is set in 1856, the same period in which the quilt was made. This quilt, newly visible to Cather's readers, is another text that testifies to the intricacy and pervasiveness of Willa Cather's southern connections.

Introduction

Willa Cather's Southern Connections

ANN ROMINES

Almost since its scholarly beginnings, the critical enterprise of Cather studies has been closely tied to place. For many readers, Willa Cather—who lived in Nebraska between the ages of nine and twenty-two—has long been identified with and by the Great Plains settings of several of her best-known fictions. The small town of Red Cloud, Nebraska, where the Cathers eventually settled, has become what may be the largest U.S. historic district devoted to sites related to a writer's life and work,[1] and for the past twenty-five years, hundreds of Cather scholars have assembled and reassembled there and at Cather's alma mater, the University of Nebraska in Lincoln, which has become a major center for Cather scholarship. Canonical Cather biographies (the most influential and comprehensive of which is currently James Woodress's *Willa Cather: A Literary Life*) have also emphasized matters of place, and particularly of Nebraska.

Willa Cather herself sometimes seems to have supported such emphases. In the preface to *My Ántonia*, two autobiographical characters agree that place is "a kind of freemasonry" (x), a secret communion shared only by people who have inhabited the same geography and space. Through pilgrimages and geographically inflected readings and criticism, many scholars have attempted to join such a society of freemasons, or at least to acknowledge its power in Cather's fiction.

Willa Cather was seventy-three when she died in 1947, and only thirteen years of her long life had been spent in Nebraska. After several years in Pittsburgh, her permanent residence for the rest of her life was in New York City. She traveled frequently, notably in Europe, the Southwest United States, and Canada. The only house she ever built and owned was in Canada, on Grand Manan Island, and she is buried in New Hampshire near a favorite inn. In recent years, Cather readers have also met to consider the writer's relations with most of these sites, and their discussions have generated an important, ongoing tradition of scholarship.

One fact has been strangely neglected by this tradition, however. It is this very simple and central one: Willa Cather was born a southerner, in Virginia. She spent her first years, between 1873 and 1882, near Winchester, in Frederick County, in the Shenandoah Valley. Members of her family had lived there for several generations, and many remain there to this day. The first Cather in the area, Jasper (Willa's great-great-grandfather), who

immigrated from northern Ireland, had purchased land on Flint Ridge by
1786. Willa's paternal grandmother was descended from an even earlier
local settler, Jeremiah Smith, who had come to Virginia about 1730, built
a (still-standing) house on Back Creek, and was deeded land there by Lord
Fairfax circa 1750 (Kerns 9–10). The Seiberts, ancestors of Willa's maternal grandmother Boak, were also early settlers; according to family tradition, they kept a flour mill on Back Creek. Both Charles Fectigue Cather
and Mary Virginia Boak Cather, Willa's parents, were fourth-generation
Virginians.[2]

   Willa Cather was born in Back Creek Valley only eight years after the
Civil War's end, and her family, like many others in this northernmost Virginia county, had divided loyalties to both Confederate and Union causes.
Although he opposed slavery, her great-grandfather, James Cather, supported the Confederacy; his son William, Willa's grandfather, supported
the Union; and when William's son Charles, Willa's father, became old
enough to be subject to the Confederate draft, he and his brother were sent
to West Virginia (only a few miles away) until the war ended in order to
avoid conscription. Willa's maternal grandmother, Rachel Seibert Boak,
also opposed slavery (although her parents were slave owners), but her
three sons fought for the Confederacy: one of them, James William Boak,
died of injuries received at Manassas. Mary Virginia Cather passed on heroic tales of this brother to Willa and her other children, and Willa claimed
to be his namesake. The war's end left the Cather family with many enmi-
ties among Virginia family members and neighbors. After Willa's parents
married in 1872, one of the intrepid bride's projects was to "bring her divided families together again" with a large Christmastime party in 1875
(Woodress, *Willa Cather* 20), when her first child, Willa, was two years old.
By then the young couple were living in Willow Shade, a substantial, sym-
metrical, three-story brick house about a mile from the village of Back
Creek Valley, which had been built by Charles Cather's parents in 1851.
This ambitious Virginia house, vividly evoked in the epilogue of Willa
Cather's last novel, *Sapphira and the Slave Girl*, was the first home that the
child Willa remembered.

   Thus young Willa Cather spent her first years in a southern family surrounded by southern controversies, southern speech, southern customs,
southern architecture, southern food; she was imprinted by southern relations between whites and African Americans (some of whom worked for
the Cathers at Willow Shade), many of whom had recently been enslaved.
In a famous anecdote, five-year-old Willa is supposed to have expressed her
rebellious impulses by naming herself a "dang'ous nigger" (Lewis 13).

   Although Willa's parents moved their young family to Nebraska in 1882,
following other Cather relatives, they remained in many ways a southern

family. Willa grew up there surrounded not only by the Scandinavian, French, Bohemian, Russian, German, and other European immigrant communities and individuals that recur in Great Plains fictions such as *My Ántonia* and *O Pioneers!* but also by southern-born parents, grandparents, aunts, uncles, and cousins. In fact, the rural community where the Cathers first settled, before Willa's parents moved into the town of Red Cloud, was so heavily populated by Virginia emigrants that it was known as "New Virginia." Detailed and frequent letters, as well as Virginia newspapers, kept the transplanted Nebraska Cathers in close and constant touch with their Virginia kinfolk and customs. Grandmother Caroline Cather, for example, often told Civil War tales, and Mary Virginia Cather, who had brought a Confederate flag and her dead brother's Confederate sword to Nebraska, continued her stories of his wartime exploits. The most-used cookbook in the family library appears to have been a worn 1850s volume published in Baltimore, almost certainly transported to Nebraska from Virginia.[3] The southern-inflected routines and rituals of the Cather household in Nebraska were kept in motion by Willa's mother, doubly Virginian by her birth and her name; by Willa's maternal grandmother, Rachel Seibert Boak; and by servant Marjorie Anderson, who traveled with the Cathers from Virginia. Cather's 1931 story "Old Mrs. Harris" is her closest fictional portrait of the Cather family in Red Cloud; in it, the Templetons— a family with parents, several children, a maternal grandmother, and a "bound girl" who came with them from the South—maintain many "feudal" southern domestic customs in a small Colorado town, customs that often put them at odds with their neighbors in "a snappy little Western democracy" (133).

Other emigrant midwestern families in Cather's fiction—the Burdens of *My Ántonia*, the Herberts of *A Lost Lady*—are, like the Templetons and the Cathers, transplanted southerners. Singular southern characters also turn up unexpectedly: the African American musician Blind d'Arnault in *My Ántonia*, or Doña Isabella Olivares in *Death Comes for the Archbishop*, for example. In addition, several early Cather stories draw specifically on the history and culture of Frederick County, Virginia. "A Night at Greenway Court" (1896) evokes the estate of Lord Fairfax, the ancestral patron of Cather's family, who is buried in Winchester; and others, such as "The Namesake" (1907) and "The Elopement of Allan Poole" (1893), draw from Civil War history and Blue Ridge mountain life. Most of these stories are products of Cather's Pittsburgh years, 1896–1906, when she had returned to the eastern U.S. and, despite her homesickness for Red Cloud, was enjoying landscape and plants that resembled the Virginia of her early memories, and where she was able to make occasional visits to family members and friends in Virginia and Washington, renewing her southern ties. One of the most subtle of these early stories, "The Sentimentality of William Tavener" (1900), considers how Virginia memories affect the life of a Nebraska farm family.

Most important, the last of Willa Cather's twelve novels, *Sapphira and the Slave Girl*, published in 1940, is set in her birthplace in the 1850s and is specifically, centrally concerned with the racial and gender politics of Frederick County. Characters are based on her great-grandparents and grandparents, her mother, an aunt, and other locals; Willa Cather herself appears, as a five-year-old child, in the epilogue, which takes place in the (still-standing) Cather house, Willow Shade. Following the late 1930s phenomenon of Margaret Mitchell's *Gone with the Wind*, *Sapphira and the Slave Girl* was initially widely read; it was a popular and widely publicized selection of the Book of the Month Club.

Nevertheless, this persistent and significant southern strain in Willa Cather's life and work has received relatively little critical attention. In the burgeoning Cather bibliographies, *Sapphira* has routinely generated fewer entries than most other Cather novels, while other southern strands, such as the few I have mentioned, have gone almost entirely unattended. If Willa Cather is a southern writer (and, based on her birth, upbringing, and concerns, one can make a strong case that she is), she is one of the best-known and least acknowledged southern writers in the canon of twentieth-century American fiction.

It is not hard to imagine reasons for this state of affairs. Other regions have consolidated strong institutional claims on Cather; in Nebraska, particularly, she is both a well-cultivated strip of scholarly turf and a civic investment, as well as a source of well-placed local pride and concern. Cather's major southern text, *Sapphira and the Slave Girl*, with its troubling, challenging racial politics and charged language, is a problematic chapter in the Cather story, and it is unlikely to be an easy hit in midwestern (or other) classrooms; relatively few teachers report having assigned the novel.[4] And as interest in Cather's career has expanded in recent years, it has played down the freemasonry of place to foreground other concerns, for which we have recently developed a more capacious theoretical/critical vocabulary: gender construction (Sharon O'Brien, Eve Kosofsky Sedgwick, Judith Butler), authorship (Merrill Maguire Skaggs, Hermione Lee), nation (Walter Benn Michaels, Guy Reynolds), mobility (Joseph R. Urgo). More than anyone else, it is Toni Morrison whom we might credit with turning the expanding vision of current critics to Cather's South, with her incisive and highly influential reading of the charged dynamics of *Sapphira* in *Playing in the Dark: Whiteness and the Literary Imagination* (1992). As readers, challenged by Morrison, turn back to *Sapphira and the Slave Girl* in a climate of cultural studies, interdisciplinary scholarship, and new- and posthistoricist

readings, it now seems impossible to ignore the dense, subtle web of southern relations woven throughout this novel and Cather's entire career.

In such a climate, in June 1997, Cather scholars at last met in Winchester, Virginia—165 strong—to turn their attention to "Willa Cather's
Southern Connections" in the seventh of a series of international Cather
seminars. In a week punctuated by ham biscuits, Virginia gospel music,
Shenandoah Valley quilts, Blue Ridge stories and songs, Cather family
visits, and explorations of the lush countryside and substantial southern
houses described in *Sapphira*, we saw "southern connections" as a central
concern (not a fugitive afterthought) of Cather's career. What began to
emerge was a version of Willa Cather that is more complex, more problematic, more ambitious, more fully engaged with the most divisive issues of
her American life, which spanned the years between Reconstruction and
the end of World War II. The essays in this collection all start from the
premise confirmed by Cather herself when she chose to write her last
completed novel about the Virginia world into which she was born: the
premise that southern connections *matter*, persistently and deeply. The
Willa Cather that emerges from this challenging new scholarship is a
writer more consistent, more troubling, and more engaged than we have
yet realized, one who, in her last years, was still working to discover what
southern connections might and must mean, in American history and in an
American writer's life.

Contributors to this volume are various; they include both seasoned and
occasional Cather scholars, southern scholars new to Cather studies, and
scholars just beginning their careers. I have grouped their essays to suggest
major issues that emerged from the seminar, issues that seem especially
pressing as we begin to excavate the full implications of Willa Cather's
southern connections. As prologue, I have placed Judith Fetterley's "Willa
Cather and the Question of Sympathy: An Unofficial Story," a provocative
speculation about what might happen if we rethink the shape of Willa
Cather's career and place her southern origins and *Sapphira and the Slave
Girl*—her major southern text—at its center, not its peripheries. The first
grouping of essays, "Cather's Problematic Southern Novel: New Views
of *Sapphira and the Slave Girl*," begins with cultural critic Joseph R.
Urgo's "'Dock Burs in Yo' Pants': Reading Cather through *Sapphira and
the Slave Girl*," which takes cues from Cather's last novel to suggest a reading strategy grounded in the troubling, disruptive moments that occur in
Cather texts. In "Political Silence and Hist'ry in *Sapphira and the Slave
Girl*," Tomas Pollard grounds his new historicist reading in the novel's
minute attention to abolitionist politics of the 1850s, a subject critics have
previously neglected; while Shelley Newman, in "No Place Like Home:
Reading *Sapphira and the Slave Girl* against the Great Depression," views

the novel through the revisioning of *home* and *memory* engendered by the
Depression years. Several essays in this group are primarily concerned
with issues of race in *Sapphira*. Roseanne V. Camacho's "Whites Playing in
the Dark: Southern Conversation in Willa Cather's *Sapphira and the Slave
Girl*," places Cather in the regional (North/South) politics of race in the
thirties and forties, situating her "among southern white contemporaries
who were already testing the limits of their privileged voices." Mako Yoshikawa, in "'A Kind of Family Feeling about Nancy': Race and the Hidden
Threat of Incest in *Sapphira and the Slave Girl*," focuses on the "slave girl"
of Cather's title and, for the first time, explicitly explores the possibility and
presence of incest in the racial dynamics of the novel. Two additional,
briefer essays were generated by one of the seminar's most provocative ses-
sions, a discussion of *Sapphira* in the context of recent African Americanist
scholarship, by a group of well-known African Americanists. Marilyn Mobley McKenzie, a Toni Morrison scholar, traces the politics and implications
of Morrison's influential discussion of Cather's novel, while Gayle Wald,
through a fresh reading of a crucial scene, places the novel's female slave/
owner relations in the context of African American women's labor history.

A second group of essays, "Cather Texts in Southern Contexts," ranges
wider in Willa Cather's oeuvre, showing the breadth and persistence of
southern connections in her work. Lisa Marcus's "'The Pull of Race and
Blood and Kindred': Willa Cather's Southern Inheritance" looks at an
early Cather poem and story, both titled "The Namesake" and related to
a Civil War soldier ancestor, showing how Cather probed and reinvented
her southern ancestry as a young writer and then returned to these issues
at the end of her life, in *Sapphira*. Robert K. Miller, in "'A Race without
Consonants': *My Mortal Enemy* as Reconstruction Narrative," discovers reconstruction concerns embedded in the language of Cather's 1926 short
novel. Mary R. Ryder focuses on paternal inheritance in her "Henry Colbert, Gentleman: Bound by the Code," as she examines the workings of the
Virginia gentleman's code of conduct in the major paternal figure of *Sapphira*. And Patricia Yaeger's essay, "White Dirt: The Surreal Racial Landscapes of Willa Cather's South," theorizes Cather's language of landscape
and, in *Sapphira*, finds Cather's southern landscapes permeated with gra-
dations of race.

Next, four essays look at "Cather and (Other) Southern Writers." (In
addition to those discussed here, references to southern writers—William
Faulkner, Eudora Welty, Lillian Smith, Carson McCullers, and many others—are frequent throughout this collection.) In "The Interlocking Works
of Willa Cather and Ellen Glasgow," Merrill Maguire Skaggs argues that
these two Virginia women writers maintained a nearly lifelong rivalry that
nourished both their fiction. Elsa Nettels's "'Aeneas at Washington' and
The Professor's House: Cather and the Southern Agrarians," alluding to Allen

Tate's poem, views Cather's text through a major southern literary-political movement of the twenties. In "O'Connor's Vision and Cather's Fiction," John J. Murphy considers the relation of Flannery O'Connor's version of a Christian grotesque to several Cather novels and stories. Finally, Janis P. Stout looks at Cather and Toni Morrison, drawing on both authors' southern maternal histories and their rethinking of southern homeplaces in "Playing in the Mother Country: Cather, Morrison, and the Return to Virginia."

Last, as "Epilogue: Leaving the South?" I have placed Cynthia Griffin Wolff's illustrated biographical essay, "Dressing for the Part: [What's] The Matter with Clothes," which views Willa Cather's childhood and adolescent experiments with clothes and "masculine" personae as responses to her mother's versions of (southern-inflected) feminine style and to contemporary theater and fashion.

These seventeen essays represent a rich variety of fresh approaches to Cather texts. They are variously theorized, complexly historicized, grounded in both traditional literary criticisms and cultural studies. Taken together, they begin to present a complex and challenging picture of Willa Cather's southern connections, and they claim an indelible place for that topic on the ongoing agenda of Cather studies.

Notes

1. The Willa Cather Pioneer Memorial and Educational Foundation, with headquarters in Red Cloud, reports that the Willa Cather Thematic District, which is listed in the National Register of Historic Places, encompasses twenty-six individually significant sites and four historic districts, including a 610-acre tract of native grassland owned by the Nature Conservancy. More than 190 sites are included in the district.

2. For information on Willa Cather's family history, I have relied primarily on Woodress, Bennett, Lewis, and O'Brien.

3. Elizabeth Ellicott Lea's *Domestic Cookery* was published in Baltimore by Cushings and Bailey in 1853. Frederick County had close connections to nearby Baltimore in the mid-nineteenth century. In addition, Lea was a Quaker, and there was a strong Quaker community in the Frederick County area, as Cather indicates in *Sapphira and the Slave Girl*. This book is the earliest of the three surviving Cather family cookbooks from the Red Cloud household that are in the archives of the Willa Cather Pioneer Memorial and Educational Foundation in Red Cloud. See Welsch and Welsch on the importance of Lea's cookbook, although, as Nebraska folklorists, they tend to understate the importance of southern survivals in the Cathers' Nebraska households.

4. In his 1997 essay, "Cather Syllabi: A Study," Virgil Albertini reported on a study of seventy-two syllabi for graduate, undergraduate, high school, and other classes including texts by Willa Cather. Of these, only twelve included *Sapphira*, while the most frequently taught novel, *My Ántonia*, was included in thirty-eight syllabi, followed by three other novels with midwestern settings, *A Lost Lady*, *The Professor's House*, and *O Pioneers!* (50).

1

Prologue

Willa Cather and the Question of Sympathy

An Unofficial Story

JUDITH FETTERLEY

At the outset of *Cather, Canon, and the Politics of Reading*, Deborah Carlin raises a series of questions: "Why, for instance, are the majority of Cather's late fictions rigorously unread? Why are they either ignored in or excluded from canons? What is it exactly that renders them, if not absolutely non-canonical, then conventionally unclassifiable in the prevailing critical assessments of Cather's work? Why, in other words, are they difficult to read?" I would like to add to this string another more specific question that I think shadows the question of Cather's southern connections: Why would Cather choose to end her career with *Sapphira and the Slave Girl*, a text that seems so foreign in setting, subject matter, and tone to either her earlier *or* her later work and that has presented a serious problem of legibility to those who read and write about Cather? Though I wish to acknowledge this question at the outset, let me also hasten to add that I have no intention of trying to answer it. Rather, I wish to focus on the form this question takes. Of course Cather could not know that this would be her last published work, and indeed she was working on a novel at the time of her death, yet the question is not illexical in the context of Cather. What this tells us, I would suggest, is how very successful Cather has been in controlling how we think about her and how central to that control is the image of her as being in charge, as always consciously choosing. As Merrill Skaggs has put it, "She is neurotically controlling and self-conscious about her work, but she knows at all points what she is doing. Above all else, she is self-conscious" (*World Broke in Two* 187).

Without question, Willa Cather was a control freak. She sought to control the reading of her texts while she was alive, directing, for example, readers who were "not under forty" away from her collection of essays and by so doing seeking to ensure that all those who did read it would do so with sympathy. Moreover, as Sharon O'Brien has noted, "She limited the excerpts from her fiction that could appear in anthologies and refused permission to include any of her work in anthologies intended for use in high schools or colleges; she also successfully prevented the publication of cheaper editions of her books. As Alfred A. Knopf recalls, Cather did not want her books to be read in the classroom, because if readers were exposed to her in a coercive environment they might 'grow up hating her'" ("Case against Willa Cather" 252). And she sought to extend this control after her death by the provisions of her will that stipulate, for example, that none of her work can be made into movies and that no one can quote from her letters. Evidence of Cather's continuing control appears in the contortions critics go through to present the content of her letters while avoiding direct quotation.

Indeed, Cather's success at controlling the way she is read seems quite extraordinary. Deborah Carlin tells how Betty Jean Steinshouer, when she first began touring her one-woman Cather performance, tried to present a Cather "who liked to dress up and wear hats and all that." Rather quickly she realized that her audiences were upset because "they had a different vision of Cather in their minds' eye." So she decided "to give people what they wanted and what makes them feel comfortable." Along with the middy blouse, red tie, and dark skirt, the image she agreed to convey of Cather is that of someone "fully balanced," "self-actualized," "well-adjusted," in a word, wholesome, personable, and frank (3–4). Others who try to challenge this image, like Steinshouer at the outset of her show, also feel distinctly uncomfortable, as witness the many moments of discomfort in the texts of those who try to write about Cather's lesbianism, as if she were there in person looking disapprovingly over the critic's shoulder. Indeed, in an eerie way this ghostly Cather most closely resembles Sapphira, whom we might thus construct as a monitory figure presiding retroactively over the whole of Cather's life and work, reminding us that if we mess with her we will be mighty sorry, coercing us to accept the official story even as that story insists on the radical disjunction between Cather and Sapphira. For I would argue that there is an official Cather story, one that exerts enormous pressure on those who write about her and one that was constructed by her. I would like to begin my reflections by outlining, briefly, what I see as the elements of this official story.

According to the official story, Cather's Virginia background is insignificant, formative neither of her personal nor her authorial identity. If the Virginia years are mentioned, it is usually to trot out the anecdote of how she horrified her mother by declaring to a visiting patriarch, "I's a dang'ous nigger, I is" (Lewis 13). This anecdote serves as proof that Cather was not "really" southern. Cather constructed this element of the official story by her comment that what matters to a writer are the years between ages eight and fifteen, a statement that excises her Virginia years from possible significance.

Then there is the issue of her first novel. According to the official story, *Alexander's Bridge* represents a false start, a novel written in imitation of James and Wharton and on the assumption that certain subject matter is inherently interesting regardless of whether the writer "knows" it or not. According to this story, Cather's career as a novelist officially begins with

O Pioneers!—the moment when, writing only for herself, she found her original and unique content and form. The control for this reading of her work comes from a 1931 piece called "My First Novels [There Were Two]," in which Cather manages to excise *Alexander's Bridge* from her oeuvre just as she had excised Virginia from her history.

A third element of the official story has to do with the question of sympathy. According to the official story, the guiding principle of Cather's work is a broad and deep sympathy; without sympathy she simply cannot write well, hence the failure of *Alexander's Bridge*. Even after her world broke in two, so the story goes, she never lost her faith in humanity, and so at the most profound level all her novels are filled with hope. However, there is nothing personal in this sympathy; rather, as the Blooms put it, paraphrasing Cather's Bread Loaf lecture of 1922, it is "an identification so intense that in its ultimate transmutation it becomes the essence of impersonality" (172). While the control for this position could have come from Cather's scathing attack on Defoe for his lack of sympathy in *Roxanna* (surely one of the strangest prefaces ever written), the critical persona Cather reveals here contradicts the image of her to which the official position is committed; and so the control comes from the preface to her edition of Jewett's stories in which she asserts that if a writer is to achieve anything noble or enduring, "it must be by giving himself absolutely to his material. And this gift of sympathy is his great gift" (*Cather on Writing* 51). There is a further reason why this preface exerts such control over the official reading of Cather, for in it Cather constructs the relation of reader to writer as inherently sympathetic. Though Cather is rarely as explicit as she is in the preface to *Not Under Forty*, by a variety of mechanisms she makes sympathy on the part of her readers a requirement for her legibility and intelligibility. Thus there is little space in the official Cather story for lack of sympathy or critique (one reason why difficult texts like *Sapphira* have to be dropped); if you are not sympathetic, you in effect disqualify yourself as a reader— you were not supposed to read the book anyway, and so whatever you may have to say is suspect.

A fourth feature of the official story, one that grows out of this issue of sympathy, assumes that Cather and her work are characterized by a singular sense of unity and wholeness. To quote again from the Blooms, whose *Willa Cather's Gift of Sympathy* perhaps best represents the official story, Cather's "moral, philosophical, and critical attitudes are virtually all of a piece with her esthetic practice" (ix). In the official reading of Cather, then, each novel takes the form most appropriate to its content and thus each work emerges as essentially perfect. In this story there are no mistakes, for nothing gets written that has not "teased" the mind for years until the idea for it is whole and clear and it writes itself in the only way possible, the right way. Even contemporary critics like Sharon O'Brien reflect the pressure exerted by this story, for in her reading of Cather in *Willa Cather: The Emerging Voice*, that which might be seen as troubling, disjunctive, fissuring becomes coherent once one recognizes the ultimate unity of her desire to let concealment serve as revelation. Since the assumption of wholeness operates only at the level of the individual text, readers have not felt pressured to find a logic, coherence, or unity to the sequence of her work; thus it has been fairly easy to drop from consideration those Cather texts that do not fit the official story, such as *Alexander's Bridge* and *Sapphira* or even, again following Cather's lead, *The Song of the Lark*. Though the control for this piece of the official story comes from virtually everything Cather wrote about her own work and those of others, Edith Lewis has also set the tone by describing Cather as one who "had not one of those divided natures that sometimes turn on themselves and what they have cherished, that hate where they love, and find in betrayal itself an ultimate truth. . . . All her impulses were simple, direct, unswerving, as if they came from some changeless center of integrity" (1976 ed., 165).

The last element of the official story that I wish to draw attention to is the assumption that Cather herself constitutes the best authority on herself, that she *should* be in control of the interpretation of her life and her work, that indeed this is morally right, and that any effort to challenge her view is simply wrong, almost immoral, and ought to make us uncomfortable.

But what would happen if we refused to be sympathetic readers, if we refused to pay attention to her warning signs, if we refused to let her control who should read her and how she should be read, if we drove down that road marked OFF LIMITS and still threatened to sue for damages? What might an unofficial Cather story look like?

For starters, it might focus on Cather's Virginia roots, and might suggest that Cather was far more southern in her "sympathies" than she was either Western or Eastern, that she had more affinity with southern culture than has previously been acknowledged, indeed that her attitudes toward race and gender and even human nature and history derived from this context— for where else did the world so clearly break in two as it did in Virginia in 1861? And it might further suggest that Cather never would have written about Nebraska if she had in fact been born there, that she could construct Nebraska as a subject for art precisely because she came to it at a certain age and as an outsider, an immigrant.

For another, an unofficial story would focus precisely on those texts Cather sought to deflect attention away from—for example, *Alexander's Bridge*. Perhaps no figure in all of Cather, with the exception of Sapphira Dodderidge Colbert, is so clearly a "control freak" as Bartley Alexander. Yet in this first and unofficial novel Cather tells the story of someone essentially out of control. Bartley Alexander has become the victim of his own success, finding constraint where he thought he would find freedom; he has agreed to a project he knows he should have rejected and is building a bridge that will never make it to the other side. Above all, he is out of control of himself, having started an affair that he cannot stop even though he knows it will destroy what he thinks of as his life. Hopelessly divided against himself, he knows he will continue to do what he says he won't, and that whatever he does he will end up hating both himself and those whom he has professed to love. Possibly a parable for turn-of-the-century gay identity, he represents precisely that kind of person whom Edith Lewis said Cather absolutely was not. Unofficially, however, we might ponder the degree to which Cather identified with Bartley and projected through him her vision of human nature and history as composed of irreconcilable conflicts and divisions, even as we might appreciate why she would wish to deflect our attention away from this perception.

Unofficially speaking, it would be far easier to make a list of all the things Cather despises than of those for which she has sympathy. Indeed her work, both early and late, seems characterized by an excess of negative energy that almost defies explanation; she consistently constructed herself as a heroic David hurling stones at an endless succession of Goliaths. That she understood art as being of necessity cruel seems as clear from her own behavior as from her work. Even Edith Lewis, indefatigable in her effort to construct Cather as sympathetic, acknowledges that relatives of the Garbers took offense at Cather's portrait of Mrs. Garber in *A Lost Lady*, and even the equally indefatigable Blooms acknowledge that she cared little for the feelings of the inhabitants of Brownsville when as a journalist she "intentionally exaggerated the town's deterioration" to make her point about the materialism of the West (57). More recently we have Mark Madigan's discovery of the source of the rift between Cather and Dorothy Canfield Fisher. When Fisher objected to Cather's use of a personal friend as the basis for her story "The Profile," fearing it might lead the friend to suicide, Cather refused to omit the story from her about-to-be-published first collection. Though the story did not in fact appear in *The Troll Garden*, the decision to remove it was apparently not Cather's, and she may well have retaliated against Fisher for her interference by changing the name of one of her nastier characters to that of Fisher's mother in the retitled "Flavia and Her Artists." Though this may seem like nit-picking, my point here is that we might discover a rather different Cather if we could escape the control exerted by the official story, one whose voice, like that of Sapphira, "could be," as Edith Lewis notes, "harsh, hard, when she felt scornful of something" (xvi).

As for the question of unity, Cather was clearly obsessed with the notion of aesthetic wholeness, of the great work whose form emerges suddenly and completely at some magical moment in the creative process, as witness her description in *The Professor's House* of St. Peter's discovery of the shape his history would take. And while I do not wish to contend that Cather's work is not characterized by this quality of aesthetic unity and wholeness, I would like to suggest that something might be gained by a different reading of Cather. For, like Merrill Skaggs, I suspect her world broke in two long before 1922, indeed that it was always deeply divided, and that her primary aesthetic derived from the effort to make a whole out of pieces. If this be so, then an unofficial approach to Cather might postulate not an aesthetic of the fragment—for she clearly did not like to leave things in pieces—but an aesthetic of the cracked-and-glued, one that focuses less on unity and more on the forces threatening to break things apart. And this unofficial reading might take as its sign the fissure so apparent in the young Bartley before he learns how to make himself unreadable: "a big crack zigzagging from top to bottom . . . then a crash and clouds of dust" (15).

While this unofficial view of Cather might provide an interesting approach to many of her texts, I wish to use it as a frame for reflecting on her last novel, *Sapphira and the Slave Girl,* for this text seems resolutely illegible from the perspective of the official story. Describing *Sapphira* as "a book that has always startled Cather's readers," Susan Rosowski finds in the criticism a "startling silence" on the subject (*Voyage Perilous* 233). And Toni Morrison finds, if not total silence, references that are "apologetic, dismissive, even cutting in their brief documentation of its flaws," and describes it as a text "virtually jettisoned from the body of American literature by critical consensus" (*Playing* 18). Edith Lewis set the context for this dismissal, providing the rationale that would insulate *Sapphira* from the rest of Cather's work and allow the official story to continue in defiance of the troublesome fact of its existence. Claiming that "it was a novel written against circumstance," in a context of successive catastrophes, and that Cather's approach to the task of writing was "a sort of fixed determination . . . different from her ordinary working mood," Lewis describes *Sapphira* as "uncharacteristic," possessing "little of that warmth and generous expansion of feeling so many of her readers delight in" (184, 185).

Recent studies of Cather have sought to remedy the "startling silence" that surrounds this text, seeking to make it legible within the context of Cather's oeuvre (for example, Carlin, Rosowski, Skaggs) or reading it within a larger framework whose terms make it legible (for example, Gwin, Morrison, Romines). Yet the words "troubling" and "disturbing" recur like a chorus throughout these and other readings of the text, reminding us of the pressure exerted by the official story even on those approaches, such as Carlin's and Skaggs's, that are explicitly designed to free us from such pressure. What, then, might *Sapphira and the Slave Girl* look like from the perspective of unofficial Cather?

My "unofficial" reading of *Sapphira* begins with the hypothesis that

Cather may have waited so long to write about Virginia not because it played so little role in her development but because it was so crucial. I would like to argue that Virginia was formative for Cather not because it represented traditions of order and social stability that attracted her conservative imagination, nor because it represented a set of smothering conventions against which she rebelled to form her own "dang'ous" identity, but rather because it was here that she first learned a set of home truths— basic, elemental truths about the nature of human relationships and what it takes to survive. Perhaps most troubling from the perspective of the official story, this knowledge is profoundly amoral; it is not about right and wrong or about values, whether enduring, endangered, or gone. It is about survival, and its "morality" emerges in *Sapphira* in those moments of textual slyness when, for instance, Jezebel reveals her history of cannibalism or Sapphira acknowledges the appropriateness of one granddaughter's death and the other's survival: "And, Henry, Mary will get *so much more* out of life."[1] Above all, *Sapphira* is not about slavery or race in any directly legible sense. Though one has to wonder about the implications of Cather's appropriating the story of Nancy and Till to tell her own story of the relations of mothers and daughters, and though one notes the imperialism of her assumption that their story was hers to use, from the perspective of unofficial Cather (those who threaten to sue) perhaps the most devastating thing one can say about her is that she did not think race mattered. She did not believe the color of her characters would materially alter the story she was trying to tell, making Nancy's situation as a daughter significantly different from Rachel's or Till's situation as a mother significantly different from Sapphira's; and she did believe she could deal with the historical issue of slavery by inserting a few facts gleaned from reference books documenting the horrors of the middle passage. The moral outrage that *Sapphira* has elicited from such readers as Minrose Gwin, Toni Morrison, and particularly Deborah Carlin can, I think, be traced to this home truth, but I must admit to finding a certain relief in this text from the pressure of official morality. Perhaps as I get older I find articulations of how things are more useful than proclamations as to how things ought to be. But of course this position has its own kind of morality, for with the recognition of what it takes to survive can come a kind of grudging respect for all those equally struggling and the possibility of some kind of reconciliation with one's mortal enemy.

Having saved Casper Flight from a beating at the hands of his cousins, Rachel Blake reflects, "I don't know whether that boy's strong enough to master what's around him . . . A man's got to be stronger 'n a bull to get out of the place he was born in" (130). And she could easily have added, "and to hold onto the place he gets to if he does escape." For the first home truth Cather learned in Virginia was the ferocity of life—and consequently, the ferocity required for survival. Jezebel fights like a tiger, takes a ferocious beating, and lives to eat sugar and work side by side with Sapphira planting a garden in the wilderness. Mary defies medical authority and her mother's passive acceptance of it to get the soup that saves her life. Rachel deals her mother the worst humiliation possible, refusing to invite her to Washington and helping Nancy escape, in order to keep from being destroyed by her mother. And Sapphira has to drive her children away in order to maintain her control over home and husband, for Nancy is as much her daughter as Rachel is, and both are equally stand-ins for those amazingly absent other siblings who are barely mentioned and perhaps were eaten. Meanwhile, Betty, the sweet child, the angel in the house, her grandpa's darling, dies easily. Tansy Dave can't handle Baltimore or love and comes home an idiot. Tap had one too many toddies and ends up hung. And, if left to her own devices, Nancy would probably commit suicide.

If one learns about the ferocity of life in Virginia, one learns from Virginia, at mother's knee, that in the struggle to survive you can count on no one but yourself, and most certainly not on the family whom you might expect to help. It is Casper's family, after all, that is trying to destroy him; and as for mothers, Tap's joke says it all—there is no titty as good as a toddy, and of course a toddy is not all that good. Mothers can disappear in a moment, as Till's did, but Till's horror at this event may be less a response to loss and more a recognition that her mother was never there in the first place. For in this text mothers are more anxious to get rid of their daughters than to keep them. And, pace Toni Morrison, this has nothing to do with race, since the only mother who wants to keep her daughter is Lizzie, the black cook.

A second home truth delivered by Virginia, and absolutely counter to the official story, is the uselessness—indeed, the counterproductivity—of sympathy. If Casper Flight is not "stronger 'n a bull," Preacher Fairhead's sympathy for him will most likely get him beaten or killed. Love made a mess of Tansy Dave, and Nancy would have been better off not caring so much about pleasing the miller. And luckily for Nancy—and Rachel too—Rachel did not contact her sympathy for her mother before she helped Nancy escape, because if she had "a-thought about how much she suffers and her poor feet," she might have "waited" (247).

Indeed, the critique of sympathy emerges most clearly in the treatment of Nancy. By all the conventions of Gothic romance, of the sentimental novel and domestic fiction, indeed of Western and Christian culture, Nancy ought to be the object of authorial and readerly sympathy. But instead she is pathetic, and in her utter inability to fight for her own survival she verges on becoming an object of contempt. Despite the difficulties such a reading presents because of our assumptions about how race matters, the truth is that Nancy serves less as a testament to the horror of Sapphira's ability to control the lives of African others and more as an instance of the colossal stupidity of those who refuse to learn the truth about the ferocity required for survival.

The critique of sympathy, however, emerges at another point in this text, further revealing how truly unofficial this story is. As I have noted above, the only mother in the text who comes close to fulfilling conventional notions of ideal motherhood is Lizzie. Yet her absolute devotion to her daughter has had the effect of permanently infantilizing Bluebell and making herself permanently manageable through the mechanism of her devotion. Though the novel is so amoral as to make the term "evil" inapplicable, Lizzie and Bluebell, far from representing an ideal, are about as slimy as Martin Colbert. Given this context, we might imagine that Till found her own escape from a proliferation of such relationships more than acceptable. Though Morrison claims that "Cather was driven to create the exchange" between Till and Rachel over the fate of Nancy "because at some point the silence became an unbearable violence, even in a work full of violence and evasion" (*Playing* 22–23), I would argue that the exchange is a false note, evidence of the violence exerted by the requirements of official cultural stories, a violence that forced even Cather to capitulate to conventional expectations as to the nature of mother-daughter relationships.

And here we come to a third home truth Cather learned in and from Virginia, one equally unofficial: namely, that while writers may wish to create aesthetic wholes, and while novels may be made to appear unified, they are in fact composed of irreconcilable stories, of points of view glued together to look compatible; and, moreover, that to read such texts actually requires a reader to become as deeply divided as Bartley Alexander, to adopt one point of view only to have to switch suddenly to another, completely different, perspective. *Sapphira* has remained illegible, however, not simply because it deviates from the official story in the ways I have already mentioned but because one of the points of view we are required to adopt in order to read it is the most unofficial perspective of all, that of the mother. Even if we can accept the idea that *Sapphira* is not about race or that Cather despises sympathy, can we ever shed our commitment to the idea that the story begins and ends with the child's need to defy, destroy, and escape from the mother? Can we ever really get past our belief in the essential illegitimacy, and therefore the essential unrepresentability, of the mother's story—always white mistress over slave girl?

It can be said that Western civilization is a story written from the perspective of the son, and that women have participated in writing this story by casting themselves as the sisters—not the mothers—of those sons, and by writing daughter stories. Cather herself wrote some of these, and her official story, when it treats of Virginia, casts her in the role of rebellious, defiant daughter. Thus, nothing prepares us for the fact that *Sapphira* articulates the mother's position as much as, if not more than, the daughter's. Nothing prepares us for the fact that in this text Cather identifies with Sapphira as well as with Rachel and Nancy, and that she represents her own situation through Sapphira's as well as theirs. Yet in a certain sense nothing could be more obvious.

Sapphira Dodderidge Colbert had the strength it took to get out of the place she was born in. Taking advantage of her father's paralysis, she learned how to manage a farm, and she married a man willing to let her be the master. She emigrated to the backwoods, lived down the dislike of her neighbors, and built a successful economic and social entity over which she exercises control, returning home each year as the master, not the mistress. She got rid of the daughter who threatened her control and retained the services of those women who, while ultimately under her control, share her values, seek control themselves, and work with her as well as for her. Now she is old, infirm, virtually immobile (recall Lewis's statement that "It was a novel written against circumstance"). The difficult daughter has returned, threatening her control over her household, and this daughter refuses to grant her mother the courtesy and consideration she automatically accords to others, as if to make the cultural point that from the daughter's perspective the mother is not a person. Another "daughter" is threatening her control over her husband, a control based on his desire to construct an identity other than *Colbert*, one of restrained rather than rampant sexuality. Henry is Sapphira's version of a capon man, something we need to take into account if we wish to avoid misreading Till's situation as just another example of the horrors of slavery; and if Henry does become just another Colbert, Sapphira's entire life project will be undone. Indeed, one could argue that she brings Martin on the scene to remind her husband of what he himself does not want to be.

Sapphira, then, asks us to consider what it means to have to be "stronger 'n a bull" to hold onto the place one has gotten to. And if we do not like what we see, that is because nothing in our culture prepares us to read this story. We have been trained to read like Rachel, to view mothers as non-persons and, therefore, as without story. And we have been trained, like Nancy, to read anything that looks like a mother's story as incoherent and to suppress it instantly by labeling it as "crazy," especially if it seems antagonistic to the daughter's story: "Oh, she's a-wanderin' agin! She wanders turrible now. Don't stay, Missy! She's out of her haid!" (89). Thus when Sapphira's voice cuts through Nancy's whimpering, reminding her that "I know your granny through and through" and "She is no more out her head than I am," we instinctively recoil from it. But if we can for a moment step outside the official cultural story, might we not appreciate the fact that mothers may want to eat their children and that it is possible to understand why? If we can't "take" *Sapphira*, is it perhaps because it forces us to adopt the position at least temporarily of Jezebel, who can think of nothing Sapphira could give her that she would "relish, lessen maybe it was a li'l pickaninny's hand" (89).

Yet the pressure to identify with the daughter is truly overwhelming, and even as I write this last question, I recognize the eruption of protest my words may produce. Cather herself created the conditions for such protest when she made what I consider the enormous mistake of not recognizing the significance of race. By making Nancy a slave and Sapphira a master/mistress, she weighted her novel, whether consciously or not, on the side of the daughter and reinforced the sense of the illegitimacy of the mother's position. But if we consider the figure of the "Double S" that structures this novel and even appears in its title, we might be forced to pause in our headlong rush toward the legitimacy of the daughter's point of view. If we identify with and applaud the daughter's story of escape, how can we not identify with and applaud the mother's story of control? No story really ends with escape; it must go on to tell of what one has escaped to and for; and so the story of escape leads to the story of control. And while the stories are not the same, at a certain point they touch, like the "Double S," and daughters become mothers. Thus Rachel and Sapphira can inhabit the same house only after Rachel has "killed" her child. Chomp! Chomp!

I am obviously not interested in arguing for the essential coherence of this text, for that would be just another version of the official story continuing to do its work of making unities appear everywhere. Rather, as I indicated earlier, I am interesting in proposing for our reading of Cather an aesthetic of the broken-and-glued, the irreconcilable, even the incoherent. For ultimately the mother and daughter stories cannot be reconciled, since they are personally oppositional, and one has to choose between them. In the figure of the miller, both husband and father, we see the pathetic limitations of the failure to choose and the ridiculousness of a sympathy that tries to encompass both. It is pointless to berate the miller for failing to choose the right side, for there is no right side. There is only the essential incoherence of incompatible stories—the mother's, the daughter's, and the miller's own, a story only hinted at but one that clearly threatens to render incoherent both mother's and daughter's stories. For perhaps a final home truth learned from Virginia is that life is not only ferocious but incoherent.

In *Alexander's Bridge*, Cather writes a history of desired illegibility by creating a character who desires to remain illegible. Bartley writes a letter to his wife but does not mail it; when she discovers the letter after his death, it is so water-soaked as to be unreadable, and she is free to imagine that it says whatever she wishes. Is Sapphira such a character? Does Cather in this text wish to remain illegible? Or is she here consciously deconstructing the official story she herself constructed? Or is she "simply" in this last work interrogating her own obsession with control, casting a clear, cold eye on what it has taken for her to get out of the place she was born in and to maintain the fiction of the official story? I have no answers for these questions, but ironically I feel more sympathy for the Cather of *Sapphira and the Slave Girl* than I do for the official Cather, perhaps precisely because the text does not coerce me into sympathy or mandate an official reading, perhaps even more because it offers some explanation for Cather's obsession with control. I do believe the text forces us to think about the question of control, about what it takes to create and maintain an official story. If we look for a justification for this obsession with control beyond the simple fact of the ferocity required for survival, we may find it in the precept Mrs. Matchem taught Till—namely, that there is all the difference in the world between doing things exactly right and doing them somehow-or-other. Till makes the connection between control and art, for one needs to be in control in order to do things exactly right and not somehow-or-other. If Sapphira's story is culturally illegible, Till's is still more so, since assumptions about race are added to assumptions about gender. Yet clearly Till has more in common with Sapphira than she does with Nancy. Indeed, what she may share most with Sapphira is the sense that daughters present a threat to one's ability to do things exactly right—and as a result, they may need to be gotten rid of. Jezebel, Till, Sapphira, Cather: the mother's story as the artist's story? Amazingly unofficial, almost illegible. CHOMP! CHOMP!

Note

1. Willa Cather, *Sapphira and the Slave Girl* (New York: Knopf, 1940), 266. All further citations are to this edition.

2

Cather's Problematic Southern Novel

New Views of *Sapphira and the Slave Girl*

"Dock Burs in Yo' Pants"

Reading Cather through *Sapphira and the Slave Girl*

JOSEPH R. URGO

"You ain't got no call to be comf'able, you settin' down de minute
a body's back's turned. I wisht I could put dock burs in yo' pants!"
— Willa Cather, *Sapphira and the Slave Girl*

Reading Willa Cather

Cultural critics are sometimes accused of ignoring the aesthetic qualities
of a text, or at best of giving these qualities too little attention. Still, cultural criticism has arisen in part because formalism, from New Criticism
through deconstruction, seems too little concerned with how the text functions in social and political discourse. It's an old argument, really. Even
back in 1937 social critics would say Willa Cather was politically irrelevant—wasn't she the one who wrote about seventeenth-century Quebec in
the midst of the Great Depression?—and New Critics would say she was
pleasant but rather simple, lacking the dense passages worth explicating. By
her own testimony Cather sought to leave the most vital elements of her
fiction—the very thing she was writing about—off the page.

It is futile, and potentially destructive to literary study, to attempt to
separate formalist and cultural concerns, and debates on the issue are
more often questions of emphasis, not exclusion. Literary artists of the
breadth and range of Willa Cather often instruct readers in how to see
cultural concerns within new forms, and thus may redefine the terms and
limitations of what it is possible to know, through their writing. Let's take
another southern example. William Faulkner entered the canon on the
strength of his aesthetics; when critics first wrote about Faulkner, they employed phrases like "frozen moment" and "reader participation" to indicate
that the *experience of reading* Faulkner was the primary thing to be valued in
Faulkner's work. That was the thing that catapulted Faulkner into the canon despite charges that his writing contained misogynist and racist content and that he participated in what was called "the cult of cruelty." More
recent criticism has challenged these indictments by claiming that Faulkner's work explores racism and misogyny in heretofore unprecedented
ways. Hence, we can say that Faulkner has instructed us to see racism, for
example, as a matter of social and linguistic construction (as he does in

Light in August), and to see misogyny as a manifestation of male hysteria (as he does in *Sanctuary*). The point to remember in this process of canonization, however, is not that critics can explain away anything—although of course they can. Rather, we should recognize the way in which meaning follows form, and literary ethics emerge from formal textual engagement. Engagement, in turn, can begin only *after* a reader is captivated by a text's literary quality. First comes Benjamin Compson, in other words, full of sound and fury, and then comes puzzled attention, the suspicion of the significance, making a pattern out of obscurity.

But where is Cather's Benjy section? Where are those dense passages wherein we create our own euphoria by acts of heroic exegesis? It was not until the 1970s that Cather began to be read as more than a sweet old lady, that old-fashioned, Victorian "Miss Cather" we have all heard about. Fifty years after her death, we continue working to align form and content in Cather. However, Cather instructs her readers as definitively as Faulkner, and it is within the texts themselves that we find their cohesive logic. For Cather's Benjy section, I nominate *Sapphira and the Slave Girl*, Cather's most challenging narrative, and one that most clearly encapsulates those narrative strategies identified as Catherian.

The act of reading *Sapphira and the Slave Girl* must not be decoyed by the seemingly transparent prose, or daunted by the need to make its politics comfortable in the present era. We do not wish to emulate Henry Colbert, reading and rereading the same book but still failing to perceive its challenge to do difficult thinking. Colbert was unable to find "a clear condemnation of slavery" (110) in his biblical text, despite the anachronistic status of the institution in 1856 Virginia. Colbert, to his credit, suspects, "Perhaps our bewilderment came from a fault in our perceptions" (111). Our perceptions are precisely what Cather is concerned with in all of her works, including this novel. If we read Cather's whole career through the lens provided by *Sapphira and the Slave Girl*, our perceptions of that career alter considerably. Critics have tended to read *Sapphira* as a minor work because, frankly, in some aspects it doesn't sit too well with us. Cather readers are far more likely to place *My Ántonia* at the center of the oeuvre, leaving *Sapphira* on the margins. However, contemporary valuations of multiplicity suggest infinite potential centers, successively revealing enriched understandings. Cather was a Virginian, and *Sapphira* claims its right to the center by virtue of its Virginia setting and by the signature Cather placed upon it herself, on its final page.

Old Jezebel would mete out justice through her sewing; to lazy boys she would provide a rough trouser seat, and to hard workers she would stitch a smooth one. Cather is easy to read; even a lazy boy can do it. But on all readers she stitches an occasional rough seat, such as when she refers to Nancy's "dreamy, nigger side" (178) or describes Sampson's head as "full behind the ears, shaped more like a melon lying down than a peanut standing on end" (109). We all know what it's like to come across one of those Cather passages and think, "She oughtn't-a done that." Remember what old Jezebel said to one boy who complained about his rough-seated pants: "You ain't got no call to be comf'able, you settin' down de minute a body's back's turned. I wisht I could put dock burs in yo' pants!" (97). Throughout Cather's fiction there are "dock burs" that stick when you start to relax, prickly things that cannot be accommodated easily or explained smoothly, things that don't sit right. Not all of these are embarrassing moments. Equally important are eruptions of the inexplicable, such as the fact that Krajiak's ax fits so perfectly into the gash on Mr. Shimerda's head; or when the soon-to-be-fired accompanist Mockford turns up after four months on Sebastien's Italian vacation, in *Lucy Gayheart,* to accompany him on the capsizing and the drowning. These are things to remember, incidents when secret fears or suspicions are revealed, when what someone really thinks or what the hidden truth is slips out, spilling revelation across polite veneers of custom.

As Carl says in *O Pioneers!,* "It's queer what things one remembers and what things one forgets" (160). Sometimes it's queer what Cather considers an appropriate detail, like the appearance of the malevolent sniper in *One of Ours* who "kept his nails so pink and smooth," the better not to snag on the "gorgeous silk dressing gown" (348) he wore when he was not shooting American soldiers out his window. These are moments that can be elided quickly in Cather, unless one wishes to think about them, in which case they stick. But I suspect that these dock burs are very important, and must be recognized and incorporated into the way we know Cather. It's queer what Willa Cather remembered when she let herself remember Virginia, to write her "southern novel" of reminiscence and recognition. Alexandra explains this process of recognition to Carl: "It's by understanding me, and the boys, and mother, that you've helped me. I expect that is the only way one person ever really can help another" (35). Each of Cather's novels, as with each novel written by any author who possesses a substantial body of work, provides a way of seeing the career as a whole. To view Cather through *Sapphira and the Slave Girl* is to look through the dock bur—but let's not pursue that image any further. Nonetheless, we should keep in mind that inside a bur is another thing entirely, a seed that grows into something else. Readers of Cather are accustomed to dramatic shifts in conceptual levels, moving into "Tom Outland's Story" in *The Professor's House* or into narratives of the miraculous in *Death Comes for the Archbishop.* These little disturbances of the text operate like dock burs, making the reader aware of physicality—the physical act of reading—but also pushing the reader into alternate casts of mind, to levels of comprehension only accessible through literary modes of thought.

Very often in Cather an everyday occurrence is raised out of its literal significance to achieve a kind of transcendent timelessness; to enter the world of art, yes, but also to command a different level of perception. Because so much of Cather's writing is rooted in memory and autobiography, we can be assured that Cather depended upon such moments for aesthetic inspiration. We might think of these as points of verticality, where the historical, material world intersects with the aesthetic or spiritual world of art, escape, and inspiration.[1] In Emersonian terms, it is the intersection of materialism and idealism, a crossing between the world that contains consciousness and the world produced by consciousness. In his essay "The Transcendentalist," Emerson says, "It is the quality of the moment, not the number of days, of events, or of actors, that imports" (104). Cather, I suggest, fits Emerson's definition of the transcendentalist, as one "who looks at [her] life from these moments of illumination." As such, "Much of our reading, much of our labor, seems mere waiting," waiting for the illumination, the moment of passage (106). When Nancy returns, after young Willa Cather's long wait, and has her reunion with Till, the scene is indeed described in the language of transcendence: "There was something Scriptural in that meeting, like the pictures in our old Bible" (283). I would stress the possessive pronoun "our" because it is crucial to see how Cather grounds the cosmic, scriptural moment in local, private memories. Her claim is not access to some secret truth, some Gnostic revelation or esoteric insight; rather the claim is to a practiced, accessible way of seeing the world around us. Such moments—picture making, cliff dwelling, eagle flying—mark Catherian connections to a dimension of existence that is mysterious, otherworldly; but it is equally within the grasp both of those who work the plot of world empires and those who work, modestly, at what Ann Romines calls the home plot. Cather's novels are replete with these moments. Sometimes they appear through a window (as to Professor St. Peter) or in a specific place (as Latour's cruciform tree) or, romantically, in a remembered moment or gesture that fills the present with inspiration or longing. Nancy's return is the genesis both of the novel and—if we take Willa Cather at her word—of the author herself, of what might be described as the "named and name-collecting adult writer" in this novel (Swift 24). Motion is central to this transcendence, but Nancy's mobility in space is nothing compared to the spiritual journey she has made, signaled by her dress, her speech, and her demeanor.

Of all writers this century, Cather demonstrates the profit to be gained by moving outside of what we today would call our "comfort zone." The dock bur is as well a signal of constant attentiveness, especially to those phenomena that are troublesome, foreign, or other. The idea of engagement, of sustained and varied interest, the ability to be, like Thea Kronborg, "a soul obsessed by what it did not know" (*The Song of the Lark* 174), is central to everything Cather wrote, and indispensable to reading her books. Again I take my model from *Sapphira*, where Mandy Ringer is described as one who lives engaged with her world: "Mrs. Ringer was born interested. She got a great deal of entertainment out of the weather and the behavior of the moon. Any chance bit of gossip that came her way was a godsend. The rare sight of a strange face was a treat. . . . Mrs. Ringer couldn't read or write . . . but the truth was she could read everything most important: the signs of the seasons, the meaning of the way the wood creatures behaved, and human faces" (119). Mrs. Ringer, though illiterate, is what country folk call a "reader." She models the kind of discernment Cather demands. According to Mildred Bennett, Mrs. Ringer might also provide a model for the kind of narrator Cather once wished to become. Bennett says that "Miss Cather told [Bread Loaf] students that her first teacher in narrative was an old mountain woman in the hills of Virginia . . . [,] a woman who could neither read nor write, but who knew the life of the mountain, the folk phrases which no one had written or could write, but which are the product of years and generations" (208–9).

Cather's mentor in narrative method was someone with wide interests who read not for simple validation but who saw the other, as we say today, as a treat, something to look forward to and to enjoy, a godsend. A dock bur feels good, intellectually speaking. We cannot read Cather unless we are willing to get interested in a lot of things we do not know: operatic careers, Southwest settlement, orchard planting, theology, slave management. She beckons interested readers to migrate outside the self.

The dock bur thus takes many forms in Cather's fiction, sometimes troublesome, other times revelatory—as if to stop you in your tracks—and very often the bur serves to give flight into a kind of intellectual migration. The Catherian dock bur is a narrative road sign, something that arrests; it works much the same as Cather's explanation of the title of her book of essays, *Not Under Forty*. That title functioned as a sign meaning ROAD UNDER REPAIR, because the world had broken in two and only those over forty would understand (v). Naturally, this would cause people under forty to pay attention. Dock burs mark breaks in the road, and sometimes they mark breaks in the world. Worldly breaks are scriptural or transcendent moments in Cather, when the stuff of ordinary life impinges on, or intersects with, the realm of art—when the real detail (the Bohemian immigrant girl's attempts to learn English, the misfit who enlists in the army, the archbishop's journey through the desert) fires the imagination of the artist and becomes the touchstone to an aesthetic possession. To be "brushed by the wing of a great feeling," as Jim Burden says, is to see the potential for greatness in the mundane, to apply the mind to Nebraska, as it were, or to the coast of New England, or Back Creek, Virginia and the likes of Mandy

Ringer. Someone, in other words, has to engage deeply the toothless, battered woman and see what it is that "could stop one's breath for a moment" and reveal "the meaning in common things" (261). The dock bur, like the scriptural moment in Cather, defines her aesthetics, which is indeed an aesthetics of common things raised to the level of great significance.

Dock Bur No. 1
The Breakfast Table at McDonald's, 1997

As I explained recently to another homeless academic over Egg McMuffin, what I really want to say is that Cather writes about slavery and doesn't make it into some grand tragedy but rather draws it as a simple matter of household regulation, like who is going to sleep where and who has the right to have sexual relations with whom. My colleague chewed. I kept talking. For Willa Cather it is not a matter of cosmic justice or the sins of the fathers or the shame of the nation—just a simple matter of who gets to decide when certain people are going to have sex, and what it is going to mean when they do, you know, are they going to get rewards— presents and property—or are they going to lose everything because of it. The people who are comfortable with those rules are the people who really are at home in this world; the others are just a-wanderin'. How Willa Cather came to think this is a long story, too long for a breakfast-table fast-food exchange.

A-wanderin' Agin

But Cather does not stay in flight. Her narratives also become suddenly grounded in the grit of vernacular reality. An emblematic dock bur occurs in *Sapphira and the Slave Girl* when Sapphira visits Jezebel on one of the few missions of mercy she takes in the novel, and asks the bedridden old slave woman what she would like to eat. Jezebel replies, "No'm, I cain't think of nothin' I could relish, lessen maybe it was a li'l pickaninny's hand." Cather sticks her readers this way all the time. One thinks of blind D'Arnault in *My Ántonia* or the comments about Marsellus in *The Professor's House*, to name some of the more notorious. But there are also incidents such as Ivar's compulsive need to wash his feet, Cécile's priggish behavior at the Harnois household, Father Lucero's commentary about the shape of Father Martinez's nose and chin, or "the lost American" who cannot remember the women in his life, in *One of Ours*. At such points we are likely to say what Nancy says to Sapphira after Jezebel's reply: "Oh, she's a-wanderin' agin! She wanders turrible now. Don't stay, Missy! She's out of her haid!" (89). Cather must have been out of her head, we think, to dream up the plot of

Sapphira, and certainly out of her head in the various discussions of heads in the text. What does she mean by writing that Rachel had "the same set of head" as her father, indicating an "enduring yet determined" (11) character—what is this, phrenology? Sapphira is crippled, Lawndis is lame, and Colbert is blind to Nancy's predicament. How are we to read this sustained attention to physicality, often brutal in characterization, in a book where race plays so prominent a role? "When kindness has left people," Cather writes in *My Mortal Enemy*, "we become afraid of them, as if their reason had left them." Reading Cather provides the repeated experience of being startled by the absence of secure moorings to which the reader can cling. In fact, to borrow again from *My Mortal Enemy*, "we drop from security into something malevolent and bottomless" in Cather's Virginia novel (42). As Merrill Skaggs phrases it, Sapphira Dodderidge is "one of [Cather's] most startling characters," and the novel as a whole makes us "deeply uncomfortable" (176, 177). There are many places where a blue pencil could make this text a lot more palatable. Nonetheless, or rather, all the more, Cather has something very interesting to say *about* race in this novel, something grounded in the relationship between physical reality—the mundane, the everyday, the black and the white—and transcendent meaning, or significance.

Reaction to racial difference is very often sensual, sensory, and immediate. Race consciousness interferes with cognition, rationality, and common sense. To society at large it is crippling; it complicates any issue in which it factors. Cather's novel about the antebellum South thus compels interest: what is it about race that could make these people behave this way? Think of the ways in which the deck was stacked against Sapphira Dodderidge. First, Frederick Law Olmstead had warned the world about Virginia in 1856: "Under no circumstances can I recommend anyone in the free states to choose in Virginia a residence for a family, unless a move southward be deemed particularly desirable, as offering a chance to prolong life, imperiled in our harsher atmospheres" (340). Olmstead made this assessment based on comparative real estate values in Virginia and Pennsylvania, pointing out that the market price of a farm in Pennsylvania was roughly three times that of an identical farm in Virginia ($25 an acre in Pennsylvania as opposed to $8 an acre in Virginia). Second, the limitations on female inheritance and property management make Sapphira emblematic of Fox-Genovese's statement that women in the plantation South were subordinated "to the domination of male heads of households" (39). Often, not even death could wrest control of property from men. "Slaveholding women might inherit households from their fathers or husbands, but they almost invariably turned the management over to men in practice, even if a will or marriage settlement had left them legally in the women's control"

(Fox-Genovese 203). Third, Cather's novel captures the complexity of relationships carried out by the female slaveholder, between herself and her
slaves, and among herself, her slaves, and her husband. In the words of
one historian, "It was a task at once urgent and disturbingly abstract"
(Steven M. Stowe 131).

Reading *Sapphira and the Slave Girl* calls for a combination of formalist
and culturally sensitive methods of scrutiny. Cather was interested—very
interested—in the complex legacy of race, sex, and property that contrib-
utes to the current matrix of class and status in the South and throughout
the United States. Given the exactitude with which she presented historical
and natural detail (phrases like "oak leaves no bigger than a squirrel's ear"),
we must be on the lookout for dock burs, we must examine very closely
those historical incidents that are described on "scriptural" terms, the details that Cather selects to transcend the confines of the historical. Second,
we must examine elements that leave no historical or natural traces, places
where Cather's engagement led her to imagine rather than recall. Finally,
we must attend to aspects that cause us some discomfort, the points where
we might say, "she's a-wanderin' agin." For with Cather, the cultural critic
is interested not so much in checking the facts or celebrating the invention
but in the peculiar institution in Cather of blending these two realms of
existence. A close look at Sapphira reveals this method.

In Acts 5 of the New Testament, the biblical Sapphira and her husband,
Ananias, are among the new Christians selling their property and giving
away all the proceeds to join the Church. But these two supplicants attempt
to keep back part of the purchase price. Their cosmic real estate swindle
falls through, and Ananias and Sapphira are caught and then struck dead
for trying to beat Christ in trade. Sapphira is cross-examined by Peter:
"'Tell me whether ye sold the land for so much?' And she said, 'Yea, for so
much.'" Then she, like her husband, is struck down for the offense of having "agreed together to tempt the Spirit of the Lord" (Acts 5:8–11). Sapphira's is thus a triple offense: once, for lying to God; twice, for holding
loyalty to her husband above her obligation to the Lord; and thrice, for her
attempt to own property *and* be a member of a community that holds property in common. The central points in the biblical Sapphira's life thus center on misrepresentation, idolizing marriage vows, and holding property
above sacred duties.

The story of Sapphira and Ananias is a tricky one for contemporary
Christians. "This Jesus would strike you down dead for lying," claimed one
Web page devoted to such objections. "Is this the 'love,' 'compassion,' and
'forgiveness' of this Jesus of yours? It looks to me as though you people are
lying not only to yourselves but to everyone else that hears you preach
about this Jesus" ("Sapphira"). The episode of Ananias and Sapphira is a

dock bur in the Good News, to be sure. Acts 5 is an uncomfortable moment in the New Testament; it is scriptural, disturbing, and engaging. By choosing this name for her main character, Cather makes it impossible to read the woman as a simple villain. After all, what kind of people would name their daughter Sapphira? How did this name affect Sapphira's sense of herself, knowing that she carried in name the legacy of a woman struck dead by God for not telling the truth, for wanting to hold back something for herself? Like Melville's Ahab, Sapphira (both the Acts' and Cather's) defied her time and place and our God, and we are thus justifiably fascinated.

At the same time, voices from the antebellum South in support of slavery are equally unnerving. Throughout the nineteenth century, slave management studies were published in the southern agricultural press. Although these studies are not easily found today, they are crucial to an understanding of a major American ideology that, although defeated in war, is far from irrelevant to the nation's historical legacy. "Between 1819 and the outbreak of the Civil War approximately two dozen agricultural publications were started in the South," containing advice on conducting plantation business, managing slave labor, and theorizing slavery. Some of these titles were *American Cotton Planter* (Montgomery, Alabama, 1853–61), *American Farmer* (Baltimore, 1819–61), *Farmer's Register* (Petersburg, Virginia, 1833–42), *Southern Agriculturalist* (Charleston, South Carolina, 1828–46), *Southern Cultivator* (Atlanta, 1843–61), and perhaps the best known, *De Bow's Review* (New Orleans, 1846–61) (Breeden xii). Students of American history are understandably more familiar with abolitionist writing, the word of the victors, than with defenses of slavery, except those filtered through a secondary historical or fictional lens.

We have the tendency, I think, to overly historicize statements such as this one by Robert Collins from his *Essay on the Treatment and Management of Slaves,* published in 1853: "Slavery was established and sanctioned by divine authority; and ever since the decree went forth, that the descendants of Canaan should be 'servants of servants,' slavery has existed in a variety of forms, and in nearly all nations; until now, in the midst of the nineteenth century, we find ourselves the owners of three and a half millions of this peculiar race, *without any agency on our part*" (4; emphasis added). Collins's statement becomes palatable through extreme acts of historicization. However, efforts to historicize often act as apologia, as if all people at all times are not merely products but victims of their time and place. If this were so—if historical figures are essentially *without agency*, trapped by their times—we would have no sense of history, because time would stand still and progress would be impossible, if not inconceivable. Collins's denial of agency signals a universal sense of abject victimization, of having inherited a social and economic system and now being left to maintain it, or at least cope with it. The statement is as pathetically self-serving as Henry Colbert's Bible study, searching for a condemnation of slavery in textual materials written when enslavement was a historical commonplace, along with various forms of sanctioned cruelty, like crucifixion. Cather's slave owners are far from victims, however, but rather emerge as beneficiaries of a system absent which, it seems clear, they could not imagine existence. Nonetheless, they are surrounded by alternatives to slave agriculture, and cannot by any stretch of the imagination claim to have become slave owners without any agency on their part.

In Virginia in the 1850s, it took tremendous managerial skills to make any profit within an agricultural system so at odds with industrial progress. Because her husband was an ambivalent slave master as best, nearly all managerial decisions were left to his wife. Like her biblical namesake, Sapphira grapples with a conflict between the bonds of marriage and the establishment of economic independence. Comments by "Cecilia," a Virginia planter's wife, writing in 1843, are instructive because they suggest the historical context that engages Cather's antebellum novel. Cecilia, a contemporary of Sapphira's, writes: "the turmoil and labor of the mistress of a family, in the management of her servants seem to warrant the conclusion, that the trouble of housekeeping more than counterbalances the comforts and enjoyments procured by the labors of her domestics. Indeed, very few Virginia ladies, comparatively speaking, are brought up in a way calculated to make them what we call *good managers*" (Breeden 38). Nonetheless, Sapphira *was* a good manager, and she was able to emerge as an effective slave master despite the handicaps of gender, physical health, a countermanding husband, and poor land quality. As such, she is one of the "very few Virginia ladies" Cecilia mentions, those who are raised to manage slaves. No victim, Sapphira is a woman of remarkable agency.

DOCK BUR NO. 2

The Trash Receptacle, 1997

I was throwing over my fast-food trash and my colleague asked me what I was going to say, then, about these wandering folk, the ones that are like caged birds held captive by a narrow set of circumstances (we'd been discussing Jewett, also) and I said I didn't know, I hadn't decided yet whether to say that I found Sapphira truly heroic, that if only through the control of property could she achieve independent agency, then she did the best she could, and qualifies, in my mind, for the mantle of Faulknerian common hero, a genuine "poor son of a bitch"[2] she was, because all she wanted to do was to keep her husband from making a fool of her. And she was successful, you know, she got what she wanted, though it cost her a bit more than she had planned. A runaway slave is a lot better than a husband fussing over one like she was his daughter or niece or worse—Anyway, I wouldn't say Sapphira was disabled by her circumstances.

Back Creek

Unwed at twenty-four years, unwed even after her two younger sisters are married, Sapphira accounts for her spinsterhood by claiming an obligation to care for her crippled father. Although Cather says that Sapphira "usually acted upon motives which she disclosed to no one. That was her nature" (22), her story reveals a woman who refuses to be trapped by circumstances. After her father dies, at the moment "when the property was divided, Sapphira announced her engagement to Henry Colbert" (24). The announcement astounds her friends, but it shouldn't; if Sapphira does not get married, she won't inherit property and will in all likelihood be compelled to move in with one of her married sisters. "It was not uncommon for spinsters to receive smaller inheritance shares and then to be farmed out to sibling households and expected to sacrifice themselves for the needs of their reproductive kin" (Clinton, *Plantation Mistress*, 85). To avoid this fate, Sapphira obtains her inheritance before her father's death, and selects a husband to secure her property holdings. Rachel thinks "she herself was by nature incapable of understanding her mother" (219), and given the marriage Rachel experienced, this is not surprising. Her mother would never settle for what Rachel had in Washington, where, for example, Rachel would take "the whole day to prepare [her husband's] favorite dishes" (138). Her mother, on the other hand, went to Back Creek with twenty slaves and sold them back to Loudoun County when cash was needed.[3] Her success is marked by the loyalty of her slaves, as shown when Sampson refuses manumission and Nancy has serious doubts about leaving home. In an era of masculine privilege, Sapphira is in nearly complete control of her destiny. "You think me the child of my circumstances," says Emerson; "I make my circumstances. . . . You call it the power of circumstances, but it is the power of me" (95). Sapphira may be Cather's transcendentalist, a form of Virginia revenge on New England.

   In the final section of *Sapphira and the Slave Girl*, Cather claims to have been sung to sleep each night by the same lullaby Martin sings in his efforts to seduce the slave girl. Young Willa says she "never doubted the song was made about our Nancy" (281), although she informs us that she had never heard of Martin or, presumably, of his connection with the slave girl (290). But it is the adult writer, grown-up Willa Cather, who places "that old darky song" in Martin's mouth when he pursues Nancy at the cherry tree, and thus has young Willa unknowingly sung to sleep by Martin's song of

sexual aggression. Is there something soothing in this song? Or is Cather
playing the role that Cynthia Griffin Wolff identifies with her, that of the
"dang'ous nigger," referring to an outburst young Cather once made to a
visitor at Willow Shade. "How can we understand the complete meaning
of this eruption?" Wolff asks. "What untellable story does it intimate?"
(229). It may intimate that Cather knew as a five-year-old child what Faulkner would write in *The Sound and the Fury*, "that a nigger is not a person so
much as a form of behavior; a sort of obverse reflection of the white people
he lives among" (95). Cather could thus imagine the "dang'ous nigger"
who put dock burs in your pants and the "dreamy nigger" who attracted
and almost welcomed the very action she feared most. In each case, the
woman departs from one form of behavior—safe, scripted—and engages
in another, "a-wanderin' agin" toward some more deeply felt need, even
courting danger, like the diphtheria patient who feeds herself in the middle
of the night, marking "how sometimes in dreams a trivial thing took on a
mysterious significance one could not explain" (259).

Two dock burs are sewn into the narrative of *Sapphira and the Slave
Girl*: the character of Sapphira, the woman of agency and of much cruelty
as a slave owner; and the author herself, who sews herself into the narrative
in the last chapter. The two threads are cross-stitched, really. Sapphira
Dodderidge has succeeded in a traditionally masculine setting; she has
transcended gender and emerged as a property owner and plantation manager. She does with impunity what male slave owners were known to do:
she buys and sells her slaves, she sexually abuses then, and she punishes
them harshly. This dock bur compels us to think about the structure of
gender differences. Her husband, Henry, is feminized in the novel; he
seems ineffectual, acts only passively to help his daughter, and reminds Sapphira that she, not he, is master. It is almost to say that a wife is not a person
so much as a form of behavior; a sort of obverse reflection of the husband
she lives with. In this case, Henry reflects a master in Sapphira, and becomes wife himself. Sexual dominance is among the master's functions, and
hence the dock bur of Sapphira's actions against Nancy. Out of this gender
confusion emerges young Willa Cather, author, name giver, and witness.
Who knows what songs of sexual aggression were sung to Sapphira as a
young girl, but Cather's closing section ("The Return") makes clear that
the lullabies that were meant to soothe her childhood fears (*Down by the
cane brake, close by the mill, / Dar lived a yaller gal, her name was Nancy Till*)
have emerged, in the mind of the author, as unspeakable horrors. The dock
bur of what Sapphira Dodderidge had to do to maintain her role as Master
may contain within it the psychic struggles experienced by young Willa
Cather as she emerged as Author.

Sapphira may have been temporarily outmaneuvered by her husband and
daughter, but she is successful in ridding herself of the slave girl. She exiles

Nancy, absorbs the loss, and manages to "forgive" everyone involved and reunite the family. Rachel also gets away with defying her mother. Nancy gets away with running away. And Willa Cather gets away with inserting herself into the novel, in an encore display of her career-long intersection of biographical, historical, and literary materials. In addition to incorporating remembered events and researched facts, *Sapphira* incorporates its author in the act of writing, making of her, too, something scriptural. In Willa Cather's fiction, there are no clear borderlines among the real, the remembered, and the imagined. These dimensions of existence continually intersect and vivify one another. Common incidents may transcend their actuality and take on a mysterious significance; figurative, literary qualities may attach to common events like dock burs. In 1921, Cather claimed that "if a person is wide awake and not self-centered he can see those interesting things in the life of those about him" (Bohlke 27).

It is commonplace to observe that the simplicity of Cather's prose is deceptive, and must be traversed with care. To this we must add that where the narrative signs say ROAD UNDER REPAIR, readers must prepare to be catapulted out of simplicity; they must not allow their own "foolish, dreamy, nigger side" to let them walk into something without comprehension. Such moments require all the intellectual armaments we can muster. Cather refers to the geological structures that interfere with road building: "The road followed the ravine, climbing all the way, until at the 'Double S' it swung out in four great loops round hills of solid rock; rock which the destroying armament of modern road-building has not yet succeeded in blasting away. The four loops are now denuded and ugly, but motorists, however unwillingly, must swing around them if they go on that road at all" (*Sapphira* 170–71).

The reader encounters such obstacles throughout Cather's fiction. Plowing into them can be dangerous, even "dang'ous," if one does so unprepared for the encounter. Modern road building may blast away much of the mystery and smooth our journey tremendously, but some roads remain impassable.

One can always "swing around" the impasse, ignore the dock bur, and be untroubled by what one elides. When Henry Colbert reads, we are told, he does so "with his mind as well as his eyes," raising questions and finding contradictions that "troubled him" (66). The question that arises is how to confront narrative troubles. Colbert endured his; what shall we do? Reading brings pleasure to those who love literature, and pleasure allows a process of comprehension to begin. As pleasures of the body open it to seduction and to encounters with other bodies, so too pleasures of the mind make it intellectually receptive, receptive also to ideas and perspectives it might otherwise reject. Catherian dock burs function this way, to push the reader past pleasure toward transcendence by means of temporary roughness, or discomfort. How much smoother on the seat had Henry raped Nancy and Sapphira risen to her defense. How much easier for us all had Martin been violent and not so mesmerized by Nancy's beauty and her scent. These details are troublesome and stand like denuded rocks, blocking the way toward easy conclusions. If the destination of readers is contemplative, these narrative burs are ends in themselves, imaginative outcroppings, where the mind of the author achieves full exposure, rubbing up as it were against something deeply disturbing, revelatory, and transcendent.

The author claims that on the day of Nancy's return she was ill; she had a cold and was not allowed to go outside. Surely, in a novel where physical incapacitation plays such a central role, the illness is not insignificant. Young Willa Cather is placed in her mother's bed, her body ministered to by others as Sapphira's had been. Cather's is the privileged body, her eyes the privileged eyes, set as they are in a manner to serve as witness to the events that inspired the novel. Master in her own right, the author has suffered for this privilege. To this day, we don't know how well or to what extent young Willa Cather ever recovered from the childhood illness afflicting her on the day of Nancy's return; but judging by the lifetime of writing that followed from it, we know that she did not, like some hurried motorist, swing around those seemingly insurmountable obstacles to comprehension.

Notes

1. Sven Birkerts explores the idea of vertical reading at some length.
2. See Faulkner, *The Mansion*.
3. The fact that Sapphira was selling slaves to raise money is further indication of the declining economy in Virginia during her lifetime. Olmstead explains that "the cash value of a slave for sale, above the cost of raising it from infancy to the age at which it commands the highest price, is generally considered among the surest elements of a planter's wealth" (60). Selling slaves to raise money thus parallels the selling of any asset (such as landholdings), and is thus an indication of declining economic status.

Political Silence and Hist'ry
in *Sapphira and the Slave Girl*

TOMAS POLLARD

In *Sapphira and the Slave Girl* (1940) Cather attempts to reconstruct the southern past using the language of the military and moral victor, the North. This effort is a difficult challenge, since a northern language cannot recapture the meanings of southernized terms like *master* and *slave*, because the moral assumptions behind our language define slavery as an unnecessary evil. Cather, however, needs to call these assumptions into question to create historically authentic characters. Focusing on Cather's attempt to cope with the loss of a southern language, I will explore Rosowski's comment that this novel "may well be the most directly political of all [Cather's] writing" (*Voyage Perilous* 244) and expand on Stout's idea of Cather's "strategies of reticence" to locate political silences. For instance, the political silence of the narrator can be seen blatantly when Sapphira and the abolitionist Mrs. Bywaters greet each other "with marked civility" at the post office because, the narrator explains, "They held very different opinions on one important subject" (*Sapphira* 37). The one unnamed important subject is clearly slavery, and erasing different southern opinions on slavery would be like erasing West Virginia. To express southern differences in a northern language, Cather's narrators often encode passages with political silence, an enriched, intricate silence mostly about slavery. In order to penetrate that silence we must become readers not only of but through the text, as Cather teases us, with dropped hints and carefully placed details, to ask questions about historical contexts or her characters' motives. Political silence does not evade politics; rather, it is an event in Cather's text that reconstructs the tensions in Virginia in the 1850s.

Without some historical background to the politics of the 1850s, readers cannot bridge the imaginative distance in Cather's fiction and certainly cannot sort through the many uncertainties about the main characters' motives. For the reader without a historicized imagination, Cather writes a story about a jealous, vengeful wife who sets up a slave girl to be raped and a cowardly husband who, at most, grudgingly helps the slave girl escape. For the reader aware of the political events of the 1850s, the motives of the characters seem much more complicated. Ignoring historical contexts robs Cather of the materials used for characterization and plot.[1] The text mainly focuses not on Cather's own past but on the meanings created by the narrative silences in memory and the privacy of the characters' minds. For example, the narrator speaks of the opacity of Sapphira's motives: "Sapphira Dodderidge usually acted upon motives which she disclosed to no one" (22). Another instance of Cather's focusing on the gaps between minds occurs when Sapphira, looking out at the light burning in Henry's window, tries to imagine what he is doing: "Was the man worrying over some lawsuit he had never told her about, she wondered? Or was he, perhaps, reading his religious books?" (107). When the text focuses on the characters' motivations, Cather's narrators circumscribe politics by encoding passages with silences that often place a thin veneer over the political debates of the 1850s. According to Edith Lewis, Cather explained that the novel "suggests more by what it omits rather than what is specifically narrated" (paraphrased by Harrison 66; Lewis 183). I believe Cather narrates a novel of jealousy, as the blurb on the cover of my paperback copy calls the book, to omit a political novel. Her novel suggests that politics plays a role, however minor, in shaping her characters' emotional life, as if laws provide part of the framework for the range of their feelings. She creates a highly evocative political text sparsely filled with politicians, politically suggestive settings, and cryptic allusions to laws. These political trappings allow her to bring politics into the emotional life of her characters—or rather, to present the contexts that shape their often low-key, restrained effusions and actions.[2]

To include politics in her work, Cather must have balanced her need for characterization against her fear of appearing too circumstantial. Her essays on fiction demonstrate the tension she must have felt when writing *Sapphira*. In "The Novel Démeublé" (1922) Cather argues that material descriptions in imaginative art should help to depict the emotional life of the characters. Holding Tolstoy's descriptions to be more appropriate than Balzac's, she explains that in Tolstoy "the clothes, the dishes, the haunting interiors of those old Moscow houses, are always so much a part of the emotions of the people that they are perfectly synthesized; they seem to exist, not so much in the author's mind, as in the emotional penumbra of the characters themselves" (39–40). At the same time, in "Escapism" (1936), first published as a letter to the editor of the *Commonweal*, Cather attacked journalists who wrote articles on reform "to collect material for fiction." She explains that "the man who has a true vocation for imaginative writing doesn't have to go hunting among the ash cans on Sullivan Street for his material" (24). Somewhere in between the reforming journalist's search in the ash cans and Tolstoy's sensitive use of dishes must lie Cather's sense of the role of law in the emotional life of her characters. For instance, to deny totally the importance of the Fugitive Slave Law for Nancy would seem solipsistic in the extreme, but overstating its importance might feel like digging through ash cans to Cather. So, Cather constructs a text in which a suicidal Nancy reluctantly leaves her home because a rapist is stalking her and a brave daughter can talk her into leaving. Her characterization requires that the politics of the 1850s surface as background noise for the emotional universe of her characters.

Cather's heavy excising of the original text shows her desire to dampen any political heavy-handedness. Woodress reports that "Cather told Bruce Rogers when he was preparing to add the novel to the *Autograph Edition*, that she had been so afraid of being diffuse that she had cut the manuscript severely" (481). Her editorial cuts, which weighed "a good six pounds" (Bennett 7), could have also been motivated by a desire to highlight the thoughts and actions of her characters that rarely give a clear indication of any political motives or mix national politics so freely with other concerns that national politics rarely surface as the driving force behind their actions. For example, while Rachel clearly has abolitionist sentiments in the novel and helps Nancy escape Martin, she does not help any slave escape slavery itself. Political fervor is reined in, and political silence fills the gap between national politics and daily life. One of the loudest political silences in the novel is the national debate over slavery during the 1850s.

The text treats 1850 as a benchmark year, as if it is the backdrop for all the scenes in the novel. For example, Rachel's return from Washington places the novel within earshot of the political debates surrounding the Great Compromise of 1850. The narrator explains that as of May 1856, Rachel Blake had been at home for six years (144). This means that she departed Washington, D.C., in 1850 sometime after March 17, the date of Daniel Webster's famous speech "The Union and the Constitution." In this speech, Webster argued that even though slavery was an evil, the North must not attempt to abolish it, because it was protected by the Constitution and many other agreements, including the recent annexation of Texas in 1845. During Rachel's stay in Washington, she could have heard Webster's highly anticipated speech on the overcrowded Senate floor (Webster 600). Henry could have read the speech or reactions to it in the *Baltimore Sun*.[3] Later in the novel, when a group plans Nancy's escape during harvest, the narrator briefly mentions the "severe Fugitive Slave Law, passed six years ago" in September 1850, that makes Nancy's escape more likely: "Its very injustice had created new sympathizers for fugitives, and opened new avenues of escape" (222). Oddly enough, the narrator even links Tansy Dave's seemingly insane despair to the end of his courting of Susanna six years earlier, in 1850 (205). Even Sapphira seems to understand that Tansy Dave's erratic behavior is a sign of uninterrupted grief. Thus in 1850 Tansy Dave loses his love when she moves away, and Rachel loses her husband and son and returns home with her daughters.[4] Both become homeless for a spell and lose their intimate connections with the other sex. The text suggests by synchronicity a noncausal link between a slave's madness and the loss of domestic stability. And, during "The Dark Autumn" section of the novel, while Nancy loses contact with her family and friends after escaping, Rachel is banished by Sapphira until one of her children dies. Their personal losses and tragedies seem to be local signs of national disharmony after the passage of the "severe Fugitive Slave Law" (222), which seems to have led simultaneously to white grief and black despair.

Against this backdrop of the laws made in 1850, Cather sets in motion the silent act of reading to show southern differences over slavery. For southerners with second thoughts about slavery, reading was a process of moral analysis and meditation. Long before Reconstruction, southern readers were agonizing over passages in the Bible and other religious texts, testing the justifications for slavery and collecting materials for a new moral self. For example, in his close reading of the Bible, George Washington Cable discovered that biblical passages used to justify slavery "yielded to scrutiny and betrayed a literalism combined, strangely enough, with a violence of inference that made them worthless" ("My Politics" 7). Southerners who are shown reading in the novel, like Rachel Blake, Mrs. Bywaters, and Henry Colbert, read antislavery texts or question the foundations of slavery while they read. Reading becomes a very effective vehicle for silently suggesting southern differences, even while the text understates the characters' preoccupation with the issue of slavery.

Rachel's reading shows her immersion in the political thought of the day even while the text portrays her as politically indifferent at times. The narrator unconvincingly urges us to forget about Rachel's moral conscience when she moves to Washington in 1837.[5] As the narrator explains, "Once settled in the narrow rented house on R Street, she no longer brooded upon real or imagined injustices" (138). In the galley proofs housed in the New York Public Library, Cather made a last-minute deletion to leave Rachel's interest in politics an open question. The deleted sentence, coming immediately after the sentence quoted above, stated that Rachel did not actively try to follow the debates of 1850 on slavery. By deleting these lines, Cather keeps intact some of the uncertainly about Rachel's political curiosity. Perhaps Cather realized that other sections on Rachel's innate dislike of slavery as a girl would make any attempt to quell her political sensibilities later in life unconvincing. Cather does tone down the importance of politics for Rachel by implying that moving off the plantation to D.C. with her "saviour" Michael leads her to think only of his happiness (134).

However, the important debates on slavery in 1850 would have given her ample material for reflection. The gag rule on debate over the abolition of slavery in Washington, in place since 1836, was lifted in 1844 (Green 37, 44). In 1849 Abraham Lincoln caused an uproar when he introduced a bill for the abolition of slavery in Washington, D.C., a fact easily accessible in

any Lincoln biography (Green 46). Although the novel understates her obvious interest in the subject matter, Rachel Blake lives in Washington during a time of intense political debate on slavery while living with a member
of the House of Representatives (134).[6]

Rachel's reading of the *New York Tribune* confirms her interest in the
debates on slavery and her abolitionist sentiments.[7] When Rachel returns
from Washington, the narrator explains that Mrs. Bywaters was "the only
neighbour with whom she ever talked freely" (145). Mrs. Bywaters also
gives Rachel her old copies of the *New York Tribune*. The *New York Tribune*
was a highly opinionated newspaper whose editorials took controversial
stands on slavery and many other social issues. Its editorials, "by the skill
with which they were composed and the attention they commanded," became "the national prototype" (Kluger 75). Its editor, Horace Greeley, was
a Free-Soiler and a nonviolent abolitionist. As one of the most famous New
Yorkers of the time and one of the first members of the Republican Party,
Greeley must have been familiar to Cather either from her years living in
New York City or from her father, an active Republican. Greeley's publications, namely *A History of the Struggle for Slavery Extension or Restriction
in the United States from the Declaration of Independence to the Present Day*,
may have sparked an interest in his life. Biographies of his life always reprint the editorials from the *New York Tribune* during the pivotal 1856
presidential campaign, when the Republican Party first emerged as a national political force. Living in New York City, Cather would have had easy
access to old copies of the newspaper.

Greeley's writings provide an important weather vane for the rise of
northern abolitionist sentiment, because he initially argued that slavery was
a problem for the South to solve by itself. Like many of his Transcendentalist friends, including Emerson and Thoreau, Horace Greeley initially
believed that southern states would voluntarily abolish slavery after they
clearly understood its evils. For example, in 1834 in the *New Yorker*, Greeley asked, "Why should not even the existing evil of one section be left to
the correction of its own wisdom and virtue, when pointed out by the un-
erring finger of experience?" (Kluger 27).

In an 1845 letter titled "Slavery at Home: Answer to an Invitation to
Attend an Anti-Slavery Meeting," Greeley places slavery in the South on
the same level as notions of group superiority, union breaking, concen-
trated land ownership that causes high rents, and the systematic discouragement of human initiative. Although he sets out to narrowly define slavery in his letter, he often generalizes about an abstract slavery, "that
condition in which one human being exists mainly as a convenience for
other human beings," including "your own wives, children, hired men and
women, tenants, &c" (353). For Greeley, slavery exists "wherever certain
human beings devote their time and thoughts mainly to obeying and serv-

ing other human beings, and this not because they choose to do so but because they *must*" (354; emphasis in the original). In other words, in 1845 Greeley still did not see the slave economy in the South as any worse than other forms of oppression that restricted ownership of property to one group.

However, by the 1850s, Greeley's stand on slavery changed drastically, and his editorial page became one of the most passionate voices in the abolitionist movement. In 1854 "Greeley's voice led the antislavery outcry greeting congressional passage of the Kansas-Nebraska bill" (Kluger 82). By 1856 Horace Greeley was helping organize the Republican Party and began arguing that the North should push for the abolition of slavery because the South would not really secede from the Union. In October 1856, in the heat of the presidential campaign, he asked pointedly, "Is there a North?" (Stoddard 181). Not only did the paper add its voice to the growing chorus of abolitionist fervor but it also encouraged emigration to the territories and helped collect over $20,000 to aid antislavery settlers in Kansas. Along with Henry Ward Beecher, the brother of Harriet Beecher Stowe and a nationally known preacher, Horace Greeley also headed a committee that shipped rifles to antislavery settlers in Kansas in boxes marked "Bibles" (Stoddard 180).

Knowing the paper's outspoken stance on abolition helps us decode a passage laden with political silence in the novel. To convincingly render the South of 1856, the text must include a freeze-frame of the political atmosphere that would lead to the Civil War. Cather's use of the *New York Tribune* demonstrates how political silence surfaces in the novel. The silent presence of Greeley's politics underscores an oddly lengthy passage on the newspaper: "Mrs. Bywaters, though she was poor, subscribed for the *New York Tribune*. Since she was in Government employ, this was an indiscreet thing to do. Even her father, Mr. Cartmell, thought it unwise. The papers came to her heavily wrapped and addressed in ink. She kept them locked in her upper bureau drawer and often gave Mrs. Blake interesting numbers to carry home in her basket. They were handy to start a fire with, she said" (145). While the narrator reports this allusive comment about the *Tribune*—that it was handy to start the fire of abolitionist sentiments with— Cather's vague diction leaves the issue of slavery unnamed. However, Cather wants to leave no doubts about Rachel's political curiosity. We can safely assume that Rachel "often" has access to the fiery editions of the *New York Tribune* from around 1850 to 1856. The *Tribune* was definitely an indiscreet thing to read and discuss as an employee of a proslavery government in 1856. Unless we are aware of the *Tribune*'s history, the extent of Mrs. Bywaters's indiscretion is not readily apparent to us.

Other readers in the novel are more discreet. Reading by himself in the Mill House at night, Henry actively searches texts to rethink his position on slavery. Although Henry's view that the Bible does not oppose slavery seems untenable now, an important debate on the scriptural grounds of slavery occurred in 1856 as the fledgling Republican Party grew from a small group to a major party in its first national election. In fact, the narrator lingers over Henry's struggle with contradictions as he reads his Bible: "he read with his mind as well as his eyes. And he questioned. He met with contradictions, and they troubled him. He found comfort in John Bunyan, who had also been troubled" (66). Focusing on Henry's musings, Cather recaptures part of the lively debate over the biblical grounds for slavery. Quite typically, as part of the debate in 1850 over the Fugitive Slave Law, Senator Badge "showed from the Scripture that, if slavery was an evil, it was not a sin" (*Baltimore Sun*, 19 March 1850, 4). On the other hand, religious groups who had always opposed slavery on biblical grounds were finding more opportunities to speak and publish their views. In 1856, for example, George D. Cheever, a Puritan preacher, authored "The Crime of Extending Slavery: A Sermon" on October 21 and "God against Slavery: A Sermon" on October 27; both were published in the *New York Tribune* during the Republican Party's first presidential campaign. Henry's view of slavery, riddled with contradictions, actually fuses the southern legalistic, scriptural defense of slavery with the northern response that slavery violates the spirit, if not the letter, of the Gospels.[8] "Nowhere in his Bible had he ever been able to find a clear condemnation of slavery," yet even so, he doubts that God's "design" holds a place for it (110–11). The debate over the religious grounds of slavery gives an important context to Henry's struggle.

The penalties for helping a slave escape under the Fugitive Slave Law of 1850 are also important to remember when analyzing Henry's "irresolution" when Rachel asks for money to help Nancy escape. Most critics wholeheartedly dismiss Henry's supplying of the money as an ineffective, passive act of a weakling or moral cowardice on the level of an evasive gesture.[9] Contrary to a vast majority of critics who see a pattern of indecision in Henry's action, Rachel "had always known him quick to act, had never seen him like this before" (225).

Imagine Henry's dilemma. He can remain loyal to his wife, betray his daughter, and keep Nancy in a position where she might be raped by a man he despises. Or, by helping Nancy escape, he can choose to risk his marriage, his reputation, the capital accumulated in his business, and the respect of most of his friends and neighbors. Since all but two of the U.S. representatives from Frederick County elected between 1827 and 1860 were Democrats and Frederick County later chose to remain in Virginia, we can safely assume that most of Henry's proslavery neighbors would have looked down on him for aiding in the escape of his wife's own slave.[10] Even though Henry tells us that "it isn't a slave-owning neighborhood" (8),

Henry's solitary meditations on slavery may attest to the lack of open discussion of the issue in Virginia by 1856. If Nancy escapes and his compli-
ance could be shown, Henry could be imprisoned up to six months and
fined up to two thousand dollars for aiding a fugitive.[11] He worries about
more than just "the laws of hospitality," as Marilyn Arnold claims ("'Of
Human Bondage'" 335). In fact, when Henry speaks to Sapphira about
asking Martin to leave, Sapphira dismisses the idea, because Virginians,
unlike Ben Franklin, do not believe that "Hospitality like fish stinks after
three days," as is "true in the North" (198). Rachel's theft of the money
helps contain the possible damage from heavy fines. If the escape attempt
fails, at least he would only have to pay legal fees and fines for one person.
Heroic, open collaboration by Henry could have been legally and finan-
cially devastating for the whole family. Rachel's solitary walk home after
asking for the money seems to be a tacit admission of this fact (228). Henry
only agrees to supply the money after bolting the door, closing the window,
and telling Rachel that "nothing must pass between you and me on this
matter, neither words nor aught else" (227). And, even though they walk
together every Sunday after church, "Nancy's name was never mentioned
between them" (247).

   Another rich passage in the novel suggests the possible political motivations of Henry. The narrator re-creates Henry's process of reading, which
requires the reader to imagine how Henry interprets a text. When he finds
out that Nancy is in danger of being raped by Martin, Henry reads two
long passages from Bunyan's *Holy War* (reprinted in the novel) that help
him find "consolation" for "things about which he could not unbosom
himself to anyone" (211). Cather leaves the passages from Bunyan and
Henry's "things" without narrative comment, greatly increasing their allusive power. Can we assume that Henry's "things" are abolitionist ideas,
repressed sexual desires for Nancy, or guilty feelings about not confronting
Martin?[12] Other passages can support each reading of Henry's "things."
For example, Henry's silence and embarrassing irresolution after Rachel
asks for his help could allude to the same "things." His silence during Rachel's visit could also result from his shock at discovering her boldness. And
all these readings of Henry's "things" seem suggested by the villain in Bunyan's *Holy War* who "haunts like a Ghost honest men's houses at nights."
The villain could be tormenting Henry for his anguished misgivings about
slavery, sexual restraint, or hesitancy in helping Nancy. Henry's silent reading could conceal a political and religious uncertainty that shapes his initial
hesitation in helping Nancy escape. Aptly, Nancy's escape begins at the mill
with Rachel's theft of the money, as if the mill is not only the literal economic fulcrum of the community, where Henry considers the reasons for
extending credit to improvident farmers as he reviews his financial records,
but also a moral center, where Henry's conscience gathers up all its force

to turn over the religious grounds of slavery before financing Nancy's escape. In any case, the vague phrasing of the passage forces the reader to form an interpretation based on limited information or to suspend judgment. The passages place us in the position of an interpreter of the southern past, like Cather, and reenact the narrative uncertainty about the contents of Henry's mind as he interprets.

Henry's romanticized view of Nancy as Mercy in *Pilgrim's Progress* points to another of his self-contradictions. Mercy is "Christiana's sweet companion," as Cather's narrator informs us (67), a traveler who makes things for the poor (188) and actually marries one of Christiana's sons (217). Like Nancy and Rachel, she is meek and innocent (162).[13] However, Henry's linking of Mercy and Nancy implies that Nancy is equally a pilgrim who works out of the goodness of her heart and not out of legal bondage. However, when she leaves he sees her escape to freedom prefigured in the Israelites' escape out of slavery in Egypt: "She would go up out of Egypt to a better land." For Henry, Nancy is paradoxically a free slave, living in Back Creek as part of a spiritual journey, whose escape finally puts her on equal ground, where "the best that can happen to you is to walk your own way and be responsible to God only" (228). Religious texts color Henry's worldview and provide him with a wide range of images to express his self-contradictions.

Portraying Henry as a restrained, pious character, Cather also casts his relationship with Nancy in terms of one of Bunyan's allegories in *Pilgrim's Progress*, a book that Cather read many times (Woodress 487). Cather gives Henry an unusual concern with dust in order to draw on an allegory, appropriately one used by Interpreter. In Bunyan's work, Christian watches Interpreter enact and then explain an allegory in a dusty room. At first, a man sweeps the room and manages only to cloud it with dust. Then, Interpreter instructs a damsel to sprinkle water around the room before sweeping. After she does so, the room "was swept and cleansed with pleasure" (25). Interpreter explains the meaning of the sweeping: "This Parlor, is the heart of a Man that was never sanctified by the sweet Grace of the Gospel: The *dust*, is his Original Sin, and inward Corruptions that have defiled the whole Man. He that began to sweep at first, is the Law; but She that brought water, and did sprinkle it, is the Gospel" (Bunyan 25; emphasis in the original). The link between defilement and the sweeping of dust also occurs in *Sapphira*.

The flour-dust at the Mill House represents the constant temptations that Henry feels he must subdue throughout the novel. Even in our first glimpse of Henry, flour-dust plays a central part: "He was clean-shaven,—unusual in a man of his age and station. His excuse was that a miller's beard got powdered with flour-dust, and when the sweat ran down his face this flour got wet and left him with a beard full of dough. His countenance bespoke a man of upright character, straightforward and determined. It was only his eyes that were puzzling; dark and grave, set far back under a square, heavy brow. Those eyes, reflective, almost dreamy, seemed out of keeping with the simple vigour of his face" (4–5).

The tension in his eyes suggests the constant struggle within Henry to become righteous and, metaphorically, to prevent sin from accumulating like dough on his face. Like minuscule devils trying to break Henry's strength at every opportunity, the flour-dust literally converges around Henry from every angle: "The miller's furniture was whitewashed, so to speak, day by day, by the flour-dust which sifted down from overhead, and through every crack and crevice in the doors and walls. Each morning Till's Nancy swept and dusted the flour away" (47). Nancy, the sweeper and duster, comes to Henry's rescue, allegorically speaking, until he can see her as a temptation, too. Bunyan's passage on Interpreter's view of the woman sweeper in *Pilgrim's Progress* has some similarities to Cather's description of Nancy's influence on Henry: "when the Gospel comes in the sweet and precious influences thereof to the heart, then I say, even as thou sawest the Damsel lay the dust by sprinkling the Flour with Water, so is sin vanquished and subdued, and the soul made clean, through the Faith of it" (25). Oddly enough, when Henry "must see her as a woman, enticing to men" (193), water streams off his naked body unto the dust on the floor after he ends a sleepless night with an invigorating morning swim. Making "footprints on the floury floor," he, quite appropriately, shaves his face to keep the dough off (192) and leaves the Mill House before Nancy arrives as usual (66), but with a stronger disinclination to see her since "Something disturbing had come between them" (192). The allegorical cleansing represents Henry as a restrained character, although the text never quite clarifies what it is that he restrains. Cather's allegorical characterization and her focus on Henry's reading allows her to present Henry's active imagination with its doubts and distractions while maintaining a degree of narrative uncertainty about his motivations.

Cather self-consciously creates narrative uncertainty about her own motives for delving into her family past when she admits that her narrators tell stories of a past that was not her own. As a frame narrator at "The End," she openly acknowledges her distance from her subject. *Sapphira* is the only frame narrative I know of that announces its last framework after "The End" of the text instead of at the beginning, as *My Ántonia, Gulliver's Travels, Lalla Rookh, The Scarlet Letter*, and many others do. Not only are Till's last words filtered through the narrative of a young girl but they also immediately call for a rereading from the perspective of "Willa Cather." The text ends with the paradoxical statement that the "I" who has just spelled the name of Mr. Pertleball doesn't "know how to spell it." And we cannot ask Mr. Pertleball how to really "spell" it because, like our new frame narrator, we have never even seen Mr. Pertleball. The many signs of an unreliable narrator, the uncertainty of her spelling, and her distance from the past seem to preclude a strict autobiographical reading of the novel. Cather could not resist mimicking that disarming, charming southern hospitality by having a narrator named Willa Cather talk to the reader like a family friend about her parents' conversations years ago along with tidbits of gossip about dead "unknown persons" who are fascinating "merely as names" (295). The narrator of the endnote confides her intimate, offhand reflections to the reader. Ironically, this breaks the fictional spell of the text by making the reader wonder why "Willa Cather" withheld the information for so long. What caused her to be silent until the novel was over?

The endnote was a late addition to *Sapphira and the Slave Girl*. In the galley proofs housed at the New York Public Library, the note by Willa Cather does not appear. According to the stamps on the manuscript, she received the proofs on August 28 and returned them on September 13. So, apparently, sometime between September 13 and December 7 (the publication date being on her birthday), Cather added the note. Although Cather knew she was writing about a memory of events in her life over fifty-five years ago, she repeatedly stated in letters to her friends that the epilogue accurately represented her past. However, the "Willa Cather" in the endnote, seemingly Cather's public self, renounces any connection to the characters, including the frame narrator of 1881, although Cather privately claimed the story of Nancy's return as her own. Gwin points out that, "Like Faulkner in *Absalom*, Cather seems to be suggesting, particularly by her sudden change to the autobiographical mode, that we can never really know the past, yet at the same time we cannot escape it" (135). Like the details that estrange the reader from the Virginia of the 1850s, the endnote also heightens "the sense of a past so distant it must be interpreted" by estranging the reader from the narrators (222). Cather's use of the narrative frameworks suggests that she wanted to create a late-breaking gap between the narrators and the reader (and perhaps Cather's carefully narrated public self and the reader), which works like the confession of a lifelong secret at the reading of a will. If we cannot know or escape the past in the novel, certainly we cannot know or escape Cather there either.

Cather reenacts her anxiety over negotiating between many versions of the past by juxtaposing her ambivalence in two listeners, Rachel and the narrator of 1881. The narrator situates Rachel in the position of the reader as a receiver of an unknown past. When the twelve-year-old Rachel "chanced to overhear a conversation which coloured her thoughts and feelings ever afterward," she is "sitting on Mrs. Bywaters's shady front porch, behind the blooming honeysuckle vines" (135). Rachel overhears a conversation through an open door when Mrs. Bywaters turns down her father's offer of a slave to help around the house because "Peace of mind is what

I value most" (136).[14] After the conversation, Rachel realizes that "she had been eavesdropping, listening to talk that was private and personal" (137). An inexperienced young girl reacts to the conversation in a moment similar to Huck's decision to go to hell in *Huckleberry Finn*. Cather presents Rachel's denouncement of slavery indirectly through the voice of the narrator: "A feeling long smothered had blazed up in her—had become a conviction. She had never heard the thing said before, never put into words. It was the *owning* that was wrong, the relation itself, no matter how convenient or agreeable it might be for master or servant" (137). Petrie explains that "Rachel Blake finds within herself, by the agency of Mrs. Bywaters, a moral bedrock that runs deeper than ephemeral political events or ideological creeds" (35). By distancing the eavesdropper from the conversation and presenting her epiphany in third person, Cather portrays Rachel's political self-silencing, which occurs immediately afterward, in a soft-spoken manner: "Rachel was more than ever reserved and shut within herself" (137). For Cather, the political can include the quietistic self-withdrawal of a young girl. Rachel's listening and self-confirmation becomes one of the least recognizable political silences in the novel.

Rachel's silent eavesdropping contrasts with Till's oral history, which acts as the official political noise in the novel. Till turns the practice of oral history into art: the narrator of 1881 tells us that Till's "stories about the Master and Mistress were never mere repetitions, but grew more and more into a complete picture of those two persons" (292). By sheer exhilaration, Till creates the past for her young listener: "She loved to talk of Mrs. Colbert's last days; of the reconciliation between the Mistress and Mrs. Blake that winter after Betty died, when Mrs. Blake and Mary stayed at the Mill House" (292). Till's silence about Nancy's father in 1856 (43) and her willingness to talk about her rosy, unconvincing version of the past in 1881 create an ironic juxtaposition that clearly calls Till's later storytelling into question.

The political silences in the novel point out schisms between the subtle political intimations of Cather's narrator of 1856 and the naiveté of the narrator of 1881. For instance, while the narrator of 1856 relates Martin's assault on Nancy, the narrator of 1881 knows of Martin only by his monument (290). Puzzling over the past, Cather demonstrates how reading and writing about the South can produce omissions as the narrators reshape the past and create texts in terms of the present.

In one instance Cather juxtaposes northern and southern dialects while the narrator of 1881, commenting on Nancy's odd speech, speaks of history: "Whereas Mrs. Blake used to ask me if she should read to me from my hist'ry book (*Peter Parley's Universal*), Nancy spoke of the his-to-ry of Canada" (284). In a sleight of hand, Cather leaves the notion of unnarrated, "universal" history in parenthesis, setting it off as an authorial comment, while using dialect to literally show how geography affects language. *Peter Parley's Universal History on the Basis of Geography*, a children's history book that attempted to present "a clear outline of the story of mankind, from its beginning in the plain of Shinar, down to the present hour," covered the Civil War in just twelve pages ("Preface"). The narrator of the *Universal History* portrays a totally unified South and sidesteps any inclusion of a southern version of history, stating that "the people of the South feared— and it is *useless* to inquire here whether they were right or wrong—that Abraham Lincoln would, if elected, not only prohibit slavery in the territories, but in some way interfere with it in the states" (624; emphasis added). Cather uses *Peter Parley's* as the child's *Universal History* to imply that the dominant representation of the South is an immature view of history that avoids any mention of the complexities of the past by its omissions and focus. The child narrator of 1881 reproduces this view because information is consciously withheld from her. For instance, when the returning Nancy asks about Martin, "Mrs. Blake glanced at her in a way that meant it was a forbidden subject" (290). Such complexities and others, like Sapphira's strong if aristocratic and "evil" character, get lost in a gloss of hist'ry. Cather presents a troubled version of reconciliation and forgiveness of the South and North by focusing on the uncomfortable, clumsy, staged reunion of Nancy and Till, which places the reader in the position of the child as a viewer of the event. The loss of words at the reunion betrays an alienation and estrangement felt between the mother and daughter that even the child notices.

In 1987, Marilyn Arnold became the first critic to be explicitly conscious of reading *Sapphira* in a northern language. To Arnold, "the fact that neither Colbert nor Rachel would even consider running Martin off the place, an alternative that the uncomprehending northern reader sees as a much easier solution than arranging for Nancy's escape, testifies to the vise-like grip of the system [of slavery]" (335). The historical distance implicit in *universal* northern incomprehension raises a few questions for all readers of this novel: what does the construction of southern hospitality by the first self-conscious northern reader tell us about our present reading of Cather's southern novel? Aren't we in a viselike grip of a northern language that defines slavery as an indisputable moral evil and a southern, not national, phenomenon? Does the low status of this troubling, powerful work in Cather's canon reflect an unconscious desire to keep quiet anything that may embarrass the American psyche, such as the 1856 narrator's casual use of "nigger" and "darky" that causes us to flinch?

While the text produces different versions of the past and creates many political silences, it thematizes escape by making art out of the escape of a slave girl. The novel challenges the notion that politics is only public and that narratives of history can be universal, so the story of the escape is anything but escapist. In order for readers to return to places of memory as Nancy returns at the end of the novel, they must understand the historical narratives of the past. The omissions in the child's narration, such as her ignorance of Martin's significance, demonstrate Cather's interest in seeing how silences distort and obscure our sense of the past and ourselves. Kenneth Burke speaks of reading texts with terministic screens, "particular nomenclatures" that allow you "to proceed to track down the kinds of observations implicit in the terminology you have chosen, whether your choice of terms was deliberate or spontaneous" (118). Perhaps in works like *Sapphira* we should also look for exterministic screens, those screens where meaning seems to end because the language calls for a moral or historical imagination outside our trajectory. In *Sapphira* the exterministic screen contains a nomenclature that implicitly rejects some kinds of observations about the southern past and tries to reconstruct those observations with its political silences. And like frustrated owners of a defunct, incompatible computer, every time we try to reboot the system it crashes, because it does not have enough memory to support the operation of reconstructing the past.

Notes

1. In conceptualizing this essay, I assumed that Cather, living in New York at the time, had access to a few historical texts: a textbook on American history that mentions the Fugitive Slave Law and the Compromise of 1850, a Lincoln biography, a reprint of Daniel Webster's "The Union and the Constitution," and a biography of Horace Greeley with a thorough treatment of his role as an editor of the *New York Tribune*. Many Greeley biographies were available, including *The Life of Horace Greeley, Founder of the* New York Tribune (1873) by Lurton D. Ingersoll, *Horace Greeley, the Editor* (1890) by Francis N. Zabriskie, *The Life of Horace Greeley* (1896) by James Parton, *Horace Greeley, Founder and Editor of the* New York Tribune (1903) by William A. Linn, and *Horace Greeley: Founder of the* New York Tribune (1926) by Don C. Seitz. Cather could have read material from the *New York Tribune* reprinted in Greeley's biographies and other historical treatments of the times. The extent of Cather's research for this novel and her historical knowledge is an open question, but an example may suffice to encourage more historical work on this novel using Cather's unquotable letters. In 1940 Cather wrote Dorothy Canfield Fisher that in a Society Library she looked up the location of the actual ferry on the Potomac River that Nancy and Rachel use. Indeed, Nancy unnecessarily tells Henry the exact location of the ferry—"about five miles out of Martinsburg"—before he offers any assistance (225).

2. By supplying more legal and historical contexts that reveal the complexity of Cather's characters, my essay extends Petrie's convincing argument that "in no case does Cather permit a character to rest secure in a reified moral/ideological station" (35). Political silence allows Cather to include historical and political contexts in her novel without damaging the com-

plexity of her proslavery characters, like Sapphira, by appearing to use them to espouse a political ideology.

3. Henry Colbert reads about Blake's death around March 1850 in a copy of the *Baltimore Sun* that is a "week old" (143). Henry immediately goes to Washington to get Rachel around May 1850. The *Baltimore Sun*, mostly a business paper then on the order of the *Wall Street Journal*, carried slave-trade advertisements and gave the most objective, in-depth coverage of the political scene in Washington (Williams 59). On 24 March 1850, it printed this notice for capturing a fugitive: "$25 Reward—runaway or kidnapped on or about the last of February, NEGRO GIRL Nelly about 16 years old; very black: large white teeth, about 5 feet 4 or 5 inches high" (3). Whole speeches were telegraphed from the Capitol to Baltimore starting in 1846 (Williams 23).

4. In fact, a cholera epidemic occurred in 1850, killing 1,851 people (Cable, *Creoles* 292). Cable describes the blasé attitude of the newspapers during epidemics. *Sapphira* contains a similar passage: "There was something in the newspapers about an epidemic down there, but it was immediately denied" (142). Cable explains that during cholera and yellow fever outbreaks, "it was the confident convictions and constant assertion of the average New Orleans citizen, Creole or American, . . . that his town was one of the healthiest in the world" (*Creoles* 292).

5. Michael Blake dies in 1850 after being married for thirteen years (142). He marries Rachel soon after his election, and they "immediately" move to Washington, D.C. (134).

6. Although Cather's knowledge of Washington life in the 1840s cannot be reconstructed, she could have placed Rachel's house on R Street, which crosses over into Georgetown, in order to situate Rachel near a failed slave escape that caused a political controversy. In April 1848, Captain Daniel Drayton and another sailor were caught transporting seventy-six slaves from Washington and Georgetown households; "after a prolonged and fiercely fought trial," both men "were finally sentenced to long prison terms as kidnapers [*sic*]" (Green 45). Although my source of the story was not available to Cather, she may have found the story elsewhere.

7. Woodress speaks of Rachel's "Yankee ideas about slavery" (482). However, if Cather had found Webster's famous speech, she could have easily had a different view. Webster recounts "the debates in the Virginia House of Delegates in 1832": he describes with "what freedom a proposition made by Mr. Jefferson Randolph for the gradual abolition of slavery was discussed in that body. Every one spoke of slavery as he thought; very ignominious and disparaging names and epithets were applied to it" (619). In fact, Webster and many others claimed that northern abolitionists solidified southern support for slavery by tainting the moral and economic issue with regional prejudice (see 619).

8. Webster summarized the different views of southerners and northerners on the "nature and influence of slavery" (603–4).

9. Most comments place Henry in the position of a bad friend, brother, father, or lover of Nancy, all legally impossible or emotionally beset relationships between a slave girl and her owner. Many critics see Henry's risk-taking action of leaving money in his coat by an open window as a "clandestine, noncommital gesture" (Stouck 30; see also Harrison [80] and Arnold ["'Of Human Bondage'" 334–35]). Others characterize him as a moral weakling when he appears helpless against Sapphira's power (Rosowski 225) and Martin's wantonness (Skaggs 13), both of which threaten Nancy. Arnold's claim that "Evasion is Henry's life habit" ("Cather's Last" 246) could point to his use of at least some of the "various behavioral tropes of silence—mocking submissiveness, unresponsiveness, exaggerated passivity, particularly exaggerated unresponsiveness, and passivity in bed"—that Stout describes as strategies of reticence (18).

10. Michael Blake in Cather's novel must be a Democrat. From 1847 to the time of secession in 1860, both senators from Virginia were Democrats (*Congressional Quarterly*).

Richard W. Barton of Winchester in 1841 and Charles Faulkner in 1851 were the only two Whigs elected as U.S. representatives for the districts containing Frederick County. Later, Charles Faulkner became a Democrat and won the seat in the new Eighth District in 1853, 1855, and 1857. He was narrowly defeated in 1859 by Alexander Boteler (Opposition) (Moore; Parsons, Beach, and Dubin; Parsons, Beach, and Hermann passim).

11. The Fugitive Slave Law of 1850 contained penalties for those helping a fugitive in any way, even if the slave did not successfully escape: "Any person obstructing the arrest of a fugitive, or attempting his or her rescue, or aiding him or her to escape, or harbouring and concealing a fugitive, knowing him to be such, shall be subject to a fine of not exceeding one thousand dollars, and to be imprisoned not exceeding six months, and shall also 'forfeit and pay the sum of one thousand dollars for each fugitive so lost'" (May 4).

12. Although Henry does not directly ask Martin to leave, he does create at least one obstacle for Martin. When Henry sees Martin with Nancy in the laundry cabin, Henry immediately sends Sampson looking for two missing scythes, apparently knowing that Sampson will look in the laundry cabin at some point (200–201). After the cherry tree incident, Henry can probably figure out that Martin's mild sense of shame can be used to protect Nancy only if he thinks someone is nearby. Both Henry and Sapphira wish to keep Martin at a distance from themselves while indirectly influencing the outcome of Nancy's future. Henry's unspoken, possibly unacknowledged contempt for Martin can be compared to Sapphira's letter to Martin that "was meant to be cordial, but not too cordial" (30). Cather goes to some lengths to show that Sapphira cannot directly encourage Martin and that Henry cannot directly discourage him.

13. Perhaps Nancy reminds him of his quiet, subdued daughter, who was "virginal in mind as well as in body" (134) at Nancy's age and also did not seem to fit into Sapphira's household. Nancy and Rachel are despised by the rest of the slaves in the house due to their privileges and aloofness, respectively.

In Cather's text, Rachel shows the same generosity to the poor as Mercy does: "when she had nothing to do for her self," Mercy "would be making of Hose and Garments for others, and would bestrow them upon them that had needs" (188). Writing from Sapphira's perspective, Cather's narrator of 1856 explains, "Rachel was poor, and it was not much use to give her things. Whatever she had she took where it was needed most; and Mrs. Colbert certainly didn't intend to keep the whole mountain" (38).

14. The use of the wild vines to beautify Mrs. Bywaters's house and the slave cabins (197) seems to be in subtle contrast with the labor-intensive landscaping around the Colbert house. Mrs. Bywaters's maintenance-free vines that only require attention when she needs to paint her house are juxtaposed with the gardens that Sapphira plants with Jezebel.

No Place like Home

Reading *Sapphira and the Slave Girl* against the Great Depression

SHELLEY NEWMAN

In 1938, Willa Cather returned to her childhood home in Virginia as part of the process of remembering that would become her last novel, *Sapphira and the Slave Girl*. Her friend and traveling companion, Edith Lewis, recalled that it was an experience "as intense and thrilling in its way, as those journeys in New Mexico" (Woodress, *Willa Cather* 28). Cather responded to the "peculiar poignancy" of the landscape's details, changed through time but remembered intact. Willow Shade, the house she had left at age nine, denied her heart's return; shorn of its willow trees, its appearance held Cather in reserve (479). It was, to put a different emphasis on Dorothy's words in *The Wizard of Oz*, no place like home.

Returning to a sentimental historicism, for Cather and Dorothy both, was emblematic of a larger cultural process that engaged America throughout the Depression. Home became a felt place, opposed to the reality of its diminishment and destruction by unemployment, impoverishment, and the economics of loss. With home no longer seeming safely nurturing or politically neutral, if indeed it was more than a roadside camp on the way to something hopefully better, the reality of family attachments to the home frayed.[1] Powerlessness, barrenness, and the inversion of familial authority deeply threatened the idea of the home as the symbolic source of the nation's citizenry, the originating location for democratic identity in the national consciousness. And since citizenship was the idealizing principle that artificially sought to conflate and obscure class, gender, and race throughout the thirties, as a creation of popular culture and through the manifestation of cultural will, the reification of home was essential to the discovery of the individual within its protective circle, and the recovery of the citizen who moves outside the home to redeem the nation.[2]

If all this seems a long way from Cather and Willow Shade in the spring of 1938, let me make clear the connection I'm seeking and my purpose in doing so. I would like to re-place Cather in her milieu by understanding the transitive meanings and transformative powers of remembered homes in *Sapphira and the Slave Girl*, interconnected with other cultural expressions of memory in Depression America. The precariousness of home—there is not one completely safe home in the novel—fractures families and forces Rachel and Nancy to define themselves against their contemporary existence to protect their future. Rachel defies the false home built on the economic foundation of slavery that simultaneously creates and perverts the Mill Farm. Her subversion is conservative, in the sense of preserving traditional believed values about equality, and regenerative of self through moral agency, in keeping with the Depression's code of personal responsibility played against the impersonal forces of world economics. Rachel's rediscovery of her citizenship through the practice of her own freedom aligns her as midwife to the new American, Nancy—in whom black and white, past, present, and, significantly, future are joined. Nancy, who has learned her own ways of resistance in her mother's home, provides Rachel with the imperative to act. She is the locus of power through which Rachel constitutes her subjectivity, and the point of reversal of power through which Nancy begins to speak and act on her own behalf. The irony, of course, is that Nancy, the new American, is fully realized in Canada, a place like and unlike home in Cather's imagination, while Rachel returns to Back Creek, demonstrating a distinctly thirties' quest for and reaffirmation of "the promise of American life" (Susman 155).

Reading *Sapphira* in the context of the Depression extends the work done by Susan Rosowski, who recognizes that the story only "seems to offer a retreat into the past [while containing] the distinctly modern search for meaning in an estranged world" (*Voyage Perilous* 239). She interprets *Sapphira* as a Gothic novel, which suggests further exploration of the relation between Cather's use of the form and other demonstrations of the Gothic that were popular in the films of the era. Joseph Urgo's analysis of memory and migration in Cather's writing addresses the theme of "transmission and metamorphosis" in *Sapphira* and argues for a sort of geographical historicism, observing, "Memory itself in Cather is always marked by a migration into what looms ahead, not back to what has gone by" (84). Like the Depression's homeless and displaced multitudes that so shocked the nation's sense of itself, Rachel and Nancy "move to survive, either by moving physically . . . or by remembering what they need to face their present circumstances and migrate to the future" (87). I hope to connect these observations and my own with Ann Romines's interpretation, which looks at the "relation between women's domestic power and political powerlessness" (*Home Plot* 175), in a reading that integrates historical and cultural ideas of citizenship expressed across the Depression. I question Toni Morrison's assessment of *Sapphira* as a "fugitive" novel in which she maintains that Cather's "almost completely buried subject [is] the interdependent working of power, race, and sexuality in a white woman's battle for coherence" (*Playing* 19, 20). I hold that Rachel's coherence—and, moreover, Nancy's—is discovered in a reciprocal, osmotic *process*, not in "the reckless, unabated power of a white woman gathering identity unto herself from the wholly available and serviceable lives of Africanist others" (*Playing* 25). The point of all this is to make the distinction between moral citizenship and what Walter Benn Michaels calls "cultural citizenship," the mediating factor between political and familial citizenship in *The Professor's House*. Michaels concludes that the exclusivity of "cultural Americanism" results in an awareness of difference that facilitates pluralism, producing an ironic link between Cather and the development of identity politics ("Vanishing American" 238). But in the case of *Sapphira*, moral citizenship seems Cather's way of blurring identity; as Urgo writes of Nancy, "The womb of the runaway slave . . . produces transnational offspring, becoming the very image of the melting pot" (92).

When considered in the company of the activist and more representative struggles of leftist artists in the thirties, Cather's work gives an anomalous impression, but to see her and her art as isolated, her vision narrowed and removed from the *Weltanschauung* of the time, is to misread the subtle varieties of involvement and challenge implicit in her work.[3] It is also to ignore the continuum of political and cultural values that operated throughout the decade, which is more accurately characterized as "a complex, ambivalent, disorderly period which gave witness to the force of cultural continuity even as it manifested signs of deep cultural change" (Levine 222). Cather was keenly aware of the nation's suffering, and her response to the Depression as experienced in her Nebraska community was generous and personal, an individual initiative very much of the heart (Woodress, *Willa Cather* 437, 471). Cather grounded her relief efforts in a genuine empathy, autonomously demonstrated, and directed them toward the ideal of a benign community emanating from individuals acting caringly. Her gestures bespeak a desire to mend society through the actions of a benevolent citizenry rather than through adherence to a political program, putting her at odds with the means, though not the spirit, of the New Deal. While her lack of ideological commitment separated her from her critics, Cather was comfortably in sync with the mass of "Americans in the 1930s [who] may not have known much about ideology but [who] knew what they liked— and what they did *not* like. Their rejection of greed, egoism and the unfettered marketplace led them towards values through which they could 're-moralize' the American economy and society" (McElvaine 223; emphasis in the original).

Cather starts history in the moment of 1856, her multiple references to time fixing the story at the zero point before the chaos of the Civil War, the event that changed the nation. The country is in a holding pattern comparable to the economic stasis of the Depression before World War II. The year is equivocal, directing our attention to the war, implying that the aberration of slavery will be duly corrected, returning the nation to its original state of grace, but also suggesting that the "solutions" of the post–Civil War era have proven hugely inadequate. And it establishes the moral temporality of Cather's story in relation to her perception of the Depression. Her angst is not an economic expression directed at a political discourse but rather a morally driven response to the conditions and effects of the Depression. Through *Sapphira's* textual association with abolitionism, Cather suggests that moral identity and its practice—moral citizenship—precede and even preempt political identity.

Thus the story begins between two polarities: the American fiction of essential grace, on the one hand, and its opposite, a national and nationalizing code underwritten by "racial disingenuousness and moral frailty" (Morrison, *Playing* 6). Slavery is the original sin in the American garden, its discursive power an invasive, shifting, and interactive presence. Linked with slavery, the myth of origin is doubled, opposing the foundation myth with the reality that fuels it. Out of this garden are built two houses, not worlds apart but worlds within each other. Ordered, formal, reminiscent of Washington's Mount Vernon, the Mill House also evokes the vexed rhetoric of the Declaration of Independence, referring to the Jeffersonian conception of equality as "an abstract and minimalist state of nature, not a concrete condition of life-in-society" (Condit and Lucaites xv). By attaching this foundational reference to the Mill Farm, the Dodderidge household is absolved of its responsibility to continually remake its commitment to equality. Slavery exists here as a completed, singular, historical fact, enervating the possibility of change through human agency. Tucked away in the farthest reaches of Back Creek, it is an alien, out-of-time presence, housing a family that even after thirty years is not "native" (*Sapphira* 4). Politically charged and spiritually destructive, the Mill Farm exists in limbo, the representation of a "nation who *decided* that their world view would contain agendas for individual freedom *and* mechanisms for a devastating racial oppression" (Morrison, *Playing* xiii; emphases in the original).

Behind this house, whose prosperity and material comforts would be marked by a Depression audience, is the kitchen, and further still, the cabins where the slaves live. This world, whose vitality derives from its day-to-day resistance to degradation and in its affirmation of community, is built as an alternative garden, still flourishing in the growth of flowers and gourds. Cather's observation that "[w]hatever was carried away in a gourd was not questioned" (21) recalls and foreshadows the light of the drinking-gourd constellation that guides the way north to freedom. In contrast to the Mill Farm's stagnation, the "back-yard" works under a flag of red calico and blue denim, a moving, "flapping" (21), vigorous symbol of the nation, and one with which Depression readers could sympathize. This is a place of conservation and renewal that insists upon affirmation, dignity, and humanity, before and after the experience of a brutal, white, outside world.[4] Nancy's mother, Till, creates her cabin as a refuge where Nancy can return with "a glad smile on her face," where she feels "snug, like when she was a little girl" (62). Compared to the physical and psychological danger that resonates from the Mill House, Till's cabin beats with a human heart that restores Nancy's innocence and inculcates the possibility of resistance. "Nancy loved that cabin and all her mother's ways" (62)—consider the combination of affection for the generative home and the prescription for resistance in Till's determined actions. Till's "ways," her practices of self within her cabin and within Sapphira's house, signify agency and choice— however limited—within a discourse that prohibits both.

Romines suggests that Till is "a woman trying to fulfill a complex set of loyalties," her "artful housekeeping" replicating a "domestic plot" (*Home Plot* 181), a skill learned from the English housekeeper Mrs. Matchem at her childhood home in Chestnut Hill. She gives Till comfort, after Till witnesses the horror of her mother's death, as well as discipline: "Matchem impressed it upon [Till] that there was all the difference between doing things exactly right and doing them somehow-or-other" (71). Here again is another con/fusion of kinship—black American child, white English mother figure—suggesting that for Cather, identity is derivative from some human, not specifically racial, bond. Till's internalization of Matchem and things English into her psyche points to the ambivalence of metaphors of resistance, because while Matchem is complicit with a slave-holding household, she is also, in her very Englishness, associated with antebellum black culture's celebration of England's emancipation of blacks in the West Indies. England became a vexed symbol of the moral ground of antislavery, compelling what ought to be in America, contingent upon an awareness of what had gone before.[5]

For Till, an empowering sense of home resides in Matchem and in the familiar landscape of Chestnut Hill; transplanted to the "resigned, unstirring back country of Mill Creek" (73), she is un/Till who bides and waits. Till accepts her marriage to Jefferson, "the capon man," with "perfect dignity," unwilling to betray the degree to which "it hurt her pride" (72). Cather's reticence to speak openly in Till's voice suggests "that some privacies of a black woman's life may not be accessible to a white woman's imagination" (Romines 180); however, Till's actions belie her supposed passivity. In submitting to the structures of her oppression, Till uses her body as resistance. Her liaison with the Cuban painter marks her will to self-expression through the acting out of her desires, destabilizing Sapphira's authority over her. Till's contribution to Nancy's citizenship is in her ability to accept and synthesize national values of duty, work, and, in the case of the painter, art, and then to project them through Nancy as the means of naturalization into American culture. Till, who is denied political citizenship by race, provides the conditions, the cultural heritage, for Nancy to undermine and ultimately surpass the limits of self-determination and legitimization through political identity.

Till teaches Nancy a variation on Jeffersonian proprietorship through caretaking, doubling Sapphira's legal ownership. The idea of a natural right to property ownership stemming from occupation and working of the land had great currency during the Depression, when vast numbers of people lost property held for generations when they were unable to service their mortgages. Similarly, Till has no material claim to the Mill House, but she has a working ownership, a right that is perhaps more spiritual than natural. Mother and daughter bring light into Sapphira's house, possessing "the space of Otherness" (hooks 46) by demonstrating their choices within it. Till maintains not just the historical referents of the "Master and Mistress twenty years ago," set on canvas and encased in "heavy gilt frames" (42)—guilt indeed—but also the memories they represent of Nancy's father. Nancy has fantasies of herself as the painter's daughter; without asking Till about her father, Nancy still knows them together as the source of her aestheticism. Nancy admires Till's "nice ways," intuiting her mother's reverse manipulation of Sapphira. Till's caretaking of the Mill House and its occupants depends on survival skills that are replicated in Nancy's lies to avoid reprimand. Learning to lie is learning to speak back, hybridizing the language of oppression, like Jezebel's learning English, like Till's adopting Matchem's voice, and like Nancy's "tell[ing] falsehoods . . . to escape from something" (44).

If the romantic home produces the child who repeats the parent, completing a reciprocity of safety and union, then the Mill House is its antithesis, producing the child who is simply other, objectifying difference and separation from the parent. Sapphira, not Till, is "natally dead" (Morrison 21), rejecting Rachel as "glum and disapproving," "difficult," and "rebellious toward the fixed ways which satisfied other folk" (14). Rachel is never "at home" in her mother's house because slavery as an external political system infiltrates and perverts the maternal bond. Sapphira im/personates the political; contained by her adherence to a morally corrupt political system, she is the false citizen to Rachel's morally authentic one. And it is Rachel's epiphany at age twelve, that radical and astute moment of adolescence, that initiates her citizenship: "A feeling long smothered had blazed up in her—had become a conviction. She had never heard the thing said before, never put into words. It was the owning that was wrong" (136). Rachel has knowledge but no way to express it, save through silent disapproval; she becomes "more than ever reserved and shut within herself" (Cather 136). Where the power of language encodes resistance across the generations for Jezebel, Till, and Nancy, Rachel internalizes the injustice of the thing put into words, confirming her isolation in a "a home where she had never been happy" (134).

Rachel's father, Henry, is also silenced and frozen, unable to support either Rachel or Nancy beyond the limits placed upon him by history. Henry is like an immigrant, his dark appearance decidedly ethnic compared to Sapphira's Anglo purity. His speech—when he speaks—marks him, for "his lack of a Southern accent amounted to almost a foreign accent" (5). What passes for love between Henry and Sapphira is really power, their relationship a fluctuating hierarchy of control. She denies him his place as head of the family and he withholds his affection, making his home in the mill room and making his work his life. Not so much a home as a monument—"all that was left of the original building which stood there in Revolutionary times" (47)—the building is a metaphor for Henry. He is a relic of history, his ethics fixed by the rhetoric of 1776, in which a free man's natural right to liberty could justify revolution but which also need be surrendered in order to secure the compact between individual and government. He instigates his personal revolution by disinheriting himself from the lascivious Colbert blood and moving away from Sapphira, both gestures of willed morality. But fearing nothing so much as the uncharted future, Henry's understanding of the world and his place in it is confirmed by marriage contract, hinging upon acceptance of external authority in exchange for limited autonomy. All of which is not to say that Henry doesn't question or doubt the absence of morality in the forms that contain him—because he does—but that he lacks the vision to exceed those forms. Positioned like the flour mill between calm and moving waters, his example to Rachel is not of revolution but of habits of resistance. Although a free man, he is not free to slip the "bonds" (110) of moral or legal reciprocity.

Henry leaves home but does not go far enough away; Rachel's salvation is in her marriage to Michael Blake and her migration to Washington, the archetypical union of home and nation. In this most political site of memory, where citizen meets the nation and projects her will upon it, Rachel sublimates herself in her obsessive devotion to Michael, and learns through her self-denial ways to act out the moral imperative of her citizenship. Although the object of her domesticity is Michael and his patriarchal pleasure, Rachel is, to paraphrase Morrison, the subject of this dream of home (17). Making a home, nurturing and caring for one's family, is both self-abnegation and affirmation for her. Rachel creates herself *out* of the Mill Farm as resistance to its illegitimate authority; through her Washington home she begins her practice of moral citizenship. But she is still vulnerable. Michael, who brings his constituency to the nation and the nation back to the individual, personifies in his profligacy the nation's unpaid debts, unfulfilled promises, and failure to protect its citizens, the worst fears of Cather's Depression audience. As Rachel's economic and emotional fortunes rise, falter, and plummet with her husband and son's deaths, she is forced into depression, poverty, and a retreat to a home that reluctantly receives her back.

Although it is Rachel's wish "to live [at the Mill Farm] like [she] had never gone away" (145), now, having been in the outside world, she brings it back with her. Rachel maintains her connection with the idealized free nation of the North and its democratic expression through Mrs. Bywaters's contraband *New York Tribune*. The power of the people's word, accessed and disseminated through the newspaper, is "handy to start a fire with" (145), and to fuel Rachel's fantasy of escape for Nancy. As agent for the moral absolutism of antislavery, Rachel's subversion is motivated by loyalty to principles that supersede those found in legal or political conceptions of citizenship. Rachel and Nancy are outlawed by virtue of conviction and race, unrecognized by the nation and in need of a safe place to land.

Rachel and Nancy's decision to challenge the law that overlooks them— "in the double sense of social surveillance and psychic disavowal" (Bhabba 193)—is a decision made in mutual obligation and according to an alternate understanding of the law. Law operates as the codification of accepted or prohibited behaviors based on and set into historical precedent, putting the citizen into a concrete relationship with society. But law is also "a temporary compromise between competing ideological interests" (Condit and Lucaites xv), contingent and interpretable. Thus, the individual's relationship to the law is ambivalent. For Rachel and Nancy, the content of the law determines the reciprocity between citizen and society; for Henry, the form of the law imposes a contractual authority over the citizen, which he uses alternately to protect Nancy from Sapphira and to keep her enslaved. When Rachel "[can't] hold back" from sending Nancy "on the road to freedom," Henry speaks the rage of impotence, afraid even to commit thought to language: "Hush, Rachel, not another word! You and me can't be talking about such things. . . . I can't be a party to make away with your mother's property" (227). Henry's defense reduces Nancy to property; he capitulates to Sapphira's ownership and surrenders his morality to an unjust law. His acquiescence brings Rachel *under* the law; by taking the money from Henry's coat, she becomes a thief, robbing her father's empty but intimate form to fulfill her higher commitment to Nancy (Rosowski, *Voyage Perilous* 241). However, Cather's resolution of moral citizenship is in Henry's acceptance that change comes first through the individual. Her hope is expressed in his wish that Nancy will "make her own way in this world where nobody is altogether free, and the best you can do is to walk your own way and be responsible to God only" (228).

The idea of Canada provides Nancy's way out and Rachel's way back into her home and her culture. Canada is an enabling fantasy, a place of the known/unknown that "enacts a visible self-criticism or self-reflection" (Kanneh 143) for America. It is a "better place," an alternative community whose imaginative value is as "a potential land of the free" (Fabre 83). Constitutionally linked to England, Canada shared its positive associations as a refuge for black Americans before the Civil War. In Canada, "the termination point of the Underground Railroad and of the slave's hazardous life and suffering; the incarnation of the North Star; the mythic Canaan Land" (Fabre 83), Nancy will be recognized and protected by "many folks in big cities that are a sight kinder than some folks on this farm" (226). Nancy gains citizenship—and a future—in Canada through the affirmation of her human identity. And because it is Nancy in whom Cather locates the aesthetic—Nancy is art in being—her escape to freedom, in the sense of Canada as the larger community, allows us to understand her as an artistic soul at home in the world, part of and acting for a human family.

As a side note to Nancy's flight, it is tempting to speculate on Canada's place in Cather's cosmology. Michael Fellman observes that while Mackenzie King, Canada's prime minister during the Depression, was "in many respects the most explicitly American[-]influenced political leader Canada has ever had," his philosophy and practice owed more to the American Progressive movement of the teens and early twenties than to the "bold experimentalism" of Roosevelt and the New Deal; "in the late 1930s, despite a theoretical engagement with the American New Deal and an almost fawning admiration for Franklin Roosevelt, King and his Liberals were slow to adopt much of the massive government programs and expenditures of the New Deal." As a result, Roosevelt, not King, was the "beacon of hope" for Canadians during the Depression (45). However, given Cather's dislike of Roosevelt, her distrust of political solutions, and her pre-1922 ethic, it is possible that Canada was a particularly "Catheresque" site of memory, functioning as a guiding light by its very adherence to the past.

Rachel's return to the Mill Farm completes the spiral process of memory and creation. Her transgression yields reunion, breaking the cast of history over home and family. Having established the limits of her ability to act freely, Rachel effects a reconciliation of personal past as daughter and national past as moral citizen. Her expression integrates Cather's memories with a cultural valorization of authentic individual action. The redemptive value of the Mill Farm reunited secures it as a generative source; Rachel can return, muting its negative force, and Cather can emerge out of it, reclaiming her natal home of Willow Shade, taking the story back by way of the epilogue. This is, after all, Cather's story, her message of perseverance against the chaos of the Depression and the beginning of World War II. In Cather's memory of home, its particular spell is as the source of a moral consciousness that inspires conservative, individual activism. Cather romances the Mill Farm into a racially shared homespace, passing into Rachel and Till's mutual ownership. And if we understand today the inherent racism of Cather's appropriations, it is because we are able to apply our contemporary understandings to the circumstances of Cather's cultural memory. By 1940, when *Sapphira* was published, there was a need not just to ameliorate the lingering effects of the Depression but also to find a domestic rhetoric that opposed Hitler's racism with an imagined egalitarianism, a move popularized by Roosevelt. Consequently, *Sapphira and the Slave Girl* offers an exchange, a kind of cultural transference of familiar symbolic meanings between Cather and her society. Cather's novel testifies to her participation in making a collective, national memory of individual moral citizenship, restoring her voice to the many inflections heard in the thirties. The irony is that by privileging the moral over the political, Cather presupposes our now fixed notion that politics are always underwritten by the personal.

Notes

1. Robert and Helen Lynd's study of Middletown in 1935 recorded the erosion of expectations within the home. From a father, this: "I would rather turn on the gas and put an end to the whole family than let my wife support me"; and from a mother: "When your husband cannot provide for the family and makes you worry so, you lose your love for him." Most tellingly, from a working son of the generation that came of age in the Depression: "I remind [my parents] who makes the money. They don't say much. They just take it, that's all. *I'm* not the one on relief" (Degler 333; emphasis in the original).

2. Jonathan Harris writes: "Within New Deal discourse in general and that of the Federal Art Project in particular, the concept of 'citizenship' took on a special meaning and value. The Federal Art Project adopted the term 'citizen' and the notion of 'citizenship' (along with its synonym 'the people') as central elements of the national-popular ideology of the New Deal" (9). While I do not mean to suggest that Cather would have sympathized with the New Deal's ideological appropriation of citizenship, I do argue that, consciously or not, she participated in and contributed to a national psychology of citizenship.

3. This is not to deny that Cather set herself apart from her times; in the prefatory note to *Not Under Forty*, she calls herself "backward," consigning herself to "yesterday's seven thousand years." And her critics on the left agreed. In 1937 Lionel Trilling dismissed Cather as an artist content to escape to the "ideals of a vanished time in weary response to weariness." He attributed Cather's malaise to "an exacerbated sense of personal isolation [coming] from the narrowing of life to the individual's sensitivities, with the resulting loss of the objectivity that can draw strength from seeking the causes of things" (154).

4. In describing the black homespace, bell hooks writes: "Historically, African-American people believed that the construction of a homeplace, however fragile and tenuous (the slave hut, the wooden shack), had a radical political dimension. Despite the brutality of racial apartheid, of domination, one's homeplace was the one site where one could freely confront the issue of humanization, where one could resist. Black women resisted by making homes where all black people could strive to be subjects, not objects, where we could be affirmed in our minds and hearts despite poverty, hardship, and deprivation, where we could restore to ourselves the dignity denied us on the outside world" (42).

5. Cather may not have fully known the metaphorical value of Englishness to black culture; nevertheless, in her imagination of Till's Anglophilia, she touches on what Genevieve Fabre calls "an important site of memory for the black community." Fabre continues: "England, at the time of the revolutionary war, had promised black loyalists freedom, whereas by contrast, the American republic often betrayed black patriots; in the 1830s England also provided more official support to the abolitionist movement, offering it a broader international forum and an audience as well as institutional and financial help. England, which only a few decades earlier had been, in many patriotic speeches, presented as the perfidious despotic tyrant/enslaver of America, was now held up as a moral example of 'humility and honest repentance' for the United States. A country that 'still clung to the doctrine of the Divine Rights of Kings' was nevertheless ahead of the American republic" (82, 83).

Whites Playing in the Dark

Southern Conversation in Willa Cather's
Sapphira and the Slave Girl

ROSEANNE V. CAMACHO

Sapphire, if you are old enough to recall, is that strong black female voice, a memory right out of your childhood and the wildly popular radio days of *Amos 'n' Andy*. Willa Cather wrote *Sapphira and the Slave Girl* in those days, just when Sapphire became, as one radio historian has put it, a "generic folk term among African Americans for a domineering wife" (Ely 208). The radio Sapphire was scripted by Charles Correll and Freeman Gosden, whites who began their careers in blackface comedy and created *Amos 'n' Andy* in the tradition Toni Morrison calls "playing in the dark," that is, to "imagine an Africanist other" (Morrison 16).

Wife of the Kingfish on *Amos 'n' Andy*, Sapphire stands close in historical proximity to Cather's Sapphira as a dominating wife—an intelligent, extremely competent, independent, and wrong-headed woman. They seem to share a straightforward participation in the neo-Freudian representation of dominant women as shrill, controlling, and counterproductive. As creations of white imaginations, however, they are linked historically in yet another way. In the "dark" of the radio, listeners could not see that white actors voiced black characters in this contemporary minstrel show or realize that the voice of Sapphire was in fact that of the first African American actor on *Amos 'n' Andy*, Ernestine Wade. She nevertheless read a white-scripted program that paralleled Cather's last novel in the sense that Cather's southern connection, made explicit in the novel, invokes southern racial discourse of this period, in which a white speaker is authorized to speak on behalf of southern blacks, a privilege whites clung to long after slavery, indeed one that needed no articulation until after the Civil War. From T. S. Stribling's *Birthright* (1922), DuBose Heyward's *Porgy* (1925), and Julia Peterkin's *Sister Scarlet Mary* (1928) to the full canon of the Southern Renaissance, white, pre–civil rights, twentieth-century southern writing speaks compellingly in a kind of literary blackface, a classic southern presumption of voice not just to create black characters but to remind us how black has been meaningful in its relation to white. Cather voluntarily positions this late novel *Sapphira and the Slave Girl* where her writing career had specifically not been identified, in the thick of regional (North/South) politics of race in the 1930s and 1940s. And by configuring the novel to imply even moderate criticism of southern racism, Cather situates herself among southern white contemporaries who were testing the limits of their privileged voices at the very moment they appeared to break with southern racial practice.

The presumptions of southern voice are recounted by Toni Morrison's essay on Cather in *Playing in the Dark: Whiteness and the Literary Imagination*, where she claims Cather's character Till is part of a plot out of Cather's control: "Consider the pressures exerted by the subject: the need to portray the faithful slave; the compelling attraction of exploring the possibilities of one woman's absolute power over the body of another woman; confrontation with an uncontested assumption of the sexual availability of black females; the need to make credible the bottomless devotion of the person on whom Sapphira is totally dependent. It is after all *hers*, this slave woman's body, in a way that her own invalid flesh is not. These fictional demands stretch to breaking all narrative coherence" (23).

The notion of the author of *Beloved* assessing the silent black mother Till is chilling. Yet one could just as easily argue that Cather's narrative is as much overdetermined as out of control, for in either case, the rupture or distortion is race-inflicted. Demands on southern-identified narratives of the 1930s and 1940s were severe in proportion to the need for maintaining a racial status quo in the face of impending change. *Sapphira and the Slave Girl*, published in 1940 at the end of Cather's career, negotiates between a southern speaker's long-standing pressure to be at least technically loyal and the gathering momentum of white liberalism (always a race-identified term in the South) generated by journalistic and academic writing as well as the legal process. Sociologists like Howard Odum at the University of North Carolina and journalists such as Jonathan Daniels in Raleigh, North Carolina, Virginius Dabney in Richmond, Virginia, and many others across the South began new conversations about region and race that presumed an intelligent white southern readership, one that could be persuaded to progressive change, a kind of humanization of segregation, which nearly all white liberals avoided in head-on confrontation and conceded would not disappear in their lifetimes. In her autobiography, *The Making of a Southerner* (1946), Katharine Du Pre Lumpkin chronicles events in the first decades of the twentieth century that portended racial change, and even though she finishes the book with segregation fully and legally in force, she testifies, "To be sure, institutions would not melt away as could old attitudes of mind. But if human hands and brains had made them, they could refashion them again" (229). Southern white liberals in these decades prior to wider national attention of the 1950s and 1960s wrote as if change could come from within, as if the South would not again have to submit to "outsiders." These speakers were southern-identified, claiming to be loyal to and critical of the South at the same time, "tiptoeing and whispering," as John Egerton describes it in one chapter of his history of this period, *Speak*

Now against the Day: The Generation before the Civil Rights Movement in the South (1994). Whites had so meticulously negotiated their positions of criticism to exist within the demands of southern authenticity that they were left with little to no leeway to ally themselves with others, "too full of doubt that they could accomplish more as an integrated force for social change than as rival factions of true believers in their own righteousness" (Egerton 573). Southern speech, whether spoken or read as social science, fiction, autobiography, or news, was subject to the same pressures and governance of this powerful conversation. The characters Rachel and Till in their relation to Sapphira register the demands of this historical moment, in which Cather can still imagine the African American "other" circumscribed within an all-southern conversation that cautiously critiques a southern way of life without being disloyal.

The imperatives of writing narratives of the South were not lightly taken in Cather's generation of white southerners. One of the widely read texts of that period and since, Wilbur J. Cash's *The Mind of the South* (1941) describes the challenge facing any southern intellectual in the 1930s seeking to depart from or to sidestep what Cash calls "the savage ideal" of maintaining southern racial practice, for as many Souths as there were from the Piedmont to Lake Pontchartrain, Cash maintains there was also a unified South. The coherence or "mind of the South" lay in the rigidity and at the same time endless adaptability of racial practices. For all the flaws in his social history, Cash's book dramatizes the early-twentieth-century writer's need for a discursive space, still southern-identified, from which to disavow or deconstruct Lost Cause and New South ideologies, the former for romanticizing racial superiority and the latter for claiming to ignore it. Writers as varied as Allen Tate, Katharine Du Pre Lumpkin, and Margaret Mitchell recycle similar codes to southern worth that leverage the space from which to speak: the southern yeoman as a common-man hero, family "stock" as the site of common personality traits, the land as a ritualized and familial resource, and the woman manager in the male's absence.

Even though Tate and Mitchell support the racial status quo while Lumpkin and Cash question it, these same southern qualities are the currency of loyalty—a loyalty that was the price of authoritative and performative speech in southern discourse and outside of which southerners would be recognized as "traitors." From the turn of the century when academics Andrew Sledd and John Spencer Bassett were driven off their respective campuses of Emory and Trinity Colleges for complaining of racism and lynchings, and writer George Washington Cable fled the South for expressing not only the validity of Negro civil rights but the necessity of a national conversation about race issues, writers in the twentieth century were likely to fear this label and its consequences enough to negotiate ways around it (Clayton 77–78, 84–89).

Cather's use, then, of the autobiographical "I" in her final novel's signed postscript grants her text a southern genealogy with ensuing consequences. The novel's plot poses questions already present as the South approached midcentury. Where is/was the greatness of the American South? And the corollary, when/how will this region fulfill its part in the American revolutionary promise of freedom and justice? Cather's novel, as Morrison indicates, writes modestly on these questions, offering what Cather desires, "a *safe* participation . . . in justice" (*Playing* 28). Nancy escapes rape in a plot that might have been written by a nineteenth-century reformer and rendered no longer controversial by the passage of time. The novel's plot of racial justice may be "safely" conceded, but the novel's treatment of gender opens considerations of a plot more conflicted and contemporary to the 1940s. By writing *Sapphira* as southern-identified, Cather begs the questions above on America, race, and region and at the same time, as Morrison points out in a different essay, provides an "encounter with very real, pressing historical forces and the contradictions inherent in them as they came to be experienced by writers" (*Jazz* 36).

The pressing historical forces here are gendered as well as racialized. Thus in 1940, Sapphira's dominance rereads not only the cruel mistress role of a nineteenth-century plot, not only a problematized strong woman of the twentieth century, but both of them together—a character whose "unnatural" authority over the slaves and her husband characterizes the South itself, like Sapphira, as not only the old order sick and dying but as a body feminized in a popular psychoanalytical critique of strong-minded women, indicating (whether black Sapphire or white Sapphira) an unnatural order of things.

Henry, her non-southern husband, is a similar combination of historical contradictions: the Enlightenment scale of the mill house he manages, "very much on the pattern of Mount Vernon," projects a romantically simple picture of slavery, where the slave Sampson with the powerful name defers his freedom for a classically simple and honest life.[1] Henry, a man of rational conscience who equally reveres his marriage as a contract and his wife's slaves as property, is ennobled on one hand by the colonial Virginian associations created by Sapphira and diminished by his subjection to her status on the other. As a couple, Sapphira and Henry plot a genderized history of the South's legendary qualities, many of which do the work of justifying their benevolent style of slavery. Their ability to create an ordered and comfortable domestic space works to represent slavery in a generally good light and enacts the ideology of reciprocal obligations as the social and economic glue of families and communities. Slaves are owned by masters, who in turn are "enslaved" by their heavy obligations to protect and govern properly. However, like the memories of "Sweet Home" in Morrison's *Beloved*, slavery under the best of circumstances—some of which are found in Cather's Back Creek—calls even more attention, through rejection, to its fundamental offense of owning people.

The proslavery arguments favorably inscribed in both Sapphira's and Henry's characters would have been co-opted in their support of segregation at the time Cather writes and would continue to be familiar to southern apologists. Cather's Sapphira as matriarch is in fact closer to a contemporary apology for segregation than slavery primarily because of her neo-Freudian characterization. Freud's psychoanalytical theories had been widely disseminated by 1940 when, according to Mari Jo Buhle's recent study *Feminism and Its Discontents: A Century of Struggle with Psychoanalysis*, Freudian revisionists shifted their attention away from biology and toward cultural and environmental influences to account for not only individual psychic health but the psychic health of society as a whole (85–124). By appropriating the neo-Freudian claim that social ills are attributable to the "imbalance" of women dominating, Cather allows Sapphira's ability to dominate and her strong character in the pain and limitations of illness to signify more accurately a troubled South of Cather's time rather than antebellum days. In addition, adjustments made between Sapphira's aristocratic Virginia heritage and life in Back Creek parallel those made in the contemporary and widely discussed agrarian manifesto of *I'll Take My Stand* (1930), in which "Twelve Southerners" defend and valorize southern yeomen as opposed to the planter class. The defense of Sapphira's modest life with a very limited number of slaves similarly does not depend on painting a rosier than necessary picture of antebellum days. At the same time, the agrarians rejected and railed against a northern industrialization that included "all blandishments of such fine words as Progressive, Liberal and Forward-looking" as outside threats to the more "stable" and "leisurely" ways of the South, in the same sense that Sapphira's inability to marry at least her social equal suggests that her dominance may be disruptive of a more desirable order to southern life (Ransom 6). In either case, the referent of "the southern way of life," defined primarily as "other" than northern, assumes mythic yet normalized qualities to be defended from the assaults of modernity contained in economic forces and changing gender roles.

Indeed, all the relations of the women characters of the novel, not so "safely" inscribed as racial justice, provide an even more modern and conflicted link to Cather's present. The multiple mother-daughter pairs, the agency of the women, and finally Cather's girlchild all represent gender intersections in this novel with the more familiar regional (racial) questions of the period. All of the women characters are related, either literally or as southerners. This "family"-making quality of slavery lays the foundation of the character of Till, who is described as a Dodderidge first and naturally, while a mother only accidentally. Morrison calls her silence the breaking point of Cather's plot, and argues that Cather is "dreaming and redreaming her problematic relationship with her own mother" in this the end of her writing career (28). Yet if one is reading *Sapphira* as the workings of white southern identification and speech in 1940, then without considering the possibilities of personal connections, the mother-daughter pairs should suggest a significant relationship to the southern historical context.

Sapphira and Rachel, for example, invert the chronology of women's history: Sapphira the modern, phallic mother and Rachel the softened version of an abolitionist. Together they suggest generations of southern women who could get things done, from the plantation mistresses with all-encompassing obligations to the members of the Association of Southern Women for the Prevention of Lynching, white women who, although much later than African American women, did finally organize in the 1920s to prevent lynching, much in the same way that Rachel prevents mountain violence and Nancy's rape—by righteously putting a body in the way. Sapphira's instrumentality in saving at least one of her granddaughters from fever and Rachel's agency in chaperoning Nancy to the underground railroad are related in southern women's history as they dwarf Henry to inaction and his cautiously arranged contribution of money toward saving Nancy. In these two agencies as historical, Rachel is the older and more affirmed while Sapphira is the more recent and negatively portrayed. This almost anachronistic quality of Rachel in comparison to her neo-Freudian, more "modern" mother, Sapphira, is what gives the novel what Morrison calls the "shape and feel of a tale written or experienced much earlier," since it is Rachel's will that prevails (*Playing* 20).

The juxtaposition of the phallic mother with a nineteenth-century reformer daughter may seem an odd combination, but it can be found exactly at this time in the writing and career of Lillian Smith, a southern white liberal, editor, and novelist who was perhaps the first white southerner outside the Communist Party to attack segregation directly and in print in 1942 (Smith, *South Today* 7–30, 34–42). In her novel *Strange Fruit* (1944), the southern white woman is represented as a repressive phallic mother who succeeds in forcing her son to conform with conventional racial praxis and whose rebellious daughter, more modern than Rachel, proves no match for her mother, who knows and inevitably effects her children's proper social place. Smith's own political stance, developed in antisegregationist writing over two decades, both models Rachel and critiques Sapphira. In *Killers of the Dream* (1949) Smith claims that white women's child-rearing practices and collaboration with religion in the South helped ensure the cultural reproduction of white supremacy. Her analysis of white southern women, like Cather's writing of Sapphira, negotiates a sympathy with southern readers in criticism that could still be called southern and could be read from "within" southern discourse from an authentic speaker. At the same time, Smith's model for political activism is an older model of woman as moral conscience, a model informed by her family's Methodism, by the example of her oldest sister, who became a missionary in China, by firsthand observation as she taught music in a missionary school (also in China) in the early 1920s, and by women's work in the post–World War I interracial and anti-lynching movement. About the time of *Brown v. Board of Education* in 1954, Smith published a small book, *Now Is the Time*, which, in addition to outlining her thoughts on the history and dynamics of race, prescribes proper and new "manners" between white and black in a chang-ing South ("The Simple, Undramatic Things We Can All Do"), modeling the practical approach to conversion practiced by students in the Student Volunteer Movement of the early twentieth century, committed to evan-gelizing the world in one generation (82; Hunter 46–49). And although Smith adamantly put distance between herself and what she saw as the lack of critical intelligence in organized churchwomen's activities, she also felt strongly even in the 1960s that white southern women, along with the youth who were already joining the civil rights movement, should be at the forefront of racial change.

This mix of the moral power of a nineteenth-century woman, armed with a contemporary neo-Freudian analysis, parallels Cather's Rachel and Sapphira, not in the sense that Cather was arguing radical or even specific social change but that Cather, by entering into the southern conversation, negotiates her way with some of the same tools of gender assessment avail-able and attractive to Smith. The image of a phallic mother proved a potent way for Smith to characterize southern racial relations as unhealthy for whites as well as blacks, and though Cather's Sapphira is more sympatheti-cally drawn than Smith's neo-Freudian characterization of a mother, Sap-phira's pathology is clearly connected to her absolute control over others. Although Cather and Smith in this regard can be seen to negotiate their southern status as speakers, their common characterization of problematic mothers and daughters projected onto southern racial practices was not at all a typical mode of analysis, and the attraction of Cather and Smith to the dynamics of women in generations and communities suggests a fruitful dis-cussion beyond this one.

Along with phallic white mothers, Cather and Smith write parallel black women who are silenced by loyalty. Among the central characters of Smith's best-selling novel *Strange Fruit* is the beautiful and intelligent Nonnie, who like Till and Nancy is helpless and/or speechless against white racism. Nonnie is indeed an elegant nonentity, defined by her bond to a white character; as Till is loyal to Sapphira's family, Nonnie is in love with a white man. The overdetermination of black women as characters like Nonnie and Till marks the limits (silence) of southern blackface or "playing in the dark." The characters are paralyzed by their loyalties and caught in contradictions to which the novels are blind, given the white southern racial discourse they practice. Till and Nonnie, who is pregnant and abandoned by her child's white father, are precisely the opposite of radio's womanish Sapphire. In her essay "Mama's Baby, Papa's Maybe: An American Grammar Book," Hortense Spillers describes black Sapphire as "the monstrosity (of a female with the potential to 'name')" and argues that "actually *claiming* the monstrosity" of Sapphire "might rewrite after all a radically different text for a female empowerment" (480). Such an empowerment does not exist for Smith's Nonnie, Cather's Sapphira, her slave girl Nancy, or Till—who most of all in her silence asks when, *till when* must we wait, who bears a name that speaks clearly to Cather's white contemporaries. Yet Cather does name and claim the "monstrosity" of white Sapphira just by retrieving and rewriting her Virginia heritage. The reconciliation between the estranged white mother and daughter, echoed twenty-five years later in Nancy's return to Till, is filled with the rhetoric of home, as Henry comments that Rachel's return would prove that "Sometimes keeping people in their place is being good to them," words that can both concede acceptance of as well as resist entirely Rachel's strategy for justice (268). Whether Cather is reworking a relationship with her own mother or the South as "other," or both, Sapphira is the site of both praise and blame. As a strong and independent woman, Sapphira still affirms the South's power to conserve the past as surely as radio's Sapphire affirms the black woman's power to resist. The threat of rape, however, is more easily resisted in Cather's text than are the silences and conflicts between women. Sapphira and Rachel, women who have the power to act without the approval of husbands who are weakened or dead, do not have the capacity to create a revolutionizing union. Cather's novel leaves Till and Nancy disconnected for their adult lives and Sapphira and Rachel split on race, reconciled only in the prospect of death.

Cather's signed postscript, which follows an epilogue, "unmasks" her connection to the fiction as surely as it secures her southern credentials within this same discourse. Her self-reference not only is sufficient to her identification but foreshadows the examples of Wilbur Cash and Lillian Smith, who soon follow, in 1941 and 1949, respectively. Their books *The Mind of the South* and *Killers of the Dream* have been read as autobiographical/confessional writing, even though neither text admits more than the slightest autobiographical detail. Each, however, notes one anecdote of racial significance. Smith tells the story of an orphaned child taken in by her parents who, when the church ladies found she was black, was swiftly removed. Smith's anecdote begins her book at a point when she questioned

her authoritative parents and provides access to the critique elaborated in
the book's essays (*Killers of the Dream* 15–31). Cash's self-reference is far
more removed, a very unassuming connection bracketed in parentheses,
hundreds of pages into the text, where he admits that he has himself heard
university men bragging of helping roast a Negro (311). Each event is presented as autobiography, a mere detail, but significant and sufficient in establishing an "authentic" speaker in southern discourse.

Cather no doubt could have written this historical novel without a postscript and left her readers to speculate how she saw herself and her Virginia
memories connected to the details of the narrative. As a writer in this process, Cather, whose writing was then identified strongly with other places
and other times, appears to be backing her way out of this novel on the
South, shifting from the omniscient third-person narrative to the first-
person epilogue, and then to what might appear a trivial addendum about
the proper spelling of local names. Cather may indeed have worried about
"spelling" the story right, since she had left the South long ago. Or she
might have worried because an increasingly problematic system of segregation that intertwined politics, class, and culture was still in place in the
South, a system that linked race and gender in a way related to but different
from the rest of the country. Her postscript, unlike the autobiographical
anecdotes of Smith and Cash, does not specifically name race. She names
and disclaims, crediting her parents as the source of names she has taken as
points for fictive departures. Yet the postscript follows closely on the same
page as "The End" of the epilogue, which in contrast is not only its own
chapter but its own book—book 9, "Nancy's Return (Epilogue—Twenty-
five years later)." The epilogue is filled with tailored endings, happy recon-
ciliations, and the prevailing of common sense: the Civil War comes and
goes, with neighbors on both sides remaining friendly; Martin Colbert gets
his just deserts by dying in the war, and the neighborhood, to its credit, is
glad; Henry Colbert dies working in his fields; Miss Sapphy reconciles with
her daughter and granddaughter and dies in her chair, by the table prepared
for proper tea.

The source of this information for the child narrator is not her parents
but "inarticulate" Till. Till closes the book not only defending Sapphira's
image but chiding her for even coming to Back Creek ("where nobody was
anybody much") and refusing to live like the "lady" she truly was (295).
Till outpaces Sapphira in loyalty to southern status in the epilogue, a sum-
mation of the statically and pleasantly neat relations of the book's characters across the color line. Significantly, the epilogue is the only chapter
presented in the narrative "I" of the child informed by Till. If Nancy's
flight indicates the coming split of the Civil War, the story of her return
pulls Cather's southern generation into the narration, firsthand. Cather's

postscript does not claim to be the narrating child, but at a minimum the child signifies her generation's connections to the Civil War and antebellum era, a generation that had ample opportunity to know and listen to those who were enslaved perhaps as often as those who fought in the war. Cather gives the final scene to the assimilated memories of a valued and critically loyal slave. At the same time, the listening, now speaking child represents Cather's own southern negotiation, situated between the outrages of history in which the novel participates and childhood memories of absolute loyalty. Like *Sapphira and the Slave Girl*'s place in Cather's career, the child does not appear until the very end. Yet in all southern narratives, as Lillian Smith so eloquently points out in *Killers of the Dream*, racial lessons are already embedded in first awareness, and the children signify the process.

Amos 'n' Andy's Sapphire no doubt generated hearty laughs from both white and black radio audiences in the 1930s and 1940s, for wives too much in control effectively parody the persistent cultural norm. A black Sapphire naming and claiming her own "monstrosity" for resistance, as Spillers argues, constitutes another script, not ready for national broadcast. Yet claiming the relationship—to image and play in the dark—between Sapphira and her slaves Nancy and Till, was still as much Cather's privilege in 1940 as it was Reverend Atticus G. Haygood's, Southern Methodist and President of Emory College, to claim in 1896 that "the [white] people of the South will yet prove themselves to be, of all people in the world, the fittest to deal with this very difficult and delicate race-problem" (17–18). Cather's biographer once called *Sapphira* nostalgic in its "evocation of place" (Woodress 254). However, since white and specifically southern privileges of the past extend fully into Cather's present, the reading of this novel today evokes a not so nostalgic period in which Cather's final negotiations of a difficult regional and personal past take shape in the language of a pre–civil rights time, overdetermined by race and conflicted by gender.

Note

1. Willa Cather, *Sapphira and the Slave Girl* (New York: Alfred A. Knopf, 1940), 20. All further citations are to this edition.

"A Kind of Family Feeling about Nancy"

Race and the Hidden Threat of Incest in *Sapphira and the Slave Girl*

MAKO YOSHIKAWA

What is Willa Cather's relationship to blackness? To arrive at a resolution to this much-discussed issue,[1] I will take what may at first seem a somewhat circuitous route: namely, an exploration of an unacknowledged threat of incest in *Sapphira and the Slave Girl*. In this novel, Nancy, a beautiful mulatto and the slave girl of the title, is desired by her owner, Henry Colbert, and his nephew Martin. She is the daughter of Till by an unidentified white man, and very early on, even before we learn who Till is, the story confronts us with the possibility that Nancy is kin to the Colberts. Sapphira, Henry's wife, tells him that "[people hereabouts] surely talked when black Till bore a yellow child, after two of your brothers had been hanging around here so much. Some fixed it on Jacob, and some on Guy. Perhaps you have a kind of family feeling about Nancy?" (8–9). Henry quickly refutes this suggestion: "You know well enough, Sapphira, it was that painter from Baltimore" (9). Yet rumors of a biological connection between the Colberts and Nancy never quite vanish from the text, surfacing uneasily in different contexts, and so leaving open the possibility that Nancy, the slave, is related to the Colberts, with their white blood flowing through her. And this leads in turn to an even more astonishing possibility: that Henry and Martin Colbert, in desiring the mulatto Nancy, are respectively and incestuously lusting after a niece and a half sister.

The notion of incest is essential to my reading of Cather's representation of race because I will be arguing here that a preoccupation with incest is directly related to a preoccupation with another transgression, the taboo of interracial sex. As critics such as Hortense Spillers have noted (130), twentieth-century African American writers have revealed a singular interest in the subject of incest, with Ralph Ellison, Toni Morrison, Maya Angelou, Gayl Jones, Alice Walker, and Carolivia Herron all tackling the subject in their work.[2] Furthermore, the incest theme figures prominently in southern literature: William Faulkner of course springs to mind, while Dorothy Allison is another writer of the region who has focused on the subject.[3] Why does this theme recur so often in these literary traditions? Why are these two different groups—one linked by skin color, the other by region—drawn so strongly to the subject of incest; what about the taboo compels, fascinates, and even obsesses them?

The key to these writers' preoccupation with incest lies in the connection between the taboos of incest and interracial sex: the transgressions are two sides of the same coin, with the currency in question being an anxiety about blood. In other words, a horror of miscegenation can trigger a romance with incest. Thus in texts of the American South, it is the white characters' desire for racial purity, their need to police their racial borders and their eagerness to avoid pollution by alien bloodlines, that propels them toward incest. So a man marries his cousin rather than risk "tainting" his children with mixed blood—incest in this context functioning as a prophylaxis against the contamination of miscegenation. Ironically enough, this prophylaxis produces a contamination of another kind, and so the obverse of this argument holds true as well: in many texts of the American South, characters seek out members of a different race in an effort to remove themselves from the attraction of the familiar, or the familial.[4]

According to this line of logic, the taboos of incest and interracial sex are mutually exclusive, with each transgression preempting the occurrence of the other. Yet in Faulkner's *Absalom, Absalom!* the threat of both impulses is embodied in the figure of Bon, the erstwhile fiancé of Judith Sutpen, as the plot unfolds to reveal that he is at once her half brother and a man of racially mixed heritage. In *Sapphira and the Slave Girl,* Nancy is like Bon in that she is at once racially other and familially familiar: as a black woman and a possible niece, she is a doubly forbidden object of desire to Henry Colbert. On one hand, the fact that Nancy encapsulates these two threats can be read as the result of a historical phenomenon, specifically related to a common practice of slave owners: if one slave family were kept by one white family for generations, it is possible that because of the frequency of rape the slaves would come to share the same blood as that of their owners, their lineage as well as their histories steadily intertwining. In becoming what I would describe as a shadow family to their owners, the slaves inevitably begin to constitute an incestuous threat to their masters, for if a master rapes a slave woman, and if his son later repeats this act with her daughter, then the son could very well be having intercourse with his half sister. Still, given the fact that *Absalom, Absalom!* also features a mulatto character who is racially different and familially intimate, it seems acutely unsatisfying to read Nancy's embodiment of these two taboos as the mere consequence of this historical practice.

Merrill Maguire Skaggs has written insightfully on the idea of "Thefts and Conversation" between Cather and Faulkner, arguing that "at the end of her life Cather engaged Faulkner in a significant literary conversation" (115). The work that she focuses on is "Before Breakfast," one of Cather's last short stories, but I would broach the possibility that this conversation extends to *Sapphira* as well. That both Faulkner's and Cather's mulattos pose the double threat of incest and miscegenation invites and even cries out for speculation about an intertextual connection between the two texts. Yet I would underscore that I only *broach* the possibility of a conversation occurring in this instance, for in Cather's novel, in direct opposition to Faulkner's, the threat of incest remains wholly unrecognized. Cather's characters do not at any point display an anxiety about, or even an aware-ness of, the fact that the disaster they only narrowly avert—the rape of Nancy by Martin—may involve no less than the violation of the taboo of incest. Even more strikingly, the narrative does not at all gesture to the specter of incest haunting its pages: "incest" is not a word that is found within the text.

So why, then, this silence? Cather's repression of the topic of incest is very far from being a case of what has been called "the artful omissions and gaps in [Cather's] narrative" (qtd. in Urgo 73)—what critics have variously praised as vacuoles or pictures or withholding. *Sapphira* has taken a drub-bing in academic circles for its awkward ending,[5] and I would submit that a large part of the problem is that the omissions and gaps are, in this case, anything but artful; the novel would have been stronger if Cather had, at the end of the narrative, given flesh to the specter of incest. Edith Lewis observes that "[Cather] could have written two or three *Sapphiras* out of her material; and in fact she did write, in her first draft, twice as much as she used. She always said it was what she left out that counted" (183). It is tempting to speculate that an acknowledgment of the incest subtext is part of what she discarded in an earlier draft; after all, Lewis also tells us that when writing a novel, Cather "always left out its real theme, the secret theme at its heart, the thing that gave it its reason for being" (155). Yet while gauging an author's level of awareness is always a loaded enterprise, I would suggest that while Cather may have deliberately chosen to leave out an acknowledgment of the incest theme, it is equally likely that she herself missed the full ramifications of Henry's having "a kind of family feeling about Nancy"—that she was as blind to the threat of incest as her characters are. Moreover, if she did intend for the hints of incest to surface within her novel, she did so in a fashion so elliptical as to be noteworthy in itself.

Cather's cagey approach to the subject of incest is rooted in her compli-cated relationship with race. At the end of *Sapphira*, the narrator, in an abrupt shift to the first person, plants herself on the scene as a girl witness-ing the triumphant return of the former slave Nancy, and it has been docu-mented that this final scene is based on a much-cherished memory from Cather's childhood (Woodress 26). By thus inserting herself into the text,

Cather highlights her own family's complicity in the story—an emphasis that has telling implications. Not only has she concocted a scenario in which her great-grandfather lusts after a slave girl who may be his niece, but she suggested the possibility that the black slave girl is kin to her; she has left the door open for the reader to wonder whether she and Nancy have the same blood flowing through their veins. Although she does not capitalize on the explosive potential of this subtext, allowing it to remain implicit and unacknowledged in the text, that it is present even in this form is startling. Cather's ambiguous portrait of the exact nature of Nancy's relationship to the Colberts, as well as the impulse that led her to raise the possibility of kinship in the first place, can be traced to the same source: her ambivalence about blackness.

In *Sapphira and the Slave Girl*, "blackness" is synonymous with blankness. This equivalence is, indeed, fundamental to the presence and also the suppression of the possibility of incest in the novel, since the mystery surrounding Nancy's paternity hinges on the insubstantiality of the character of her mother, Till. It is impossible to know whether Nancy and Martin share a father, because Till is the only one who might possibly offer a clue on the subject, and she is not talking. In the words of Morrison, "Because Till's loyalty to and responsibility for her mistress is so primary, it never occurs *and need not occur* to Sapphira that Till might be hurt or alarmed by the violence planned for her only child" (21; emphasis added). Till never comes forward to proclaim incest as possibility or even fact, not even to protect her daughter.

Cather presents Till as a slave, first and foremost, and a mother only by default. To the reader as well as to the other characters, she appears to lack human warmth; Nancy does not even consider complaining to her of Martin's sexual harassment, turning instead to Sapphira's sympathetic daughter, Rachel. Till's silence about herself and her single-minded devotion to Sapphira render her an illegible and ultimately illogical character, and her emotional vacuity complicates not only her maternal but also her sexual identity in provocatively problematic ways. To ensure that Till places her duty to her mistress above all others, she has been married to old Jefferson, a "capon man" who is unable to have children. She accepts this marriage "with perfect dignity," and the narrator emphasizes how her appetites and emotions have been subsumed under her desire for position: "Perhaps the strongest desire of her life was to be 'respectable and well-placed.' . . . It was the right thing for a parlour maid and lady's maid to be always presentable and trim of figure. . . . Some years after she had moved her belongings from her attic chamber in the big house over to Jeff's cabin, the Cuban painter came along to do the portraits. He was a long while doing them" (72–73). Coyly evasive in its representation of Till's sexuality, this passage admits a wide range of readings. In that "long while" the Cuban painter spent at the Colberts' house, there is room for the one grand romance of Till's life—the one time in which she selfishly indulged her sensuality and fulfilled her appetites. Yet we also cannot omit the possibility that she was raped by the painter, Henry's two brothers, or all of the above. In that it functions to deny her explicit sexual agency, the illegibility of her character seems incompatible with sensuality, with the result that her body is an object of neither desire nor interest in the text.

Nancy, by contrast, is sexually irresistible to the white characters precisely because of her blankness. So passive is she that we are led to suspect she is intentionally being characterized as forgettable. As Morrison speculates, "Rendered voiceless, a cipher, a perfect victim, Nancy runs the risk of losing the reader's interest" (24); but while she is right to posit this blankness as a flaw in the text, I would also contend that this lack of a voice and a distinctive personality is where the force of black sexuality resides in the novel. Nancy's character is not of interest because it has been upstaged by her body, which rivets the white characters' attention and consumes their thoughts. Indeed, if her character and voice were any stronger, her body could not contain the others' sexual fantasies to the extent that it does.

In order to see how Nancy's body accommodates the myriad desires of others, we need first to see that a significant motif in this text involves the substitution of one black body for another, and that this exchange is made possible by the black characters' lack of individuation. Tormented by jealousy and paranoid enough to suspect that her husband is spending his nights with Nancy, Sapphira forces the slave girl to sleep on the floor outside her door, but even this preventative measure cannot completely quell her fears: "Hours ago she had heard Nancy put her straw tick outside the door. But was she there now? Perhaps she did not always sleep there. A substitute?—There were four young coloured girls, not counting Bluebell, who might easily take Nancy's place on that pallet. Very likely they did take her place, and everyone knew it" (106). The notion of the black characters' essentially interchangeable nature also undergirds the obliqueness with which Henry and Sapphira speak to each other. It has been said that Cather's narratives are characterized by the strategy of indirection;[6] these two characters certainly converse in code. Over tea, Henry complains to his wife about the slave girl Bluebell's cleaning:

> "Don't try any more Bluebell on me!"
> His wife replied with her most ladylike laugh. . . . "Poor Bluebell! Is she never to have a chance to learn? Why are you so set against her?"
> "I can't abide her, or anything about her. If there is one nigger on the place I could thrash with my own hands, it's that Bluebell!"

> The Mistress threw up her hands; this time she laughed so heartily
> that the rings on her fingers glittered. It was a treat to hear her hus-
> band break out like this. (52)

Henry and Sapphira are figured as self-contained, but this brief conversation holds within it two emotional explosions—his outbreak of anger
and her burst of laughter. The high emotional pitch in this exchange becomes understandable when we realize through Sapphira's perspective that
within this discussion, black bodies are being substituted for one another
once again. As the narrator tells us, after Henry leaves, "[Sapphira] smiled
faintly; it occurred to her that when they were talking about Bluebell, both
she and Henry had been thinking all the while about Nancy. How much,
she wondered, did each wish to conceal from the other?" (53). This constant and deliberate confusion of Nancy's body with Bluebell's crucially
functions to deny Nancy a space and an identity of her own in the text.

It is also critical to note that Nancy's plasticity is not limited in racial
terms; she can be confused with white as well as black characters. Bluebell
is, after all, similar to her in color and age, and so the fact that Henry identifies Nancy with the character of Mercy in *Pilgrim's Progress*—a white
woman, and an icon of Christianity to boot—comes as much more of a
shock. The blankness of Nancy's character is such that her body serves as
a canvas on which the white characters can map *any* of their fantasies, religious as well as sexual. This ability to project a range of desires upon her is
predicated on a certain myopia: the white characters cannot allow themselves to see Nancy as an individuated being because to do so would mean
that they could no longer see her as Henry's lover, Sapphira's betrayer,
Martin's victim, or Bunyan's Christian icon. It is as a result of this willed
blindness, too, that the notion that she is related to the white characters, as
well as the attendant threat of incest, remains shrouded from them and, by
extension, from the reader as well.

I have discussed why Cather's portrayal of blackness as blankness leads
to the occlusion of incest in the text. But equally interesting is the question
of why Cather is drawn to blackness. As Cynthia Griffin Wolff suggests,
the text pairs the figure of the narrator, the young girl who makes what is
little more than a cameo appearance at the end of the drama, with Nancy,
the oppressed and harassed slave girl who figures so prominently throughout: they are "undeniable doubles, the two women—the two children that
they once had been—reflecting one another" (228). Why does Cather end
her novel with a portrait of a doubling that cuts across racial lines; why
does she intimate the possibility, even, of a familial relationship between
these two figures? The most obvious conclusion here is the most important: implying a kinship between the character of "Willa" and the character of Nancy enables Cather to suggest a connection between herself

and blackness. She is identifying herself, on some level, with the black heroine of her novel; I would go even further and say that her hints at a shared lineage between herself and Nancy attest to a yearning for blackness on her part. That Cather blurs racial borderlines in this manner does not extricate her from the charges of racism that have been leveled at her—in fact, quite the contrary. Her attitudes toward race, as evidenced in this text, are highly complex and ambiguous: it is vital to remember here that for all that she drops teasing hints about the possibility of an interracial kinship, she never explicitly alludes to it.

A remarkable story told by Edith Lewis, Cather's longtime companion, reveals what an identification with blackness signifies for Cather. As Lewis tells us, "[Cather] told once of a old judge who came to call at Willowshade, and who began stroking her curls and talking to her in the playful platitudes one addressed to little girls—and of how she horrified her mother by breaking out suddenly: 'I'se a dang'ous nigger, I is!'" (13). This anecdote is enlightening on several accounts, with Lewis, for one, hazarding that it indicates that Cather began rebelling against the constrictions of her gender and position at an unusually tender age. Yet what I would stress most about this account is that the young Cather—and, by extension, the older Cather who remembers and tells the story—is performing a peculiar identification with the black race. The key word here is *performing*: she is acting out blackness, just as some years later, she would famously act out masculinity by chopping off her hair, dressing up as a man, and taking on the sobriquet of "William Cather." She is, moreover, performing blackness for the same reason that she cross-dresses: the performance of blackness, like the performance of masculinity, is a subversive act, allowing her to break free of conventions. Another, perhaps more telling way to put this idea is to say that blackness offers her a means of escape. Joseph Urgo avers that Cather epitomizes the restless spirit of this country's writers, and I would complicate this compelling argument to suggest that we can read blackness as yet another space of refuge in her psychic geography. Just as Cather's white characters use Nancy as a screen on which to project their sexual fantasies, so too does Cather use the character of Nancy as an embodiment of her own personal fantasies of flight. And just as she envisions a familial relationship between herself and the character of Nancy in order to associate herself with an image of flight, so too did the child Cather take on the role of a "dang'ous nigger" to escape—in this case, from the unwanted attentions foisted upon her by virtue of her age and position.

The blankness of Nancy's character and the silent passivity of Till stand in marked contrast to, and exist in uneasy tension with, the almost wistful admiration with which Willa regards the prodigal Nancy, and the story of young Cather seeking shelter in a black identity. Yet Cather's deeply con-flicted attitudes toward blackness are, finally, most poignantly betrayed by the incest plot hidden in the novel. For while we could take the presence of the incest threat in *Sapphira* as a warning against the dangers of interracial mixing, of too much intimacy between master and slave, we could also interpret the buried narrative as a cautionary tale about the dangers of refusing to acknowledge the kinship between blacks and whites. This second reading may seem a stretch, not least because the characters never do acknowledge the possibility of such a kinship, and the rape is averted nonetheless. Still, the threading of the threat of incest through the narrative at least gives us the option of believing that *Sapphira* contains a condemnation—albeit one both subtle and halfhearted—of the racist ideals and practices that constitute the institution of slavery.

Notes

1. See Toni Morrison's groundbreaking first chapter in *Playing in the Dark*. Although this article is limited to considerations of Cather's depiction of African American characters, her attitudes toward Native Americans and Jews have also productively come under scrutiny by critics such as Elizabeth Ammons, Guy Reynolds, and Loretta Wasserman. For a nuanced, thoughtful exploration of the development of an American cultural identity in light of Cather's representation of Jews and Native Americans in *The Professor's House*, see Walter Benn Michael's "The Vanishing American."

2. See Katie Roiphe, "Making the Incest Scene," *Harper's*, Nov. 1995, 65–71. I refer to Ellison's *Invisible Man*, Morrison's *The Bluest Eye*, Angelou's *I Know Why the Caged Bird Sings*, Jones's *Corregidora*, Walker's *The Color Purple* and the story "The Child Who Favored Daughter," and Herron's *Thereafter Johnnie*.

3. Allison's *Bastard out of Carolina* and the story "Don't Tell Me You Don't Know"; Faulkner's *The Sound and the Fury* as well as *Absalom, Absalom!*.

4. Werner Sollors makes a similar point in chapter 10 of *Neither Black nor White yet Both*. I would further note that these ideas on incest apply to class as well as racial anxiety. Frank Whigham, in an excellent reading of John Webster's *The Duchess of Malfi*, reaches similar conclusions regarding the way in which a preoccupation with class distinctions surfaces as incestuous desire.

5. Mostly it is criticized for the way in which it straddles the line between fact and fiction. Whereas Skaggs, for one, argues that Cather is "deliberately refus[ing] to maintain the formalist boundaries between writer narrative persona, and characters" (*After the World Broke* 180), I would echo Susan J. Rosowski's comments about the uneasiness with which the novel's last chapter does so (see "Willa Cather's American Gothic").

6. See Jo Ann Middleton, who examines Cather's cryptic style and a range of critical receptions thereof (51–65).

"The Dangerous Journey"

Toni Morrison's Reading of *Sapphira and the Slave Girl*

MARILYN MOBLEY McKENZIE

> . . . if I am not what I've been told I am, then it means that *you're* not what you thought *you* were *either*! And that is the crisis. . . . What is upsetting the country is a sense of its own identity. If, for example, one managed to change the curriculum in all the schools so that Negroes learned more about themselves and their real contributions to this culture, you would be liberating not only Negroes, you'd be liberating white people who know nothing about their own history. And the reason is that if you are compelled to lie about one aspect of anybody's history, you must lie about it all.
> — James Baldwin, "A Talk to Teachers"

> . . . only a persistent, rigorous, and informed critique of whiteness could really determine what forces of denial, fear, and competition are responsible for creating fundamental gaps between professed political commitment to eradicating racism and the participation in the construction of a discourse on race that perpetuates racial domination.
> — bell hooks, *Yearning: Race, Gender, and Cultural Politics*

> . . . it occurred to her that when they were talking about Bluebell, both she and Henry had been thinking all the while about Nancy. How much, she wondered, did each wish to conceal from the other?
> — Willa Cather, *Sapphira and the Slave Girl*

The title of this essay is taken from the phrase that ends Toni Morrison's first chapter, "Black Matters," in her now famous book of literary criticism, *Playing in the Dark: Whiteness and the Literary Imagination*. At the end of that first essay, Morrison acknowledges that at the end of Willa Cather's literary career she returned to her childhood and, though she "may not have arrived safely, like Nancy[,] . . . to her credit she did undertake the dangerous journey" (Morrison, *Playing* 28). As I reread these words, I was reminded of President Bill Clinton's recent attempt to take on race as a serious subject of national discourse. While some of his critics have viewed his decision as a waste of political time and energy, others have praised him for at least venturing down this dangerous road of domestic discomfort. As

I considered Willa Cather's southern connections, I was also reminded of an incident in my "Foundations of African American Literature" course in which a student shared an excerpt from a late 1950s Virginia elementary school textbook chapter called "How the Negroes Lived under Slavery."[1] One portion of this excerpt reads as follows:

> A strong tie existed between slave and master because each was dependent on the other. The master needed the work and loyalty of his slaves. The slave was dependent for all his needs on the master. . . . The regard that master and slaves had for each other made plantation life happy and prosperous. . . . Life among the Negroes of Virginia in slavery times was generally happy. . . . They were not so unhappy as some Northerners thought they were, nor were they so happy as some Southerners claimed. The Negroes had their problems and their troubles. But they were not worried by the furious arguments going on between Northerners and Southerners over what should be done with them. In fact, they paid little attention to these arguments. (Simkins et al., 373, 376)

I have referred to this excerpt on several occasions since my student first shared it with me because it illustrates so well the literary and cultural concerns that prompted Morrison to comment on *Sapphira and the Slave Girl*. It has particular relevance as an example of the kind of national discourse into which *Sapphira* entered when it was published in 1940. It inscribes the prevailing collective memory that has been constructed and that still circulates in the minds of many Americans, and it articulates the very narrative of nationhood that prompted Morrison to advocate for a new kind of literary-cultural criticism to transform the study of American literature. My thesis, then, is that Morrison's reading of *Sapphira and the Slave Girl* is a critique of Cather's narrative of American history, of America's narrative of its history, and of the ways in which both perpetuate myths about the racialized and gendered identities from which it has been difficult for the nation to extricate itself.

Although I was familiar with Cather's work and had quoted her preface to Sarah Orne Jewett's *Country of the Pointed Firs* in my own cross-cultural study of Jewett and Morrison, I did not become acquainted with *Sapphira and the Slave Girl* until I read *Playing in the Dark*.[2] I immediately understood this to be a significant piece of criticism because, unlike other critics and scholars who were negating the value of the canon, Morrison was advocating not only that we read and reread canonical authors but that we reenter the texts of several white authors from a New Critical perspective, and that we do so to interrogate constructions of whiteness. Ironically, it could be argued that Cather has not been considered a canonical author and that Morrison's discussion of her last novel actually resurrected attention to it and possibly introduced some readers to Cather for the first time. What is most important, however, is that she asks us to read how whiteness is constructed imaginatively around, through, and against blackness. In addition, Morrison asks us to consider how critics have replicated Cather's own narrative shortcomings by ignoring the novel altogether or by denying its connections to American racial politics. My first order of business, therefore, was to discern just how critics overlooked or omitted *Sapphira*, how often they focused on the landscape, the beauty of southern tradition, fond memories of Virginia, and the like without really taking on what Morrison calls the novel's "Africanist presence" (*Playing* 5). What I discovered is a range of readings, from James Woodress's *Willa Cather: Her Life and Art* (New York: Pegasus, 1970) to Deborah Carlin's *Cather, Canon, and the Politics of Reading* (1992). Of course, there is scholarship both before and after these two artificial signposts I have constructed, but I single them out to suggest that in 1992, the year Morrison wrote *Playing in the Dark*, a paradigm shift in Cather criticism was taking place. While early critics like Woodress sought signs of coherence between Cather's life and art in a way that is characteristic of New Criticism, Carlin argues that the book exposes the "collective memory of culture" (157). But if Cather's novel is a dangerous journey into the nation's collective memory, then Morrison's reading of that novel is in many ways more dangerous, for it calls into question the author's narrative intentions and exposes the contradictions between art and life, between the writer's expressed intentions and the ways in which language betrays and deconstructs those intentions to tell a national narrative America has not yet allowed itself to read or hear. And in acknowledging that she would take on an American Africanist project, rather than an African Americanist project, Morrison challenges the "substitute language in which issues are encoded, foreclosing open debate" (*Playing* 9). She adds that "the habit of ignoring race is understood to be a graceful, even generous, liberal gesture" and that it has become equally well established, when racial discourse is undertaken at all, to focus on the victim of racism rather than on "the impact of racism on those who perpetuate it" (*Playing* 9–10, 11). Her project, then, could be interpreted as exposing what Cather as well as many of her critics seemed to have concealed even from themselves in their representation of race. As critic Elizabeth Ammons argues in *Conflicting Stories: American Women Writers at the Turn into the Twentieth Century*, "Cather's racism and ethnocentricity undercut her attempt to create art somehow outside of or at least in dialog with inherited, conventional, white western narrative tradition" (134).

In using *Sapphira and the Slave Girl* as a test case for her critical hypothesis, Morrison calls attention to three forms of fugitive status in the novel, all of which point to a "breakdown in the logic and machinery of plot construction [that] implies the powerful impact that race has on narrative—

and on narrative strategy" (*Playing* 25). First, the narrative is in flight from itself, because it withholds the name of the slave girl until four pages into the novel. Incidentally, by the time the reader learns Nancy's name, she has also had to journey through several examples of the familiar nomenclature of the day for the Africanist presence—"coloured man," "old black man," "nigger," and "darky." Withholding her name from the title reifies her in the object position and maintains the established hierarchy of power relations, in which the white woman's identity is dependent on the black woman's otherness. As Morrison says, to have named Nancy in the title would have called attention to this interdependent identity. My own reading of this omission is that it commodifies blackness in a way that replicates the institution of enslavement, at the very moment it could be argued that Cather wanted to engage in a critique of the peculiar institution.

The second form of fugitive status in the novel is Nancy's slave narrative from bondage to freedom. This narrative is precipitated, of course, by Sapphira's need to believe her husband, Henry, has sexual intentions toward her beautiful mulatto slave. Her plot to bring her husband's licentious nephew onto the plantation to seduce Nancy is foiled by her own daughter, Rachel Blake, who helps Nancy escape. But, as Morrison points out, this slave narrative does not ring true for two reasons. Nancy has to be persuaded to seek her own freedom, and as Morrison indicates, Cather seems imaginatively ill-equipped to see Nancy in a context of concerned community or family. Thus, we as readers are unprepared for her mother's sudden interest in her, since Cather has substituted a mother's concern for her daughter with the overriding loyalty of a slave mother to her mistress. Put another way, nothing in the culture or national consciousness in the late 1930s enabled Cather to create a requisite interior life for her slave girl or her mother.

Morrison suggests that the third form of fugitive status is the novel's plot. It runs away from its status as fiction and retreats instead into nonfiction or memoir. In our own contemporary moment we might argue that the narrative desire in the text is toward creative nonfiction. But that is the subject for another essay. My point here is that the narrative voice shifts from third person to first person at a peculiar moment that places Cather at the center of her own narrative. In book 9, "Nancy's Return," the reader suddenly must negotiate this shift in narrative voice and accommodate it to the author's need to tidy up the conclusion. Yet as Morrison brilliantly points out, "things go awry. As often happens, characters make claims, impose demands of imaginative accountability over and above the author's will to contain them" (*Playing* 28). It could be argued that what goes awry is Cather's desire to tell Nancy Till's story. At the point that the novel places Cather herself in the narrative at the age of "something over five years old . . . in [her] mother's bed" and focuses on her own mother attending to her needs, rather than on the reunion between the black slave mother and daughter, the narrative undermines its original narrative intentions and reproduces the cultural pattern of white appropriation of black bodies and black voices. In a sense, then, the slave daughter's story has been a conduit for the author to inscribe her own story. As Ammons pointedly observes: "Appearing to celebrate black and white women's shared struggle, and particularly the heroism of a black women, the novel in fact steals the black woman's story to give it to white women. At the center of the book is not Nancy Till as an agent in her own drama but Sapphira, Rachel, and vicariously Willa Cather as Nancy's manipulator. . . . Nancy, like all the other black characters in the book, is vague, stereotypic, a pawn. She exists not as a fictionalized human being but as Cather's solipsistic, racist projection" (135).

But I would like to offer a slightly different reading of the text here. I agree that Cather's "strategy of containment," to borrow a phrase from Fredric Jameson, to negotiate the subject of enslavement is an unwieldy narrative device.[3] But I believe the fact that the novel ends with Till—that Till, in other words, gets the last word—must be interrogated more carefully. If the shift to the autobiographical voice was meant as a strategy of containment, then putting the final words of the text in the mouth of Till is another strategy of containment because, in a novel that could have been an honest critique of slavery, Cather simply reproduces the popular political ideology of the day through the victims of the institution. We are back to the point of the Fairfax County, Virginia, textbook: the master (and in this case the mistress) and slave have benefited equally from slavery. Till is represented at the end of the novel as the keeper of the community history, as the storyteller who passed down this troubled but generally happy tale of slavery that the author both owns and disowns. The author recalls: "In summer Till used to take me across the meadow to the Colbert graveyard to put flowers on the graves. Each time she talked to me about the people buried there, she was sure to remember something she had not happened to tell me before. Her stories about the Master and Mistress were never mere repetitions, but grew more and more into a complete picture of those two persons" (292). What Till's words represent is the racialized Africanist presence being used to reify the myth of domestic tranquility of the southern past. Thus, while the journey may have been a dangerous one into Virginia history that no one wanted to discuss, the outcome of the journey is certainly less than satisfying. But the question might be asked, less satisfying to whom? How do white readers read this novel? How do black readers read it? What differences obtain between white women and black women who read this novel of a relationship that is historically contested terrain for scholars and critics alike, even among feminist readers? As I ask my students, what is invested in our readings of any given text anyway? Why did Cather read slavery, Virginia, her own family life, the way she did? What enabled and disabled Morrison's acceptance of Cather's reading of her own life?

For critics who need to read the Cather canon as one of coherence between art and life, *Sapphira* may be satisfying. For critics who need to focus on the Virginia landscape and Cather's desire to return to her home site at the end of her life for the fictional materials that reside there, then this novel might be satisfying. But for readers who choose the discourse of universality to discuss the American literary canon, Toni Morrison suggests they will have to perform an intellectual and imaginative feat: "A criticism that needs to insist that literature is not only 'universal' but also 'race-free' risks lobotomizing that literature, and diminishes both the art and the artist" (*Playing* 12).

Willa Cather's rendering of enslavement invokes the Africanist presence only to leave much of the unspeakable matters unspoken and the power relations and their attendant racial ideologies that sustain them intact. Ultimately, the novel rings true because of the larger untruths that go unchallenged. Those of us in African American literature are familiar with the critique of an earlier moment in literary criticism, when to focus on race was disparaged as a form of politicizing the text. Now that cultural studies is the accepted terrain into which literary studies has ventured, a reading of the text that did not account for its obvious political dimensions of race, gender, and class would be considered remiss. Morrison's reading of *Sapphira* is designed to enable us to see what happens when an author has not fully interrogated "what racial ideology" had done "to the mind, imagination, and behavior of the masters" (*Playing* 12). More importantly, she has offered us a critical map for our own dangerous journeys into the racialized past, which have not only shaped the national literature and our attitudes toward it but are also shaping the nation itself at this late-twentieth-century cultural moment. Morrison's reading of Cather's last novel tells us that our mission, should we choose to accept it, is to reread so-called white American canonical texts, this time with a goal of understanding how they inscribe *us*, the racial other. Such rereadings will render the journey no less dangerous, but they will inspire a dialogue that is sorely needed both in and outside of the academy.

Notes

1. A student gave me this excerpt in 1991 and indicated that the text was still in use at that time. It is no longer used, according to sources at the Virginia Historical Society. I do know

from conversations with students who have taken my course in subsequent years that such an excerpt is one familiar to many Virginia residents who were educated in public and private institutions in the state.

2. I quote from Cather's preface to Sarah Orne Jewett's *Country of the Pointed Firs*, in which she says, "Miss Jewett wrote of people who grew out of the soil." See Marilyn Sanders Mobley, *Folk Roots and Mythic Wings in Sarah Orne Jewett and Toni Morrison: The Cultural Function of Narrative* (Baton Rouge: Louisiana State University Press, 1991), 7.

3. Fredric Jameson, *The Political Unconscious: Narrative as a Socially Symbolic Act* (Ithaca: Cornell University Press, 1891), 52–53.

Race, Labor, and Domesticity in Cather's *Sapphira and the Slave Girl*

GAYLE WALD

In *Sapphira and the Slave Girl*, Cather's title character, Sapphira Colbert, an upper-class white invalid woman so ordinarily imperturbable that she dies sitting alone and "upright in her chair," experiences a crisis of composure only once (294). This emergency occurs—as such emergencies so often do—in the middle of the night, as Sapphira restlessly contemplates the significance of a moment of sympathetic communion that she has earlier witnessed between her husband, Henry, a plain-spoken miller, and their young "slave girl" Nancy. Her anxiety over a sexual liaison between Nancy and her husband having been fanned by the sight of a light burning in the "miller's room," Sapphira finds herself in the grip of a sudden and irrepressible panic. She sits still, writes Cather, "scarcely breathing, overcome by dread. The thought of being befooled, hoodwinked in any way was unendurable to her. There were candles on her dressing-table, but she had no way to light them. Her throat was dry and seemed closed up. She felt afraid to call aloud, afraid to take a full breath. A faintness was coming over her. She put out her hand and resolutely rang her clapper bell" (106). Nancy's prompt appearance at this signal of her mistress's need "wakens" the old woman from her "dream of disaster," restoring Sapphira's sense of domestic and sexual order; and yet, eager to save face, she fakes a medical emergency, directing Nancy to summon her mother, Till, and to prepare a hot bath for her swollen knees and ankles. When this task is completed and Sapphira is returned to her bed, "Till begged to stay with her," Cather writes. "But Mrs. Colbert, comforted by the promptness and sympathy of her servants, thanked them both, said the pain was gone now, and she would sleep better alone" (107).

I begin with this image of a sleepless and frightened white woman being "comforted" in the middle of the night by two black female slaves because it succinctly illustrates the intersecting issues of domesticity, labor, race, and sexuality that I take to be crucial aspects of the "southern" context of Cather's novel. How are we to understand the nature of the "comfort" that Till provides as she is awakened from her own dreams—the content of which lies beyond the novel's imagination—to "rhythmically stroke" her mistress's legs? What sorts of needs and desires resound so loudly that they require Sapphira to pantomime illness, and of what significance is Sapphira's "faking it" in light of the performance of solicitousness that such feigned urgency requires of Till and Nancy? How might Till's and Nancy's labor have a curative or restorative effect on Sapphira's wounded authority, the actual medicinal value of their work notwithstanding? How, in other words, does Sapphira manage to retain and even bolster her authority in a moment in which she is structurally infantilized, in need of assurance that her "dream of disaster" is merely a dream?

Cather's novel would have us believe that the importance of this scene lies in its dramatization of Sapphira's momentary surrender to a passionate irrationality born of sexual jealousy regarding the youthful and attractive Nancy. Such illustration of Sapphira's vulnerability earns her the reader's sympathy, establishing narrative point of view and recuperating Sapphira as a likeable character, despite her domineering, emotionally indifferent ways with slaves and family members alike. According to this narrative logic, our appreciation of Sapphira's "strong heart" (294) is enhanced by our insight into the ways she can be wounded. Following the examples set by Sapphira's husband and their daughter, Rachel Blake, in other words, we as readers are encouraged to grow to love, or at least to admire, Sapphira because of her dignified way of enduring in the face of adversity, real or imagined.

It is for this reason, perhaps, that Cather uses the scene of Sapphira's momentary loss of self-control as a sort of negative, or antithetical, foreshadowing of the scene of Sapphira's death at the novel's end. Whereas Sapphira's capitulation to fear and desire is what renders the earlier scene remarkable, in her dying moment it is Sapphira's restraint—her decision *not* to seek comfort in the company and attentiveness of her "servants," as she calls them—that distinguishes and putatively ennobles her. As the narrator puts it, "Though her bell was beside her, she had not rung it" (294).

Building on the structural parallels between these two scenes, I want to suggest an alternative reading, one that argues that the "crisis" depicted in the first is less a crisis of sexual jealousy (as most of the published work on the novel suggests) than a crisis of labor—indeed, of precisely those forms of sexualized and racialized labor that are meant to secure Sapphira's bodily and domestic "comfort" as a white woman. In particular, I want to point briefly to some of the ways that Cather's novel enlists a series of contradictions in its representation of black women's labor: labor that is at once visible and invisible, embodied and disembodied, both dependent upon and constitutive of "race" itself.

In so doing, I am situating my comments in the context of work done by Hortense Spillers, who has demonstrated in her essay "Mama's Baby, Papa's Maybe: An American Grammar Book" how American slavery, from the time of its inception in the seventeenth century, was organized around a series of paradoxes concerning the representation of black women's gender and sexuality.[1] Within what Spillers calls the "grammar" of American slavery—a term that she uses to refer to the myriad practices, rhetorics, and beliefs that operated, under slavery, under the sign of "race"—black women's gender and sexuality became sites of social, cultural, and legal contradiction. In a process that Spillers argues began with the Middle Passage, or the transport of human cargo from Africa to "New World" destinations, black female slaves in the United States were simultaneously denied status as "women" and exploited for their reproductive capacity—most notoriously in the border states, where the breeding of slave labor was a well-known and profitable enterprise. Black women were, additionally, both denied legal and social agency as "mothers" (insofar as they could not claim their children as their "own" to prevent them from being bought and sold) and accorded negative authority as the progenitors of offspring who were required to inherit their mothers' slave condition, whatever the status of their paternity.

Sapphira and the Slave Girl illustrates some of the issues that Spillers touches on in its depiction of mother-daughter plots that variously enact themes of loss (as in the case of Rachel and her daughter Betty, who dies of diphtheria), reconciliation (as in the case of Sapphira and Rachel), or reunion (as in the case of Till and Nancy). Yet I am more concerned here with the ways in which the novel imagines black women's labor to be the site of a different contradiction, one in which it is naturalized—that is, imagined outside of the coercive context of slavery, and thereby paradoxically figured as the product of their *own* desire and volition. Henry Colbert, for example, conceives of Nancy's work around the mill as part of the natural, pastoral order of things. Imagining that she tends the miller's room primarily because of her "love and delicate feeling" for him, Henry takes special pleasure in picturing Nancy as disembodied and "free from care, like the flowers and the birds" (67). Similarly, during her visit to the African woman known as Old Jezebel, Sapphira reminisces about "how we used to get up early and rake over the new flower-beds and transplant before it got hot" (87), her rhetoric not only falsely equating their work but nostalgically papering over the fact that they have not equally reaped either its profits or its pleasures.

One of the effects of interpreting *Sapphira* primarily through the lens of Sapphira's sexual jealousy and vindictiveness is to render black women's labor invisible within critical discourse as well. Quite literally, once the novel is read as the story of a "Virginia lady" who is "irrationally jealous" of her "beautiful slave" (as the back cover of my Vintage paperback edition advertises), black women's labor recedes from visibility as a "context" for understanding not only the eight books that comprise the bulk of the narrative but also the autobiographical epilogue, which persists in defining Till's subjectivity in terms of her work—a gesture that is symbolically anticipated in the name "Till" itself. Indeed, what the rubric of sexualized

competition between mistress and female slave most conceals, I would argue, is the way in which the slave's—in this case, Nancy's—labor is itself
violently sexualized.

The novel accomplishes this sexualization of Nancy's labor in a variety
of ways. On the one hand, by imagining Nancy to be the object of her
husband's desire, and hence an impediment to her own domestic comfort,
Sapphira can construe Nancy's potential rape by her nephew Martin as
one aspect of a slave girl's "duty" to her mistress. Insofar as she comes to
mediate and even embody Sapphira's own desires,[2] Nancy thus performs
a kind of sexual(ized) labor *for* Sapphira, even as Sapphira imagines that it
is Nancy who renders *her* the victim of sexual one-upmanship: she imagines, as she puts it, that she is "deceived and mocked by her own servants
in her own house" (105). On the other hand, and as the scene of Sapphira's
"crisis" of composure demonstrates, her agency as a white woman derives
from her ability not merely to extract labor from black women's bodies but
to use black women to serve as compensatory, supplementary, or even pros-
thetic appendages of her own desire. Hence Sapphira plots Nancy's rape as
the expression of her own frustration at not being fully able to master either
her own body or the eroticized body of her female "servant."[3]

In short, as a white woman, Sapphira is able to exploit the expectation
that black women make their bodies available to satisfy the needs and desires of white men, and to do so as an indirect means of satisfying her own
needs and desires (desires that might here include being a privileged spectator of a rapidly unfolding drama of sexual violation of her own design).
As I have been arguing, the "rape plot" explicitly dramatizes the manner in
which Sapphira ruthlessly extracts a kind of sexualized labor from Nancy,
by acting the "pimp" to Martin's "john." Likewise, the scene of Sapphira's
nighttime crisis of composure theatricalizes labor relations between mistress and slave—relations that Cather's narrative otherwise naturalizes under the sign of the slave's, rather than the mistress's, desire. In feigning the
need to have her own body tended to in such an intimate manner, Sapphira
perhaps unwittingly creates the conditions in which we can better realize
the nature of her own habitual performance of such need, a performance
that daily secures her position within the domestic hierarchy. We can see,
as well, how Nancy's and Till's rapid dispensation of "comfort" to their
mistress constitutes a different kind of exigency (and, perhaps, a different
kind of performance), one that ironically reifies their position as "natural"
workers and caregivers.

By way of closing, I want to exploit the ambiguity in the novel's title
to examine the character of Old Jezebel, another "slave girl" in Cather's
novel. In book 3, the book named for her, Jezebel makes a brief and haunting appearance—quite literally so, since it is her narrative function to die.

Drawing upon familiar Christian tropes of reward in the hereafter, Cather would seem to be encouraging the conclusion here that death is the privileged form of agency for an enslaved black woman, who is compensated for her earthly labor in a "beautiful" funeral that doubles as an occasion for the Colberts to display their benevolence and generosity (as one of the slaves notes, the master and mistress "were more animated than usual, expressing their satisfaction that things had gone so well" [102]). But book 3 also contains the narration of Jezebel's earthly voyages, first from Guinea to Maryland, and later from the possession of Dutch planters to the possession of the Dodderidges, Sapphira's kin. Jezebel's history, which Cather lays out in dispassionate and apparently well researched detail, belies the narrative of "shared labor" that Sapphira's well-intentioned reminiscences of their work together in the (not Edenic) garden would retroactively construct. In particular, through descriptions of the process of Jezebel's "breaking in," we are offered an illustration of that process of simultaneous dehumanization and ungendering that Spillers elaborates, and which is ultimately the precondition of her construction as a laborer, still tending the garden at age eighty.

Although Cather never fully or explicitly explains the links between the two events, we may nevertheless attribute some significance to the fact that Sapphira experiences her unique moment of discomfiture on the night of Jezebel's funeral. The most obvious conclusion to be drawn is that "Old" Jezebel's death occasions Sapphira's own musings on her dwindling health. Yet whereas Jezebel, the "loyal" slave, is laid to rest in one of Sapphira's old nightgowns, it is Sapphira, helped into her own "ruffled nightgown" later that night by Till, who ironically cannot fall asleep. In particular, she cannot banish from her mind the image of her own "crippled and incapacitated" father (105), with whose bodily suffering she was previously unable to empathize. It is here, lost in the "far past," that Sapphira's mind eventually turns to the present and to Nancy.

In retrospect, Till attributes her mistress's unexpected need for bodily soothing to a chill that she imagines Sapphira has caught "waitin' out there by the graveside" (107). Imagining that Till has diagnosed Sapphira correctly, it would thus appear that Sapphira's brooding derives from some unconscious speculation sparked by the passing of the "slave girl" who also had a hand in raising her. At that very moment, as we later learn, Henry is himself being kept awake in the mill by discomfiting thoughts of Jezebel's life, and of the peculiar institution that kept this proud woman in a perpetual bondage from which she could only be emancipated in death. Who knows, as these chilling thoughts of Henry's suggest, but that the waking "dream of disaster" from which Sapphira anxiously seeks release has anything to do with the dreams and the desires of *this* slave girl?

Notes

1. Hortense Spillers, "Mama's Baby, Papa's Maybe: An American Grammar Book," *Diacritics* 17.2 (1987): 65–81.

2. For a more detailed elaboration of this argument, see Morrison, *Playing in the Dark*, 18–28.

3. Critics have noted the parallels between Cather's novel and Harriet Jacobs's *Incidents in the Life of a Slave Girl* (1861), a slave narrative that devotes an entire chapter to a description of the "jealous mistress" who demands that her "slave girl" sleep outside her bedroom door. See, for instance, Annalucia Accardo and Alessandro Portelli, "A Spy in the Enemy's Country: Domestic Slaves as Internal Foes," in *The Black Columbiad: Defining Moments in African American Literature and Culture*, ed. Werner Sollors and Maria Diedrich (Cambridge and London: Harvard UP, 1994), 77–87.

PART

3

Cather Texts in Southern Contexts

"The Pull of Race and Blood and Kindred"

Willa Cather's Southern Inheritance

LISA MARCUS

> Born theoretically white, we are permitted to pass our childhood as
> imaginary Indians, our adolescence as imaginary Negroes, and only
> then are expected to settle down to being what we really are: white
> once more.
> — Leslie Fiedler, *Waiting for the End*

Imagining the Other: Indians, Negroes, and Confederate Soldiers

Edith Lewis, Willa Cather's longtime companion, tells a now famous legend of Cather's childhood that illustrates the psychic process that Leslie
Fiedler describes—a process of consolidating white identity through momentary identifications with racialized others. A community patriarch was
visiting the Cathers' Virginia family home and made the mistake of patron-
izing the young Cather with southern parlor platitudes. Five-year-old
Willa, voicing her rebellion against the visitor's condescending attentions,
brazenly exclaimed "I'se a dang'ous nigger, I is!" This fleeting imaginary
identification with the racial other enabled the young girl to perform race
instead of surrendering to a customary *and gendered* curtsey of politeness.
As Edith Lewis tells it, "Even as a little girl she felt something smothering
in the polite, rigid social conventions of that Southern society—something factitious and unreal. If one fell in with those sentimental attitudes,
those euphuisms that went with good manners, one lost all touch with
reality, with truth of experience. If one resisted them, one became a social
rebel" (13).

The young Cather's startling ventriloquized[1] performance of blackness
reveals an urgent desire to disrupt the veneer of southern social customs and
marks her entrance into racial othering, a process that Toni Morrison, in her
compelling study *Playing in the Dark: Whiteness and the Literary Imagination*,
has called "American Africanism." "The fabrication of an Africanist persona," Morrison illustrates, "is reflexive; an extraordinary meditation on the
self; a powerful exploration of the fears and desires that reside in the writerly
conscious" (17). As Morrison explains, the Africanized "other" figures as a

symbol that allows white Americans to both project and police "matters of class, sexual license, and repression, formations and exercises of power, and meditations on ethics and accountability" (7). For Willa Cather, performing the "dangerous nigger" in the drawing room deflects the performance of gender (and sexuality) called upon by the social visit.

Cather's early penchant for destabilizing gender by performing race in the ventriloquized voice or assumed guise of the other is evidenced not only by the story Lewis relates but also in a number of photographs from Cather's youth. Portraits of the crew-cutted Cather dressed up in military garb in imitation of her Confederate uncle, or as "Hiawatha"—fully accessorized with bow and arrow—indicate her often simultaneous interest in contested subjectivities. Her childhood experiments with disguise allowed her to try on different and frequently conflicting identities.

In the "Hiawatha" portrait, taken after the young Cather gave a dramatic recitation from the famous Longfellow poem, little Willa indicates her ability to play the wild Indian without giving up her whiteness or her femininity (see figure 9.1). The bow and arrow and the extravisible cross seem to duel for attention in the photograph, and ultimately the girlish outfit and cross neutralize Cather's attempt at wildness. In fact, Morrison's suggestions about the adoption of the Africanist persona seem particularly applicable here as well. Cather's adoption of the Hiawatha costume and her public delivery of the Longfellow poem are attempts to use a racialized Native American persona to disrupt the conventions of white southern femininity. But if Leslie Fiedler is right (and I think he is), these performances are designed for white children to playfully transgress their boundaries, all the while knowing that they can reassume their whiteness when the games are over.

It is well known among Cather scholars that Cather frequently crossdressed; while conventional women wore shirtwaists, corsets, and long skirts, Cather cropped her hair in short crew-cuts and frequently wore "mannish" attire.[2] Indeed, in juvenile photographs Cather is represented in masculine suit and tie as often as she is beribboned in feminine garb. At an early age, Cather seems to have been fascinated with her body as a site of gender performance—in Judith Butler's terms, "a cultural locus of gender meanings": "Becoming a gender is an impulsive yet mindful process of interpreting a cultural reality laden with sanctions, taboos and prescriptions. The choice to assume a certain kind of body, to live or wear one's body a certain way, implies a world of already established corporeal styles" ("Variations" 131). Cather's shifting corporeal styles are interesting not only because they explore the cultural mechanisms that inform gender production but because her corporealization of gender is often racially and ethnically coded. For Cather, the performativity of gender entailed a performative racialism as well. Extending Butler's insight, I want to suggest

9.1. Willa Cather as Hiawatha. By permission of the Nebraska State Historical Society.

that, particularly in America, "becoming a gender" simultaneously entails becoming a race. Cather's body, while certainly a locus of gender meanings, is also a locus of racialized meanings, even, and perhaps especially, when she dons the Confederate garb to masquerade as her Confederate uncle. The appropriations of racial and ethnic identity revealed in Cather's gender crossing have yet to receive significant attention by her critics.[3] Neverthe-less, the stylized corporealization of herself as other—as "dang'ous nig-ger," as "Hiawatha," as Confederate soldier—dramatizes the manner in which racially "other" bodies frequently come to represent gender trans-gression for Willa Cather.

Nowhere does Cather more daringly explore the intersections of racial and sexual otherness than in her remarkable 1940 novel *Sapphira and the Slave Girl*, a text that explicitly employs "American Africanism" to expose the intricate entanglement of race, sex, and power in the antebellum South. In this novel Cather rewrites the master-slave rape story, documented his-torically and dramatized so frequently in slave narratives, by reinscribing the menacing master as a sadistic and powerful mistress. Re-marking this relationship as a threatening scenario of white female power, Cather, like other modernists,[4] wrote explicit sexuality onto the body of the black woman—for Cather, the black woman is both desired object *and* stereo-typically desiring subject. Critics of Cather who seek to claim her as a lesbian writer frequently lament that she identifies her desire for women through conventionally heterosexual relations, and always through her supposed identification with her male characters (e.g., Jim Burden of *My Ántonia*).[5] However, *Sapphira and the Slave Girl* presents an even more com-plex projection of desire. Cather not only scripts a female character who, through a surrogate, seduces a woman: she makes her authorial identifica-tion with this character explicit by entering her own text as a character in the final pages of the novel. Cather thereby metonymically aligns herself with a tyrannical southern heritage and, simultaneously, establishes a trou-bling connection between sexual and racial alterity that gets mapped out within the violent parameters of master (and mistress)/slave relations.

The South in *Sapphira* provides the staging ground for Cather's remark-able exploration of how race and gender intersect in the constitution of particular American subjectivities. For Cather, the region becomes the fo-cus of national questions about civic identity as the South comes to stand synecdochically for the nation. Cather is not frequently acknowledged as a southern writer, though she was a southerner by birth, born only eight years after the end of the Civil War in a state that had seceded from the Union. Though she is embraced as a Nebraska writer, she did not move to the Nebraska plains until she was nine, and she lived most of her life (and wrote most of her fiction) while living in the very cosmopolitan Greenwich Village. Cather's final novel, however, marks her quintessential return to origins in its Faulknerian obsession with the problems of southern inheritance. Indeed, Faulkner wrote of southern writers: "we need to talk, to tell, since oratory is our heritage" (222). Substantiating her southern roots, Cather in 1938 was drawn back to her birthplace of Back Creek Valley, Virginia. During this visit, she contemplated the stories that she had inherited from her childhood, one of which became *Sapphira and the Slave Girl*. This tale of the antebellum South is Cather's confrontation with her own genealogy, with the troubling connections between white southerners and their inherited history of slavery. Moreover, it is an account of the manifestation of white power and surveillance over black subjectivity. Along with Toni Morrison, and in contrast to most Cather scholarship,[6] I find that what compelled Cather's return to her native southern soil in her final novel was "her struggle to address an almost completely buried subject: the interdependent working of power, race and sexuality in a white woman's battle for coherence" (20).[7]

In order to understand Cather's confrontation of race and sexuality in *Sapphira*, it helps to see the novel as the culminating act of a lifelong affiliation with her southern heritage. As is particularly evident in the photograph of Cather as a Confederate soldier (the third in my trio of Cather personae), Cather's relationship to the fraught history of the American South and slavery gets played out in her performances of racial and ethnic others. Like her experiments with cross-dressing and disguise, Cather's allegiance to the South reveals her impulse to explore contradictory subjectivities. Indeed, there were significant contradictions within the southern allegiances of Cather's family. Both sides of Cather's Virginia family were Unionists, although some of their sentiments still remained with the Confederacy during the war. But Cather as a youngster very explicitly identified herself with an uncle, William Seibert Boak, who fought and died for the secessionists. Calling herself William or Willie as a child, she liked to think she was named for this uncle who died for Dixie. Cather penned a poem and a short story, both entitled "The Namesake," to honor this ancestral "hero." The conflictual nature of Cather's southern identity is illustrated in her ability to both rebelliously ventriloquize the voice of the imagined "dang'ous nigger" and proudly identify as her "namesake" the soldier for whom she wrote:

> proud it is I am to know
> In my veins there still must flow,
> There to burn and bite alway
> That proud blood.

In this poem, Cather joins most white writers of her era in mythologizing a romanticized South, in which brave Confederate youths fought and died to free the South from the imposing North and dangerous emancipated slaves (perhaps the "dang'ous niggers" she rebelliously envisioned as a child). Cather shifted and revised her allegiances a number of times until, in her final novel, she mapped out an affiliative kinship with the mythical southern mistress. Before exploring that final metamorphosis, however, I want to look at how Cather's early romance with the South is played out in "The Namesake" poem and short story.

Pledging Allegiance: Dis-membering and Re-membering National Subjectivity

Willa Cather's self-naming has been perplexing to most of her biographers. Arguing that Cather's shifting names destabilize gender and sexuality at the site of the name, Judith Butler suggests, "For women . . . propriety is achieved through having a changeable name, through the exchange of names, which means that the name is never permanent, and that the identity secured through the name is always dependent on the social exigencies of paternity and marriage. . . . Identity is secured precisely in and through the transfer of the name, the name as site of transfer or substitution, the name, then, as precisely what is always impermanent, different from itself, more than itself, the non-self-identical" (*Bodies That Matter* 153). Willa Cather, to be sure, performed her identities through her shifting names. Originally named Willela Cather after an aunt, Cather had this name erased from the family Bible and replaced with Willa. Her middle name was given as "Love" for the doctor who assisted in her birth, but she changed this too, latinizing it when she was in college to "Lova." Finally, she changed her middle name altogether to Sibert, claiming the shift was due to recognizing that her "namesake" was her uncle William Seibert Boak, a Confederate soldier killed in the war.[8] After all, Virginia Boak Cather, Willa's mother, "cherished her brother's sword, and the confederate flag," thereby keeping this secessionist namesake operative for her children (Brown and Edel 15). Willa had long been transfixed both by the surviving flag and sword and by the southern cause itself. The photograph of the young Cather, with a close-cropped masculine haircut, wearing a Civil War military cap, initialed "W. C.," indicates her identification with this uncle and his cause; whether the initials on the cap were original (perhaps a military insignia) or a monogram sewn on by Cather herself, we can recognize her explicit identification with her namesake (see figure 9.2).[9]

Cather biographer Sharon O'Brien has argued that Cather's nominal investment in her uncle was an act of maternal identification, bringing her closer to the mother who cherished the Confederate flag (110). I want to suggest, however, that his memory allowed Cather to reconstruct a romantic and particularly masculine southern genealogy. In both the poem

9.2. Willa Cather in Confederate cap. By permission of the Nebraska State Historical Society.

and story "The Namesake," Cather aligns herself with a southern citizenship that is achieved through a masculine, military initiation. Cather portrays citizenship as a homosocial union, in which the masculine subject achieves an abstract membership in the nation only by suffering a bodily dis-memberment.

Cather's poem "The Namesake" was written in 1902 and published in *April Twilights* in 1903. In a nationalistic version of the pathetic fallacy, Cather opens her poem by enlisting the trees in the Confederate cause: the "poplars sigh / Where Virginia's thousands lie." As the wistful trees sway above the buried Confederate dead, the poet finds among the "stones . . . that mark their bones" a "lad beneath the pine / Who once bore a name like mine." The subsequent story of the young soldier reveals a fascinating confusion of gender and nation. Cather's masculine gender identification is conflated with a southern militaristic patriotism:

> Ah! You lad with hair like mine,
> Sleeping by the Georgia pine,
> I'd be quick to quit the sun
> Just to help you hold your gun,
> And I'd leave my girl to share
> Your still bed of glory there.

Most critics agree that Cather's speaker is a young man with whom Cather identifies—the poem is dedicated to her maternal uncle, "W. S. B. of the 33rd, Virginia." Cather's cross-identification in this poem enables a lyrical ballad of both homosocial and nationalistic bonding; glorified death is equated with romance, linking war and eroticism. In a simultaneously homoerotic and self-annihilating desire, Cather's speaker yearns to share the soldier's "bed of glory" and help him "hold his gun." Ostensibly, this union is achieved through the speaker's renunciation of heterosexuality and of life itself—his willingness to leave his girl and embrace a patriotic death. But the punning phrase "leave my girl" also refers to Cather as author, to the fact that her masculine southern identification is achieved through leaving behind the girl in her.

In the poem's first version (1902), the story is passed on to the poet in the lines "once my mother told me" of this soldier relative; however, the lines published in 1903 read "often they have told me." [10] Cather belatedly balks at originating the story with the maternal voice: upon revision, she links the story's origins to an anonymous "they." Rather than celebrating the maternal in choosing this namesake, Cather was choosing to write herself into a masculinist, nationalist heritage and history—a history of male camaraderie and gallant heroism. At the same time, she was adopting a southern history and allegiance fraught with racial implications.

Willa Cather's second "Namesake," the short story published in 1907, complicates the southern identification dramatized in the poem. The story demonstrates, even more strikingly than the poem, Cather's identification of citizenship with a masculine, military logic of self-sacrifice. However, while the story clearly pays homage to Cather's dead Confederate uncle, she rewrites him as a Unionist, politically masking her progenitor's southern allegiance. The story is narrated by the quintessentially American Lyon Hartwell who "seemed, almost more than any other one living man, to mean all of it from ocean to ocean" (52), even though he is an expatriate artist in Paris. The tale is primarily about the genesis of his American national consciousness; he admits that his "citizenship was somewhat belated and emotional in its flowering" (54). Hartwell, like Cather, is an artist (a sculptor), whose nationalism is expressed through an artistic rendering of symbolic identification with a heroic uncle. Hartwell's most recent sculpture depicts the patriotic gore of this uncle's battlefield dismembering and death. This young uncle enlisted eagerly at fifteen; a year later, bearing his unit's flag during an advance on a fortified hill, he had his right hand and forearm shot away. Transferring the flag to his left hand, the boy kept plunging forward—as if in a Stephen Crane novel—until his left arm was blown away too, and "he fell over the wall with the flag settling about him" (60).

Hartwell hears this remarkable story when he is literally compelled to return to his family and national heritage—called home to care for a deteriorating aunt. He complains that he "could feel no sense of kinship with anything there" (59); the portrait of his boy uncle thus becomes "the only thing to which [he] could draw near, the only link with anything [he] had ever known before" (59). Hartwell is so drawn to his uncle that he searches for some relic of the dead soldier by which to know him better. A Memorial Day observance becomes for Hartwell a patriotic epiphany, triggered by his discovery in the family attic of a string of nationalist, military symbols that Cather describes in florid sentimental detail. Hartwell finds "a leather trunk with my own name stamped upon it" (61). Of course, the insignia is both his own and not his own—literally, it belonged to his soldier uncle, who proves to be his literal namesake and progenitor. Hartwell's misrecognition of the insignia tellingly foreshadows his (and Cather's) identification with the dead hero. He discovers in the chest all of the artifacts that he had been searching for to flesh out the uncle's identity, and thereby his own: clothes, exercise books, boots, riding whip, even toys emerge from the cache, as well as a dog-eared copy of *The Aeneid*, illustrated with boyish doodles of bugles, bayonets, and artillery cartridges. On the flyleaf of the book is a trio of symbols—the uncle's signature, a portrait of the Federal flag, and lines from "The Star-Spangled Banner"—explicitly marking the relationship between individual identity and national citizenship.

This moment becomes, for Hartwell, an anthem to the nation, as his Americanness is aroused. Lauren Berlant has theorized citizenship as a process in which the nation prophylactically protects the citizen while also suppressing his local historical body.[11] In Cather's logic, however, national membership requires corporal dis-memberment and dissolution. Hartwell's climax of artistic and national sympathy is depicted in terms that re-create his uncle's battlefield death:

> The experience of that night coming so overwhelmingly to a man so dead, almost rent me in pieces. It was the same feeling that artists know when we, rarely, achieve truth in our work; the feeling of union with some great force, of purpose and security, of being glad that we have lived. For the first time I felt the pull of race and blood and kindred, and felt beating within me things that had not begun with me. It was as if the earth under my feet had grasped and rooted me, and were pouring its essence into me. I sat there until the dawn of morning, and all night long my life seemed to be pouring out of me and running into the ground. (63)

Hartwell is "a man so dead" because he is alienated from his citizenship, whereas the dead uncle lives in nationalist martyrdom. Hartwell can only come alive by being emotionally "rent in pieces": his individual self bleeds out of him, "pouring out" and "running into the ground," while a new nationalist self feels "beating within" the "pull of race and blood and kindred." Hartwell dissolves as a body and becomes united with the body politic, erasing his individual self. The race and blood of the nation rubs out the individual, as the expatriate is reunited with the firm American earth. As in the "Namesake" poem, Cather conflates citizenship, death, and eroticism. This is both a procreative and annihilating moment; Hartwell's homeless spirit pours out of him like semen into the fecund spring earth, a copulation that simultaneously enriches and depletes Hartwell's national body. Again as in the poem, this moment of homoerotic bonding with a dead soldier entails dismemberment and obliteration. As Walter Benn Michaels has reminded us, Memorial Day itself was "christened" a national holiday in 1868 to commemorate the Civil War dead (32).[12] It seems no accident, then, that Hartwell's epiphanic kinship with America comes on Memorial Day.

Clearly, this narrative parallels the *April Twilights* poem's homage to the soldier uncle, and yet with one fascinating revision. As James Woodress understatedly phrases it, in the story Cather "denied her uncle his allegiance to the Confederacy, for at that time she had not lived in Virginia for twenty-four years" (31). Cather not only denies her uncle's Confederate allegiance, she crucially *rewrites* him, making him not a southerner at all but a Pennsylvanian, a Unionist with Federal fervor stirring in his blood.

Why does Cather reinvent this uncle while maintaining the genealogical narrative? Perhaps Cather, more cosmopolitan and worldly in 1907, recognized that her dedication to her dead Confederate relative was problematic. This would help to explain why, when *April Twilights* was reissued in 1923, "The Namesake" poem was cut. The "Namesake" texts represent the last time, up until her final novel, that Cather explicitly rooted her writing in the South: she would not return imaginatively to Virginia until 1937, when she began working on *Sapphira*, and by then she had quite a different allegiance to her southern ancestors. Cather is best known for her work written between these framing southern texts; both these early works and *Sapphira* are considered artistically inferior. However, I feel it is precisely when Cather confronts her southern past that she most interestingly reveals the intertwined narratives of race, gender, and nation—the "pull," as Cather put it, "of race and blood and kindred."

What do these two pieces tell us about the Cather who would later write *Sapphira and the Slave Girl*? The two "Namesake"'s function as memorial pieces—they both memorialize the Confederate South in the person of Cather's secessionist soldier uncle and, too, they memorialize a masculinist patriotism with its logic of military sacrifice. *Sapphira* is a memorial of a far different sort. A novel of homecoming and going (it was her last novel), it memorializes Cather's lush Virginia birthplace, but it pays homage to a particular story that was getting told in many different ways all over the United States—the drama of American slavery. Cather had this quintessentially American story in her blood, and it is only fitting that she exited the American literary landscape with this remarkable novel—a memorial, of sorts, to the struggle over slavery that helped to consolidate American national subjectivity.

The masculine military identification that Cather explored in both "Namesake"'s freed her, at least temporarily, from the feminized southern inheritance she rebelled against by performing the "dang'ous nigger" in the drawing room. However, Cather's celebration of a masculine patriotism in both texts, and her erasure of the Confederacy from the short story, show that she had not yet confronted the racial and gendered implications of southern womanhood. As we shall see, in Cather's last, admittedly autobiographical novel, she returned to an identification with the South—only this time she did so in her "woman's weeds." [13]

Who's the Fairest of Them All?
Or, Consolidating White Female Subjectivity

Willa Cather once said that what compelled her to write was the "bliss of entering into the very skin of another human being" (Sergeant 111).

Cather's early performative self, as I have argued, enabled her to ventriloquize "Indians, Negroes, and boys," to paraphrase Leslie Fiedler. By dressing up and thus imaginatively entering into "the very skin" of these others, the young Cather could playfully transgress the constraints of her gender. In *Sapphira and the Slave Girl*, however, the mature Cather turned finally to those very constraints in an exploration of white female subjectivity or, as Morrison puts it, "the sycophancy of white identity." Here Cather confronts white southern womanhood's implication in a system of violent domination. Through the imaginative construction of Sapphira Colbert, Cather returns to her native South in the borrowed and unflattering white skin of a woman whose crippled body is a grotesque icon of the South itself. Rather than confirm the romanticized image of the mistress as tender benefactress and nursemaid to her slaves, Cather topples this myth of benignity and exposes the domination and terror that southern mistresses could and often did wield over their slaves.

Foucault has shown us that "nothing is more material, physical, corporal, than the existence of power," both in its effects on subjected bodies and in the way it implicates and distorts those who wield power.[14] In *Sapphira*, power is embodied paradoxically in the wheelchair-bound, dropsical Sapphira Colbert, who oversees the operations of the entire plantation from her chair. Sapphira is simultaneously powerful and paralyzed: she administers a network of discipline, subjection, and surveillance that renders her slaves into what Foucault calls "docile bodies";[15] however, the very productivity of these slaves, both economic and sexual, threatens the conspicuously unproductive and asexual Sapphira. Sapphira's bloated and pale body imprisons a seemingly muted sexuality, but her passions erupt suddenly over a nubile female slave who is simultaneously an object of her mistress' envy, rage, and jealousy. Even though disciplinary power is frequently invisible, as Foucault reminds us, it simultaneously "imposes on those whom it subjects a compulsory visibility" (187). Whereas the crippled body of the southern mistress seems an unlikely repository of disciplinary power or articulated desire, in contrast, the sexuality of Sapphira's pubescent slave Nancy is all too visible and readily available for consumption. In the climactic moment of Cather's novel, Sapphira asserts her "invisible" power through a surrogate, choreographing her slave's seduction. Before we get to that critical scene, however, I would like to map out the scenario at the Back Creek plantation where this remarkable American drama unfolds.

An aristocratic planter's daughter, Sapphira Colbert nominates herself the "master" of the plantation, sitting "in her crude invalid's chair as if it were a seat of privilege" (15), while her husband is merely "the miller." Engaging in numerous acts of surveillance that allow her invisibly to mastermind the plantation slavocracy, she ensures that those who serve her remain visible under her ever watchful gaze. The initial drama of the novel begins when Sapphira, through her expert surveillance, witnesses her cook, "Fat Lizzie," teasing Nancy about her custom of arranging fresh-picked flowers in Henry Colbert's mill room. However, Nancy, as Morrison puts it, is "pure to the point of vapidity"—although the "miller" lives down at the mill and only occasionally visits his wife's bedroom. To forestall any sexual liaison between her husband and slave, Sapphira commands Nancy to move her sleeping pallet from her parent's hut to the hallway just outside of her mistress's room.

The fear that her husband is sexually involved with her slave provokes Sapphira to suggest selling Nancy. The miller (who doesn't believe in sell-ing human bodies, though he does oversee his wife's slave property) stub-bornly refuses, because he sees Nancy as a guileless ingenue. Of course, this provides additional fodder for Sapphira's idle mind. As the narrator snidely comments, "such speculations were mildly amusing for a woman who did not read a great deal, and who had to sit in a chair all day" (54). Eventually, Sapphira's speculations become so pronounced that one night she fantasizes that Nancy and the miller are indeed sexually involved, and this produces "strange alarms and suspicions" in her mind. Sapphira can survey the miller's cabin from her bedroom window, and seeing his light on she thinks, "the thought of being befooled, hoodwinked in any way was unendurable to her." In order to confirm her power—that it is Nancy and not she who is sexually vulnerable—Sapphira feigns illness and calls Nancy from her damp pallet just outside of the bedroom. When Nancy, abruptly stolen from her sleep, rushes into the bedchamber, Sapphira sighs in relief: "Her shattered, treacherous house"—and by association, her very body— "stood safe about her again" (106–7).

Nancy has reached a crisis in her "coming of age," a crisis that nine-teenth-century slave narrator Harriet Jacobs aptly termed a "perilous pas-sage in the slave girl's life" (383). Though Nancy cannot understand why the mistress has turned on her, Nancy's increasingly sexual black body has become intolerable to the mistress who is imprisoned within her own white flesh. As a system, slavery rendered southern white women's bodies sanc-tified icons of chastity while ideologically constructing the black woman's body a prostituted vessel for reproducing both labor and desire.[16] Indeed, the mistress's very chastity depended upon her slave's sexual availability. Cather exaggerates this dynamic by making Sapphira a cripple to iconic chastity, while Nancy displays a stereotypical blooming, fresh sexuality.

The slave girl's "perilous passage," and the rage it provokes in the white mistress, is charted brilliantly in Jacobs's 1861 narrative, *Incidents in the Life of a Slave Girl*. When Linda Brent (Jacobs's pseudonym) turns fifteen, she enters "a sad epoch in the life of a slave girl"; haunted by her lasciv-ious master, Linda asks, "Where could I turn for protection? No matter whether the slave girl be as black as ebony or as fair as her mistress, [i]n either case, there is no shadow of law to protect her from insult, from violence, or even from death; all these are inflicted by fiends who bear the shape of men. The mistress, who ought to protect the helpless victim, has no other feelings toward her than jealousy and rage" (361). The mistress in Jacobs's narrative proves to be an "incarnate fiend" (349) whose slaves "were the objects of her constant suspicion and malevolence" (364). Like Sapphira, Mrs. Flint "watched her husband with unceasing vigilance" (364). Upon discovering her husband's designs on Linda Brent, Mrs. Flint, much like Sapphira, moves Linda to sleep within her purview. Now it is the mistress who haunts the slave girl with nightly visits: "Sometimes I woke up, and found her bending over me. At other times she whispered in my ear, as though it was her husband who was speaking to me, and listened to hear what I would answer. If she startled me, on such occasions she would glide stealthily away; and the next morning she would tell me I had been talking in my sleep, and ask who I was talking to. At last, I began to be fearful for my life" (366). These night visits take on the drama of seductive pursuit: Mrs. Flint ventriloquizes the voice of the desiring master as she astonishingly tries to provoke Linda to respond sexually and thus expose her guilt. Instead, the ghostly visits provoke fear and dis-ease: "You can imagine, better than I can describe, what an unpleasant sensation it must produce to wake up in the dead of night and find a jealous woman bending over you" (367). As this moment in Jacobs's narrative makes clear, the mistress's jealous rage is expressed in a sexually provocative manner—sleeping in the mistress's anteroom, the slave girl is safe from the master, yet is she safe from his wife? [17]

Southern diarist Mary Chesnut was quick to defend her Confederate countrywomen, portraying them as "the purest women God ever made," who were trapped in a "monstrous system" of sexual concubinage perpetrated by their husbands.[18] However, Chesnut ignored not only the degree to which this white aristocratic female purity depended on the economic and sexual productivity of slave women but also the certainty that many white mistresses participated directly in the systems of domination that threatened slave women. Accounts abound of mistresses who beat and tortured their slaves; in one grisly incident, a mistress decapitated a slave woman's baby after discovering the baby was the master's progeny.[19] As Jacobs notes, mistresses, rather than sympathizing with the victimized slave women, were frequently violent and cruel, especially when they saw their slaves as potential sexual threats. In *Sapphira*, Cather's callous mistress reacts to her slave's threatening sexuality on at least two levels: Sapphira is visibly disturbed at the possibility of a sexual liaison between her husband and her slave; yet in her attempt to control her conflicting passions toward

Nancy, Sapphira projects herself into the role of the predatory master that she appropriates from her husband.

Sapphira's tangle of envy, jealousy, and rage for Nancy is evidenced in a mirror scene that takes place early in the novel. Nancy arranges Sapphira's hair, coiling it into a complicated braid with "wavy wings" that frame her forehead like a crown, while Sapphira "sit[s] at a dressing table before a gilt mirror, a white combing cloth about her shoulders" (13). As Sapphira gazes into the mirror, she sees, not her withered white flesh, but the lovely slave girl who is creating her "toilet." Glancing into the mirror and seeing Nancy instead of herself, Sapphira enviously projects herself into the sexually vital body of her slave. When this fantasy is disrupted by the sound of approaching footsteps, Sapphira beats Nancy with the hairbrush.[20] Able to express herself only within the master-slave paradigm, Sapphira reconfirms her power over Nancy's docile body by punishing her slave for representing a sexual vitality that has abandoned Sapphira's own body. Like the evil queen in "Snow White," Sapphira must constantly reaffirm that she is "the fairest of them all." In fact, the ethnic aspects of snow-whiteness in the Grimms' fairy tale become magnified when transposed to an antebellum American setting. When Sapphira looks into the mirror to confirm her "fairness," what she discovers is that Nancy, her beguiling black slave, is "fairer" than her white mistress—which results in a crisis of subjectivity for the white woman. The mirror is symbolically cracked in this momentary identification, disrupting rather than consolidating the mistress's identity. Much like the evil stepmother, Sapphira can only regain her access to whiteness and femininity—combined in the notion of "fairness"—through punishing the one whose body challenges her dominion.

This scene, it seems to me, demystifies the "cult of true (white) womanhood":[21] of course Sapphira's asexuality depends upon Nancy's sexual availability—and Sapphira resents this. Nevertheless, Cather complicates this familiar relationship: not only is Sapphira envious of Nancy—desiring to be as sexually captivating as Nancy is—but her nightly surveillance of Nancy echoes the more menacing seductive overtones of Mrs. Flint's predations in Jacobs's narrative. The imaginative possession of Nancy's body that Sapphira achieves, if only for a moment, in the mirror scene is actualized later in the novel, when Sapphira projects her desire through a surrogate seducer.

I want to return to "the bliss" Cather felt in "entering into the very skin of another human being," and stress that Cather's strange expression is a metaphor for writing. If for Cather writing entailed a kind of violent inhabitation (or colonization) of another's body, then her task in this novel parallels the minstrel performances of her childhood. The novel, it would seem, is an especially powerful vehicle for analyzing racialized subjectivity, because the imaginative projections central to the novelist's art are analogous to the fantastic projections that constitute subjectivity. When Sapphira develops an obsession with her slave, the black girl becomes the repository for all of the novel's excesses—including sexuality. A similar dynamic occurs in *My Ántonia* as well, when Cather describes the pianist Blind D'Arnault as a "glistening African god of pleasure, full of strong savage blood" (123).[22] Cather, like other white American writers, embodied her Africanist characters with a vital sexuality and utilized them to dramatize carnal pleasure and transgression. There was not only bliss but violence, then, in entering into the skin of another—by writing blackness, a white writer could vicariously enjoy a stereotyped sexual excess that their own racial identification disapproved; however, the price of this transgressive pleasure is the violence of racist stereotypes.

By providing a striking example of this recurrent pattern in American fiction, *Sapphira* teaches us a larger point about the supplementarity (and fragility) of whiteness. Whiteness—as African American writers from Ralph Ellison to Toni Morrison have insisted—is literally constituted in relation to blackness. That is, in order to understand whiteness, one must see that whiteness includes, even as it excludes, a racialized other. The degraded otherness embedded in racist stereotypes of blackness is a fantastic projection of the white subject who needs that degraded other to consolidate his or her own white subjectivity. Not only does Cather's fictional rewriting of the mistress-slave relationship explore these complex dynamics of race but, as I will discuss later, Cather literally writes herself into the end of the novel, making *Sapphira* a genealogy of her own American subjectivity. In so doing, she suggests that the mistress-slave relationship is a paradigmatic case of white American subject formation: that twentieth-century white American subjectivities find their origins in the drama of American slavery.

The Pleasure (and Danger) of Surveillance

At the center of *Sapphira* is a seduction scene, masterminded by Sapphira, that most fully supports my suggestion that for Cather, the black racial body is a staging ground for the performance of white subjectivity—especially white femininity. By objectifying the black body in this manner, Cather dramatizes what Foucault has called "the pleasure of the surveillance of pleasure." In a pivotal chapter of the novel, Sapphira invites her rakish nephew Martin Colbert to visit, with the explicit hope that he will sexually compromise her slave Nancy. When Martin arrives at the plantation, he becomes a narrative surrogate for Sapphira's designs. The scene of sexual crisis takes place in a cherry tree, reminiscent of both Faulkner's pear tree in *The Sound and the Fury* (1929) and Zora Neale Hurston's blossoming pear tree in *Their Eyes Were Watching God* (1937); like these other trees, this one too is resonant with sexual secrets.

This scene is propelled by a complex relation of surveillance and surrogacy, as Sapphira attempts to affirm her own power and subjectivity by aligning herself with—and indeed acting through—a deputy of whiteness and patriarchy. When Martin, as Sapphira's messenger, traps Nancy in the cherry tree, Sapphira's invisible will behind the scene (as well as her pleasure) is made explicit, making it possible to read this troubling sexual drama as encoded with a homoerotic subtext—a reading bolstered by the sapphic pun in the name of Cather's heroine. Martin tracks Nancy to the cherry tree, where Cather has Nancy lolling about with "nothing but the foolish, dreamy, nigger side of her nature" exposed. (Of course, what really seems to be exposed here is Nancy's *underside*, as Martin looks up her dress. Here Cather quite resoundingly calls to mind Caddy's muddy underwear in *The Sound and the Fury*.) Martin almost convinces Nancy that his is a true flirtation, when suddenly "everything change[s] in a flash" and Martin pulls Nancy partially down from the tree, wrapping "her two legs about his cheeks like a frame." When Nancy begs him to stop, he tells her, "This is nothin' but to cure a toothache," and the narrative continues: "Martin framed his face closer and shut his eyes. 'Pretty soon.—This is just nice.—Something smells sweet—like May apples'" (181). This richly layered scene, where Martin seems to "taste" Nancy's ripe body, begs to be decoded: on the surface a white man, a "rake," is exercising his privilege by attempting to sexually possess his family's property. After all, this novel has allowed for such sexual liaisons in the past—it is rumored that Nancy is born of Till's rape by either one of the Colbert men or a visiting Cuban painter, who as a guest would have had sexual access to any of the Back Creek slaves. On a more subtle level, Sapphira's ventriloquized sexual performance, through her nephew, seems to infuse the scene with a homoerotic violence. Thus the ostensibly heterosexual scene of sexual crisis can be read as inflected with a problematic projection of homoeroticism. Or can it?

If one wanted to pursue the idea that Sapphira's power over Nancy might be homoerotic, how would such a reading unfold? Such an interpretation quickly runs into objections and obstacles. First, I would suggest, as I have been arguing throughout this essay, that gender and sexuality in this scene cannot be understood apart from the dynamics of race and racism—given that this is a slave narrative of sorts. Sapphira's manipulation and surveillance of Martin as sexual surrogate certainly crosses what Eve Sedgwick calls the "threshold between genders." Notably though, Cather's crossing of gender thresholds is a crossing of racial thresholds as well. As Toni

Morrison argues, "What becomes titillating in this wicked pursuit of innocence—what makes it something other than an American variant of *Clarissa*—is the racial component" (24). In her fiction, Cather frequently projects lesbian desire through a male surrogate—and other critics have noted this.[23] What has not been noted, however, is the performance of race and rape that troubles the possibility of a homoerotic drama in *Sapphira*.

Writing of the framing of desire in Cather's fiction, Sedgwick concludes that "a growing minority gay identity does or did depend on a model of gender liminality, it tends to invest with meaning transpositions between male and female homosexuality, but also between the bonds of homo- and hetero-sexuality" (68). Arguing that Cather's work displays "the shadows of the brutal suppressions by which a lesbian love did not in Willa Cather's time and culture freely become visible as itself" (69), Sedgwick concludes that "among the reasons Cather may have had for not [writing a lesbian plot] may have been, besides the danger to herself and her own enabling privacy, the danger also . . . to the early and still-fragile development of any lesbian plot as a public possibility for carrying value and sustaining narrative" (69). Sedgwick's conclusions about Willa Cather are incomplete, however, without a consideration of Cather's final novel. Cather does offer in *Sapphira* a highly coded and historically charged plot of female subjectivity and corporeality, one that offers a terrifying[24] exploration of the distortions of desire by power. The nagging question remains, however, why Cather would have conflated homoerotic desire with violence, and why a scene of potential homoerotic pleasure would be coded as a rape.

This question compels me to offer an alternative reading of this scene, one that takes into account Marilee Lindeman's cautionary advice that whatever this novel is about, it is *not* about homoerotic desire.[25] Any possible homoeroticism in Nancy's deflowering in the cherry tree is overwhelmed by the heterosexual violence of the scene. Sapphira is not projecting sexual desire through Martin so much as she is aspiring to a position of (white) heterosexual domination within the patriarchal system of slavery. Sapphira, after all, has been playing the role of "master" on her plantation. In this sense, she is simply exercising her mastery over her slave's body. Here, again, Jacobs helps us read Cather: the seductive overtones of the mistress-slave relationship—in the case of both Mrs. Flint and Sapphira— are not homoerotic then, but instead reveal the white woman's allegiance to the hierarchies of white, patriarchal southern society. Both women are conspicuously ventriloquizing the power of the master. Feminists have long insisted that rape is about power, not sex, so whatever eroticism is evoked in these two scenes between mistresses and their slaves is less about sex than about the erotics of power.

Cather's exploration of the sadistic and cruel aspects of Sapphira's powerful desire does, however, enable a plot too often suppressed in southern historiography—the narrative of relations between white mistresses and slave women. Cather seems to insist in this novel that not all mistresses were "true" women, fainting and ignorant while their husband's raped their slaves, but that mistresses too were complicit in the violent concubinage that undergirded slavery, and that mistresses too could express a troubling desire that mingled with sadism. While numerous passively cruel mistresses are offered up by fiction and slave narrative, this novel is the first to my knowledge that considers the white woman's lust for power significant enough to propel the plot, let alone the seduction plot of her slave.

Cather, in her effort to expose the violence of mistress-slave relations in her own and America's past, expresses this American narrative in complexly sexual and racialized terms. If *Sapphira*, in some sense, contains the echoes of a failed or deeply encoded homoerotic plot, I would stress that the disturbing intersection of race and gender in Cather's narrative is symptomatic of the ways in which homosexuality and Africanism were mutually pathologized in the American imagination of the 1930s.

"White Once More": Identity and the Politics of Disguise

The concluding section of *Sapphira* structurally parallels the surveillance scenes of the earlier sections of the novel. In this final segment—which takes place twenty-five years later, after Nancy has escaped to Canada and Sapphira has died—a little white girl, confined to bed, is metonymically substituted for the immobile Sapphira. Like Sapphira, this girl surveys and directs the plots of her social inferiors. Indeed, she masterminds the dramatic performance that is the reunion between Nancy and her mother, Till: when Nancy returns from her long exile, the little girl insists that the mother and daughter's reunion occur in her sickroom under her watchful gaze. Like little Eva in *Uncle Tom's Cabin*, the girl in the sickbed gathers together the white and black characters for a harmonious final vision of forgiveness and racial unity.[26] But the sick little girl is likened as well to her predecessor in the novel, the immobile and frequently bedridden Sapphira. Equally important, the omniscient third-person narrative that has prevailed throughout the novel is dropped; in this final section the narrative is picked up by the nameless little girl herself, now older, looking back on the stories of her childhood. Strikingly, Cather, in her letters, went so far as to admit that this little girl is a version of herself.[27] This youthful, unnamed narrator, like Cather, is heir to the southern heritage embodied in Sapphira's tale. Through this narrator, then, Cather seems self-consciously to place herself in a metonymic relation to Sapphira, stressing her identification with this troubling southern ancestor and, perhaps unwittingly, politicizing her self in relation to that ancestry.

I say "unwittingly" only because Cather claims to have disliked the political in novels, and though her novel rings with allusions to *Uncle Tom's Cabin*, she claims to have hated Harriet Beecher Stowe and to have found *Uncle Tom's Cabin* a failed novel. As Cather wrote in 1894, "An artist should have no moral purpose in mind other than just his art. His mission is not to clean the Augean [sic] stables; he had better join the salvation Army if he wants to do that. The mind that can follow a mission is not an artistic one. An artist can know no other purpose than his art. A book with a direct purpose plainly stated is seldom the work of a great mind. For this reason *Uncle Tom's Cabin* will never have a place in the high ranks of literature" (*Kingdom of Art* 406). Why then is *Sapphira* such a politically potent book and so resonant of *Uncle Tom's Cabin*? Ironically, Cather's novel is frequently and almost unanimously considered a failure by her critics. I agree with Toni Morrison's suspicion that "the problem with *Sapphira and the Slave Girl* is not that it has a weaker vision or is the work of a weaker mind. The problem is trying to come to terms critically and artistically with the novel's concerns: the power and license of a white slave mistress over her female slaves" (18). Fundamentally about a white woman who, as Morrison puts it, "gather[s] identity unto herself from the wholly available and serviceable lives of Africanist others" (25), *Sapphira and the Slave Girl* is a politically charged novel about how white femininity gets consolidated through the service of blackness.

Though Cather criticizes "political" novels, her act of writing herself into her own novel is the culminating political gesture of her most quintessentially American book. For by explicitly aligning her authorship with Sapphira's surveillance and ventriloquism, Cather implicates herself in the problematic genealogy of white southern womanhood. As a young child, Willa Cather expressed her unease with the southern society that expected her to act ladylike by claiming to be a "dang'ous nigger." In her final novel, Cather accepts the responsibility, in Fiedler's terms, of becoming "white once more": she acknowledges that she *can't* be "the dangerous nigger" *or* the secessionist soldier—that as a white woman with southern roots, her subject position is inescapably and genealogically aligned with the plantation mistress.

Notes

1. Judith Butler suggests in *Bodies That Matter* that identifications "are phantasmatic efforts of alignment, loyalty, ambiguous and cross-corporeal cohabitation" (105). In this sense, when the young Willa enacts the "dang'ous nigger" performance in the drawing room, she is engaging in a kind of phantasmatic "cross-corporeal cohabitation," constituting her own subjectivity in the moment of alignment with the other.

2. I am self-conscious about the way in which my use of this term invokes the "mannish lesbian" discussed so famously by Esther Newton and complicated more recently by Teresa

de Lauretis. Here I follow de Lauretis's claim that "[g]ender reversal in the mannish lesbian . . . was not merely a claim to male social privilege or a sad pretense to male sexual
behavior, but represented what may be called, in Foucault's phrase, a 'reverse discourse': an
assertion of sexual agency and feelings, but autonomous from men, a reclaiming of erotic
drives directed toward women, of a desire for women that is not to be confused with woman
identification" (146).

3. Several critical works do discuss Cather's performative racialism, however, though none
explicitly link it with her sexual performance. See Painter, Gwin, Carlin. Irving's argument
that ethnicity displaces homosexuality in *My Ántonia* comes closest to my own suggestions
about *Sapphira* here.

4. Gertrude Stein's portrait of Melanctha is perhaps the most obvious example of this. See
DeKoven for an elegant extended discussion of the eruptions of race in modernist texts.

5. This is most recently charted in Judith Butler's provocative chapter "'Dangerous Crossing': Willa Cather's Masculine Names" in *Bodies That Matter*. Though Butler offers an intriguing reading of Cather's "dangerous crossing," suggesting that "sexuality never qualifies
as a truth, radically distinct from heterosexuality—It is almost nowhere figured mimetically,"
she neglects to consider the scene in *Sapphira* of Nancy's seduction, masterminded by Sapphira, that this chapter centers on. See also Sedgwick, who similarly argues that Cather does
not directly emplot lesbian desire but only refracted cross-gender desire. Of Cather's biographers, Sharon O'Brien offers the most lengthy treatment of Cather's sexuality.

6. While most of Cather's biographers note Cather's final return to the South in *Sapphira*,
it is generally agreed to be an inferior novel or is hastily referred to in a final chapter after
a thorough discussion of Cather's more significant works. Most critics have similar responses
to this perplexing final novel. Until the Seventh International Willa Cather Seminar in Winchester, critical discussion of *Sapphira* as a southern text had been limited. For earlier discussions that address the novel's southern context, see Rosowski and Romines.

7. Cather's return to the South and her turn to the dynamics of power in human racial
relations also responds to the international racial crisis of her time. In 1938 racial and ethnic
difference made all the difference in the world between survival and extermination, and
Cather was supremely conscious of Hitler's "will to power." James Woodress suggests that
when "Hitler invaded Poland, . . . [*Sapphira*] became [Cather's] refuge from the horrible
events taking place abroad" (*Willa Cather* 480). That Cather would "take refuge" in a book
that catalogues racial tyranny and the problematics of domination makes the international
context of the book a compelling layer to our understanding of it.

8. On Cather's shifting names, see Slote's notes on "The Namesake" in her edition of the
1903 *April Twilights*. Also see Bennett 234–35.

9. Cather charts a similar identification in her story "The Namesake," where the main
character discovers what he thinks are his own initials on a chest belonging to a dead soldier
uncle. See my discussion of this story below.

10. See Slote's notes to *April Twilights* (56).

11. My argument here is informed by Lauren Berlant's theoretically rich discussion of
citizenship. She argues that "the American subject is privileged to suppress the fact of his
historical situation in the abstract 'person': but then, in return, the nation provides a kind of
prophylaxis for the person, as it promises to protect his local body in return for loyalty to the
state" (113). In Cather's drama of citizenship, however, the nation fails to prophylactically
protect the citizen and, in fact, requires his dis-memberment in exchange for his national
membership.

12. Michaels argues quite convincingly that "The Namesake" highlights Cather's "progressive understanding that [American] identity [is] essentially political, reenabled by the Civil
War as the refounding of the American nation" (34).

13. This is what Shakespeare's Viola says in *Twelfth Night* when, after cross-dressing as
a young man for the entire play, she returns to her female garb.

14. As Foucault argues, "The body is directly involved in a political field; power relations have an immediate hold on it; they invest it, mark it train it, torture it, force it to carry out tasks, to perform ceremonies, to emit signs. This political investment of the body is bound up in accordance with complex reciprocal relations, with its economic use; it is largely as a force of production that the body is invested with relations of power and domination; but, on the other hand, its constitution as labour power is possible only if it is caught up in a system of subjection . . . the body becomes a useful force only if it is both a productive body and a subjective body" (25–26).

15. Foucault suggests that "a body is docile that may be subjected, used, transformed and improved" (136).

16. For an extended discussion of this, see White and Clinton.

17. Despite the homoerotic overtones of Mrs. Flint's pursuit, I am not suggesting here that this is a moment of homosexual crisis. Rather, where Linda Brent might be hoping for a sister in Mrs. Flint, Mrs. Flint is patently not a sister but a master as she ventriloquizes her husband's sexual demands.

18. Mary Chesnut ruminates, in an often cited passage, that "we live surrounded by prostitutes. An abandoned woman is sent out of any decent house elsewhere. Who thinks any worse of a Negro or Mulatto woman for being a thing we can't name. God forgive us, but ours is a monstrous system & wrong & iniquity. Perhaps the rest of the world is as bad. This only I see: like the patriarchs of old our men live all in one house with their wives & their concubines, & the Mulattoes one sees in every family exactly resemble the white children—& every lady tells you who is the father of all the Mulatto children in every body's household, but those in her own, she seems to think drop from the clouds" (42).

19. For information on general violence toward slaves, including mistresses' abuse, see *The Suppressed Book about Slavery* 187–232. For the account of the mistress who decapitates her slave's baby, see Clinton, "Southern Dishonor," 64.

20. Sapphira's daughter, Rachel, overhears this beating: "[Rachel] heard her mother's voice in anger—anger with no heat, a cold sneering contempt. 'Take it down this minute! You know how to do it right. Take it down, I told you! Hairpins do no good. Now you've hurt me stubborn! Then came a smacking sound, three times: the wooden back of a hairbrush striking someone's cheek or arm" (13).

21. Barbara Welter coined this famous term in 1966.

22. Irving is interested in how Cather displaces sexual deviancy onto ethnic others in *My Ántonia*, yet she does not mention the symbolic function of the Blind D'Arnault scene where the particularly *Africanized* other's piano playing enables the immigrant girls' sexualized dancing.

23. See, for example, Butler, Irving, O'Brien, and Sedgwick.

24. Cather suggested in a letter to Viola Roseboro' on 20 February 1941 that in *Sapphira* she was writing "the terrible" (cited in Carlin 152).

25. My reading here is indebted to Marilee Lindemann's compelling argument about Sapphira in *Willa Cather: Queering America*. She writes, "To suggest that 'the lesbian writer' is so compelled to tell and yet to camouflage the story of her sexual desires that she would stage a vicious drama of heterosexual miscegenous rape/seduction is, in my judgment, to turn her into the pathetic, erotically obsessed creature of turn-of-the-century inversion theory" (134).

26. See Stowe, *Uncle Tom's Cabin*, particularly 256–63 and 271–95.

27. Cather suggested this in a letter to Laura Hills on 9 November 1940 (Willa Cather Collection, Pierpont Morgan Library, New York).

"A Race without Consonants"

My Mortal Enemy as Reconstruction Narrative

ROBERT K. MILLER

"We are unfortunate in the people who live over us," observes Oswald Henshawe toward the end of *My Mortal Enemy* (1926)—that elegantly un-furnished novel, so rich with "the inexplicable presence of the thing not named" ("Novel Démeublé" 41). His wife elaborates in a passage worth examining by readers interested in exploring Cather's southern connec-tions. Myra describes the people above as "The palavery kind of Southern-ers; all that slushy gush on the surface, and no sensibilities whatever—a race without consonants and without delicacy. They tramp up there all day long like cattle. The stalled ox would have trod softer. Their energy isn't worth anything, so they use it up gabbling and running about, beating my brains to a jelly" (56). She continues: "Those two silly old hens race each other to the telephone as if they had a sweetheart at the other end of it. While I could still climb stairs, I hobbled up to that woman and implored her, and she began gushing about 'mah sister' and 'mah son,' and what 'rah-fined' people they were. . . . Oh, that's the cruelty of being poor; it leaves you at the mercy of such pigs!" (57).

Readers know, by this point, that Myra often speaks scornfully of other people and that she does not suffer fools gladly. Even so, the violence of this passage is remarkable. A witty and cultivated woman is reduced to us-ing the kind of trope that an angry child might use. The "animals" (55) who live above are compared to cattle, ox, hens, and pigs. But what is it, exactly, that makes these southern women so bestial? Surely Cather can't expect us to condemn them simply because they are women, as "hens" sug-gests, or because they are "old" and good-natured enough to enjoy laugh-ing and talking on the telephone. Perhaps there is something unseemly about racing to the phone as if "they had a sweetheart at the other end of it," but is it really "silly" for the "old" to reach out for love? I can't help thinking, in this respect, of how sympathetically Cather treats another ag-ing woman who races to the phone to speak with a sweetheart—Marian Forrester, in *A Lost Lady* (1923), who risks both her health and her reputa-tion to place a long distance call to Frank Ellinger upon learning of his marriage. And what are we to make of the importance Myra gives to pro-nunciation when she dismisses her neighbors as "a race without conso-nants" and ridicules them for pronouncing *my* as "mah" and *refined* as "rah-fined"? We don't have to look far in Cather's fiction to find plenty of sympathetically drawn characters who speak with accents or faulty gram-mar. Many of these characters are immigrants with an uncertain grasp of

English, but others are native speakers. Consider, for example, how positively Cather portrays Mahailey in *One of Ours* (1922), a child of the South "brought West by a shiftless Virginia family" (21). Her speech is marked by both the absence of consonants and the substitution of alternative consonants for those that are considered correct. "I'm just a-goin' to lay on my fedder bed," she tells Mrs. Wheeler, "or direc'ly I won't have none. I ain't a-goin' to have Mr. Ralph carryin' off my quilts my mudder pieced fur me" (65). Within two short sentences, she has dropped three *g*s and one *t*, and substituted double *d*s for the *th* sound in *feather* and *mother*, in addition to using the regionalism *a-goin* for *going* and pronouncing *for* as *fur*. We also know that Mahailey is illiterate, although she can recognize the letters of the alphabet and create her own narratives out of the images she sees in the newspaper. Yet it is to Mahailey, a woman of no consonants, that Cather gives the last word in *One of Ours*. She speaks the final line of dialogue, in which she says "Mudder" instead of *Mother*—her pronunciation unimproved through 391 pages. Cather adds only one additional sentence: "Mrs. Wheeler always feels that God is near, but Mahailey is not troubled by any knowledge of interstellar spaces, and for her He is nearer still, —directly overhead, not so very far above the kitchen stove" (391). In this case, the woman closest to God is the woman "not troubled by any knowledge," and this lack of knowledge is signaled by pronunciation shaped by geography and social class.

So what, then, is wrong with Mrs. Poindexter and her sister, the women without consonants who live in the apartment above Myra and Oswald Henshawe? They do seem to have a heavy step, for Nellie Birdseye, the narrator of *My Mortal Enemy*, also hears "heavy tramping overhead" (55). It is also Nellie who reports hearing "a telephone ring overhead, then shrieks of laughter, and two people ran across the floor as if they were running a foot-race" (56–57). But Nellie's impressions are by no means foolproof in this novel, as several critics have noted.[1] And if she can hear the telephone ringing in the apartment above, other sounds from above must be carrying at least in part because of poor construction—a view taken by Oswald, who states, "These new houses are poorly built, and every sound carries" (56). In other words, the sound of heavy footsteps cannot be attributed altogether to coming from a race without consonants. Moreover, we might well ask how much quiet anyone could enjoy living in an apartment beneath such families as the Rosickys, the Templetons, or even the Miners. Families make noise—with or without consonants.

This much, however, is clear. The neighbors above are not only southerners but southerners of the wrong sort, the "palavery kind," with "that slushy gush on the surface, and no sensibilities whatever" (56). As we try to understand this passage, we need to recognize, at the onset, that there is no reason that the Poindexters had to be southerners of any sort. The apartment house in question is located in a "sprawling overgrown West-coast city" (49), which sounds very much like San Francisco; the rest of the novel is set in Illinois and Manhattan. I believe that Cather made Mrs. Poindexter and her sister southerners so that she could challenge one of the abiding myths of American culture: the belief that we can easily construct and reconstruct our lives until we produce a version that suits us. The promise of a new life is held out to us in many ways—witness the appeals of advertisers, the proliferation of recovery programs, and the popularity of self-help books. But the principal way in which Americans have sought change is to move from one location to another—the migration (even if it is only from one house to another) about which Joseph Urgo has written so persuasively. That the Poindexters are southern signals, in one sense, that they do not "belong" in the West. Then again, neither do the Henshawes, whose own roots are elsewhere. So, strictly speaking, the Poindexters are no more out of place than the Henshawes. Bearing this in mind can help us to see that the two families represent antithetical ways of living in a new home, both of which are problematic and neither of which is endorsed by Cather.

The Poindexters, of course, are southerners of a certain kind. It's easy enough to find sympathetically drawn southern women in Cather's fiction. In addition to Mahailey, there are Rachel Blake and Mrs. Bywaters in *Sapphira and the Slave Girl* (1940), old Mrs. Harris in the story of that name (1932), and the "nice little Virginia girl . . . [with] kind eyes and soft Southern voice" (205) who befriends Tom Outland in *The Professor's House* (1925). The Poindexters, however, are the "palavery kind of Southerners" (56).

According to the *Oxford English Dictionary*, to *palaver* is "to talk profusely or unnecessarily, to 'jaw,' 'jabber'; to talk . . . flatteringly." It's true that people who talk too much can be annoying. But do they lack immortal souls? Remember, after all, that these women who talk too much are reduced to the level of *cattle, oxen, hens,* and *pigs.* Or, more accurately, below this level. In Nellie's words, "the Poindexters did tramp like cattle—except that their brutal thumping hadn't the measured dignity which the step of animals always has" (59). And at least one of these women would be a danger in any stable or farmyard. When Myra last refers to Mrs. Poindexter, she describes her as having "the wrinkled, white throat of an adder . . . and the hard eyes of one. Don't go near her!" she pleads to Nellie (62). The deadly threat established through this language cannot be attributed to a tendency to talk too long on the telephone.

Nor can this threat be attributed to the corrupting nature of flattery. There is no evidence of the Poindexter sisters flattering anyone in this book. When Nellie does go upstairs to confront the women, the scene is limited to a parenthetical paragraph consisting of two sentences. The first tells us that Nellie shares Myra's aversion to Mrs. Poindexter's appearance; the second provides a summary of what Mrs. Poindexter said: "She smiled, and said that the sick woman underneath was an old story, and she ought to have been sent to a sanatorium long ago" (62). This response to Myra's situation may lack empathy, but it cannot be said to be flattering or garrulous—so *palavery* is ultimately no more helpful than *old* or *hen* when determining what makes the Poindexter sisters so disturbing to Myra's peace of mind.

I believe that the real threat to social harmony—from Myra's point of view, and possibly from Cather's—is that these are southerners who do not know their place. Sympathetically drawn southern women in Cather's fiction tend to be content in humble circumstances. Mahailey is a loyal serf who devotes her entire life to serving her superiors. Old Mrs. Harris loyally serves her family for long hours every day before climbing into a cold, narrow bed where she can be warmed by a neighbor's castoff sweater. In *Sapphira and the Slave Girl*, Mrs. Bywaters is the village postmistress, and Mrs. Blake lives in a modest cottage while ministering to the poor and ill. And as for that "nice little Virginia girl" (205) with "a pretty little fluttery Southern laugh" (207) in *The Professor's House*, she has the sense to decline an invitation to lunch expensively at the Shoreham Hotel. Mrs. Poindexter might have accepted. The key to being a southerner of the wrong sort, then, is to live without a sense of propriety, a sense that demands a clear sense of where one stands in the social hierarchy. The Poindexter sisters have the means to step over a woman who considers herself their cultural superior. Their transgression is not so much that they are noisy old women; it is that they have the audacity to live above Myra. They are able to do this because they have more money, and for this reason the disenfranchised nobility can expect no help from authority. As Oswald explains to Nellie when she proposes getting the landlord to reproach the Poindexters, "No, they pay a higher rent than we do—occupy more rooms. And we are somewhat under obligation to the management" (57).

Here then is the rub: The wrong family is not only occupying the most rooms, but these rooms are on top of a family that would have been socially superior to them twenty years earlier. There has been an inversion of the old social order. The trauma of being displaced geographically is a common enough theme in Cather's work—think of Jim's coming to terms with the prairie in *My Ántonia* (1918), for example, or Mr. Shimerda, who is brought to suicide when transplanted too far from his native soil. But Cather was also troubled by a kind of social displacement that is independent of geography. When Ivy Peters acquires title to the beautiful marsh that Captain Forester had carefully preserved, he is buying land in his own hometown. Nevertheless, readers of *A Lost Lady* have good reason to feel the land should never have gone to him. Successful entrepreneur though he may be, he is also a despoiler of the natural world who sits in a chair he cannot fill. One way to read *A Lost Lady* is to see it as a kind of Reconstruction narrative in which a scalawag or carpetbagger displaces the local gentry, and I suggest that we read *My Mortal Enemy* with this construct in mind.

By "Reconstruction narrative" I mean stories that explore how to negotiate the changes that emerge from social and political conflict—especially those stories that are set at least in part in the American South during Reconstruction (1865–1877). Such stories need not be written during the years in question, but could—like *Up from Slavery* (1901), *Gone with the Wind* (1936), or *Beloved* (1987)—be written much later. Written by a dispossessed southerner shortly after another great war, *My Mortal Enemy* is a variation on such narratives. The variation, however, is significant. Reconstruction narratives usually explore how "something or someone is reconstructed as something or someone else" (Thomas 118). *My Mortal Enemy* tells the story of a woman who refuses to change no matter how many external changes occur in the world around her.

To understand Myra's response to the Poindexters, we might benefit from recalling an important scene in *Gone with the Wind*, that amply furnished novel published exactly ten years after *My Mortal Enemy*. After she has returned to Tara and been reduced to rooting for radishes, Scarlett O'Hara finds unbidden guests at her door. Jonas Wilkerson, once a disreputable employee at the plantation, has returned with his equally disreputable bride, the aptly named Emmie Slattery, hoping to buy Tara on advantageous terms because of unpaid taxes owed by the O'Haras. They are decked out in store-bought finery and driving a carriage of their own (which reminds me of how Myra is infuriated when she sees a social rival in a carriage of her own). Unlike Myra, who walks away from her birthright, Scarlett is determined not to lose her home. Horrified by the sight of "poor white trash . . . coming up the steps of Tara," she cries, "Get off those steps, you trashy wench!" (528), and when Jonas threatens to "buy this place, lock, stock, and barrel" and to live in it, she vows, "I'll tear this house down, stone by stone, and burn it and sow every acre with salt before I see either of you put foot over this threshold. . . . Get out, I tell you! Get out!" (529). It is this confrontation that prompts Scarlett to reconstruct both her curtains and herself. Because *Gone with the Wind* is told from the point of view of the white gentry that ruled the land before the war, readers and viewers routinely experience relief when the plucky Scarlett sets about securing her title to Tara and remaking her life.

Myra Henshawe is not so fortunate. As she has learned too late, "It's better to be a stray dog in this world than a man without money" (13). Once the mistress of the best house in Parthia and the engaging hostess of a New York salon, she is, without money, forced to live a circumscribed life to which she is unaccustomed. Her torment is the result of living underneath people whom she believes to be inferior to her—the fundamental horror of a Reconstruction narrative told from the point of view of someone opposed to social change. White trash, aided by carpetbaggers, have triumphed over the old gentry. In a much-discussed essay, almost certainly read by Cather,[2] H. L. Mencken surveyed the South—studying Virginia in particular, the state of Cather's birth shortly after the Civil War—and announced, "The picture gives one the creeps. . . . The old aristocracy went down the red gullet of war; the poor white trash are now in the saddle" (138–39). As a result, Mencken laments, southerners are "now merely pushful and impudent. . . . The old repose is gone."

I trust we all understand that the "old repose" was built upon the backs of slave labor, and I have no interest in celebrating the antebellum South. But I write as someone who believes in the importance of social and spiritual change. Myra does not. Her one attempt to reconstruct her life—by defying her uncle and eloping with Oswald—has failed because it is external not internal. She is, at heart, a character in stasis. Indeed, the most telling line within this novel may be Nellie's judgment when she meets Myra in much reduced circumstances after a separation of many years. "She was . . . she was herself," Nellie reflects, "Myra Henshawe!" (53). If there is a certain nobility to the strength with which Myra retains her identity and asserts her allegiance to the past, holding on to her tea cups and refusing to turn her own velvet curtains into a dress, her resistance to change ultimately dooms her. She is fighting a battle that cannot be won. She is, as Mrs. Poindexter points out, "an old story" (62) in a world that no longer has a place for her. Incapable of reconstructing herself for life in the twentieth century, Myra is limited to a series of unattractive choices: She can cling stubbornly to the single room the conditions of which she resents, go into a sanatorium, as Mrs. Poindexter recommends, or return to her childhood home as a supplicant by invoking a clause in her uncle's will. Her only other option is to die—and that, of course, is what she does.

The Poindexters, on the other hand, seem to be flourishing. Myra is furious with them, in part, because they are so active. They move about and make a lot of noise. But the noise is significant only because it reminds Myra of lives radically different from her own, and that's the ultimate source of her rage. For Myra, the problem with the Poindexter sisters is not that they are southern, or that they are women, or that they want sweethearts, or that they talk too much. No, the real problem is that they represent that "pushful and impudent" citizenry of the New South that has destroyed the old repose as surely as cattle let loose to tramp throughout the house. The old order has been overturned because a race without consonants now has money in the bank and friends in the legislature. Reconstruction may have brought about "new houses [that] are poorly built" (56), but a dispossessed gentry hovering on the brink of bankruptcy has nowhere else to go.

Readers of this novel often question what Myra has in mind when she asks, "Why must I die like this, alone with my mortal enemy?" (78). Left to puzzle this out on their own, students usually reject the possibility that she is referring to Oswald or Nellie and conclude that Myra is her own mortal enemy. I tell them that a work of art, like life itself, is ultimately a mystery—but not a detective story in which we substitute "who is it" for "who done it." Nevertheless, exploring the southern connection within *My Mortal Enemy* reveals an alternative reading of this question—a question which, after all, gives the book its title. Instead of focusing upon the characters who are actually in the Henshawe apartment—Myra, Oswald, and Nellie—we can look to those disturbers of the old repose who have, so to speak, invaded Myra's space, an outrage suggested by their name, for *poindre* means "to break" or "to peep," and *dexter*, of course, is a breed of cattle.[3] Myra yearns to be alone—and eventually summons the resources to die alone, aided only by a "kindly Negro driver" (59), a figure associated with the ancien régime. She must escape outdoors because she no longer can expect any privacy at home. Her torment comes not from Oswald or Nellie, both of whom she bends to her will, but from the Poindexters, who refuse to do as she demands. Whatever their personal limitations may be, these two southern women are like animals to Myra primarily because they are dumb to her demands. Myra, we are told, is "not at all modern in her make-up" (76). The Poindexters, who "go to the movies" (57) and rush to the telephone, are just that—modern. These neighbors are fundamentally opposed to one another. Seen from Myra's point of view, and that of those under her spell, the Poindexters are her mortal enemy because they represent the antithesis of all that is "time-honoured" (68)—not just the "holy words and holy rites" that Myra embraces but the traditional social order associated with such rites (70). The Poindexters are the future, a future without consonance to those aligned with the old order, a future in which the ill-mannered cannot be ordered off the steps of Tara.

Myra's intransigence, her rage at the present and inability to create a new life for herself, is emphasized by the western setting of part 2. The West, after all, has traditionally represented the regenerative space in which Americans from both North and South believed they could begin their lives anew.[4] Elsewhere in Cather's fiction, it is where characters such as Lena Lingard and Tiny Soderball are able to make their fortunes.[5] Myra, however, can move but not change.[6] I recognize, of course, that she is physically disabled by the time we find her in the West, dying of a "malignant growth" (74) that seems to be cancer—her body changing even if her spirit cannot. But even if she were in good health, it is difficult to imagine her becoming a successful pioneer or entrepreneur. She is, as Joseph Urgo has argued, "a woman who has lost her sense of the future and has come to identify her destiny in her past," becoming trapped, as a result, in an

"American nightmare" (193). If the American dream is to be able to reconstruct ourselves, our nightmare is that we cannot. There are, to be sure, social and economic problems that can keep many of us from realizing that dream, but the dream itself is of great importance—as Cather emphasizes in other works.[7] Myra's imagination has failed her. If her story is "a ballad of exile" (Winters 55), it is because she refuses to adapt to a new social order. Incapable of friendship with her neighbors, she has become a bitter recluse. We can only imagine what her life might have been like if she were capable of overcoming class bias and began chatting with the Poindexters on the telephone.

As we have seen, Myra's rejection of her neighbors is rooted in her conviction that they are southerners of the wrong sort. She is more troubled by their social class than by the region from which they come. Nevertheless, she is responding to *southerners* whom she believes to be her social inferiors and doing so with a degree of antagonism that suggests she knows something about southern manners. Parthia is set in "southern Illinois" (3), a location that could easily be further south than towns in Kentucky and Virginia. Whatever assumptions we may have about how people behave in other regions, we are often more keenly aware of social differences within our own region. In other words, Myra Henshawe—who lives in Parthia well beyond the age of nine—could be more southern than Willa Cather. Unlike the "palavery kind" of southerner, she seems more like a southerner of the old guard; a Sapphira-like character who can fascinate as well as horrify.

Although *My Mortal Enemy* is not specifically set in the South, it evokes the kind of displacement that many southerners felt during Reconstruction—the period in which Myra comes of age.[8] Myra is unable to reconstruct herself because she rejects a reconstructed social order, turning herself into a kind of monument to the manners, values, and hierarchies of the past. Telling her story gives Cather the opportunity to celebrate aspects of the past that were close to her own heart and to challenge aspects of modernity that became increasingly troubling for her after her own world broke in two. At the same time, however, she has the wisdom to show the high price paid by anyone who is determined to resist change. If we accept Myra's pronouncements uncritically, *My Mortal Enemy* seems the most reactionary of Cather's novels. But the story itself demonstrates the horror of being unable to embrace the present and envision a future. It is a sign of Cather's genius that she could convey Myra's dark vision with majestic force while also conveying how that vision leads to paralysis and death.

The Poindexters, however, do not represent an ideal alternative to the Henshawes. If Myra's response to them is excessive, they nevertheless seem determined to live entirely on their own terms without being at all willing to accommodate the needs of their neighbors. Their southern accent signals that they too have simply moved from one place to another without truly reconstructing themselves. As different as the two families may be in terms of values and manners, they are similar in this: both seek to live without being bothered by the other. Busily engaged in the present, the Poindexters may be more successful than the Henshawes in positioning themselves for life in a new century, but both families lack the imagination to reconstruct a social order that can accommodate diverse needs. Cather is using this West Coast apartment house to illustrate a house divided. The division is no longer along the Mason-Dixon line; it is carried across the country by Americans who are determined to protect the integrity of their own space at the expense of community. A kind of civil war continues beneath the surface of a nation apparently at peace.

My reading of *My Mortal Enemy* as "Reconstruction narrative" is based, then, on the significance of the southern references in the text as well as the period in which the book is set. If this novel is, as Merrill Skaggs has argued, "Willa Cather's most brilliant—in the sense of technically astonishing—tour de force" (91) or "a brilliant technical success" in which all excess detail has been stripped away (Middleton 125), then we must account for the association, within the book, of southern characters with civil discord. Having done so, we should also reflect upon what kinds of reconstruction would resolve that discord.

In *My Mortal Enemy*, Cather shows us characters who are incapable of overcoming the divisions that separate them—hence the frequency with which this text is described as troubling. To envision ways to heal at least some of the divisions that continue to rend our nation, we can look to her other works for inspiration—considering, for example, how Ántonia Shimerda successfully reconstructs her life or how Archbishop Latour patiently reconstructs his diocese. And, of course, we can look to sources unrelated to Cather studies. But this much is clear: It is too easy to blame social dissonance on neighbors who speak with accents different from our own and to judge too harshly those who do not seem to the apartment born. The era of Reconstruction may be long past, but the challenge to rebuild remains before us. Rather than complaining, "These new houses are poorly built" (56)—and either resentfully living where we don't want to be or changing our address without changing our selves—we should build better houses and make ourselves more worthy to dwell within them.

Notes

1. See Rosowski, *Voyage Perilous*, 147–55; Skaggs, *After the World Broke in Two*, 94–105; Middleton, *Willa Cather's Modernism*, 122–23.

2. This essay, "The Sahara of the Bozart," appears in the same collection as "The National Letters," an essay Cather praises in a letter to Mencken dated 6 February 1922, which can be found in the Mencken Collection of the New York Public Library. Although relations between Cather and Mencken would later sour, they were still cordial at this time. It is certainly possible that she chose not to read what this influential critic—who had helped to advance her own career—had to say about the South, but I think it unlikely given Mencken's reputation, Cather's interest in the South, and the notoriety of the piece in question.

3. Responding to an earlier version of this paper, Evelyn Harris Haller notes that *poing* is French for "fist" and *dexter* is Latin for "right." If we read Poindexter as "right fist," the name conveys the violence that Myra experiences from this family.

4. One of the key texts in shaping our understanding of the West and the American imagination is Frederick Jackson Turner's "The Significance of the Frontier in American History." Brook Thomas describes this essay as "part of a general project at the end of the nineteenth century by which American historians dramatically revised accounts of the era of Reconstruction. . . . Turner constructs an opposition *between* Europe and America based on the latter's ability to avoid the former's history of dialectical confrontation. But that opposition helps to minimize conflict *within* the United States that a generation earlier had threatened to tear the country apart: the Civil War and its Reconstruction aftermath. Rather than construct a narrative of American history that focusses on the Mason-Dixon line separating North and South, Turner focuses on a frontier common to both" (131). By placing southern characters in the West and showing that they have irreconcilable differences with their neighbors, Cather is challenging a revisionist view of American history. No matter how important the West has been, it did not eliminate conflicts between the North and South.

5. It should be noted, however, that Cather never promises a fortune to those who head West. Like Oswald, characters such as Carl Linstrum in *O Pioneers!* and Hillary Templeton in "Old Mrs. Harris" suffer disappointments in the West.

6. Her inability to change can be traced in part to her belief in the determining power of race, a topic that I have addressed elsewhere. See my essay "Strains of Blood."

7. As Captain Forrester declares in *A Lost Lady*, "a thing that is dreamed of in the way I mean, is already an accomplished fact" (44).

8. When reading from a volume of Heine to Myra, Nellie notes the inscription on the flyleaf: "'To Myra Driscoll from Oswald,' dated 1876" (65).

Henry Colbert, Gentleman

Bound by the Code

MARY R. RYDER

Willa Cather's *Sapphira and the Slave Girl* (1940) has traditionally been considered somewhat of an anomaly in the Cather canon not only because of its Virginia setting but also because its female protagonist is so markedly different from her predecessors. Critical attention has focused largely on the moral ambiguities present in the novel or on the character of Sapphira. More recent studies have shifted to analysis of women's relationships in the novel, with particular emphasis on those of mother and daughter or of slave and mistress.[1] What has received too little attention, though, is the role of Henry Colbert, perhaps the most complex, if not the most enslaved, character of the book. His moral dilemma is vastly more complicated than simply wrestling with the question of slavery, for Henry Colbert is caught between two concepts of being a gentleman—the nineteenth-century view, which his wife embraces, and the Jeffersonian ideal of the yeoman aristocrat. The readiness to dismiss Henry Colbert as a weak man of vacillating values (Woodress, *Willa Cather* 487; Stouck, *Cather's Imagination* 230; Rosowski, *Voyage Perilous* 241) or as a man of stultified thinking and conscience (Brown and Edel 316) is mitigated if his struggle to find his "place" in antebellum Virginia is fully realized.

Cather generated *Sapphira and the Slave Girl*, in part, as a kind of tribute to her parents, and Henry Colbert is an affectionate portrait, in temperament rather than in visage, of her father, Charles. Charles Cather, as Mildred Bennett notes, was "a Southern gentleman refined almost to the point of delicacy," a nonaggressive man who was uncomfortable in the limelight (22–24). When as a college student Willa Cather wrote a sketch of a southern gentleman for the *Nebraska State Journal* (17 Dec. 1893), she no doubt had her father in mind, emphasizing the delicate sensibility and generosity of the southern gentleman. She concluded, "That man had better go back to the South; it does not pay to be a Southern gentleman in the hustling Northwest" (*World and the Parish* 21). Henry Colbert is such a man, and, interestingly, western Virginia was in his day referred to as the Old West. Like Charles Cather, Colbert is not obsessed with profit making or getting ahead. He grinds grain and gives it to those who are in need or ignores the debts of even the most shiftless of his neighbors.

The ideals that both Charles Cather and his literary double embrace—courtesy, honor, modesty, and personal integrity (the elements of Renaissance *virtu*)—are the standards of a gentleman, and Cather was well aware of the necessary struggle to retain those virtues in a fast-changing world. The nostalgic, retrospective approach of her Virginia novel has even led critics like John H. Randall III to assume that Henry Colbert is more a profile of the aging Willa Cather than of her father (367). Indeed, Cather employs a kind of "Double S" curve in exploring the place of a gentleman in her world. She brings a pre–Civil War gentleman into a 1940 novel and then projects into the past a contemporary struggle with values.

Cather's background and reading, however, provided her with the materials from which she could sympathetically develop her portrait of Henry Colbert. She was, after all, a daughter of the South until age ten and, from an early age, was exposed to romanticized accounts of Virginia gentlemen. She heard the oral histories of her region from older relatives and from neighbors who visited Willowshade and knew the literary conventions of the popular novels, which characterized the South as a place of refined manners, beautiful women, and dashing gentlemen. The Cather family library boasted the works of John Esten Cooke, a writer from the Shenandoah Valley, whose 1850s novels are set in pre-Revolutionary Virginia and present tantalizing tales of privileged landowners of high culture and impeccable virtue. Cather, on occasion, wrote under the pseudonym of John Esten, and her little brother Jack was named John Esten Cather (Skaggs, *World Broke in Two* 169). An 1890 edition of Dinah Mulock's *John Halifax, Gentleman* also appears on the list of family-owned books, and Cather in her January 1897 column for the *Home Monthly* described the novel as "that dear old romance of the last generation" (*World and the Parish* 335). George Cary Eggleston's *Two Gentlemen of Virginia* (1908) later graced the family bookcase, as did Martha Frye Boggs's *A Romance of New Virginia* (1896).

The Cathers' love affair with Virginia and her writers flourished, and Cather was undoubtedly acquainted with the works of Thomas Nelson Page, at least three of whose novels the family owned. Page's fiction, and especially his stories *In Olde Virginia* (1887), provided a "vision of antebellum magnificence" (Watson 168) and "justified the slave plantation" system (Hubbell 802). As Theodore Gross has pointed out, Page provided a "suitable setting for his Southern gentleman by evoking a dream-like past in which realism is not demanded" (119). His protagonists are kindly masters who are admired by their slaves because they enforce the gentleman's code of manners, courtesy, and hospitality (Gross 21–22). But in a later novel, *Gordon Keith* (1903), which the Cathers also owned, Page sets the stage for what Cather would deal with in *Sapphira*, namely the struggle of a new generation of southerners to "bring their old code of conduct into contact with new social problems" (Watson 178).

Moreover, growing up west of the Fall Line, that imaginary line separating the Tidewater region from up-country, Cather was conscious of a distinction between the Cavalier gentleman of the Tidewater plantation system and the yeoman aristocrat of her own area. The former, with roots in seventeenth- and eighteenth-century England, ascribed to a code of conduct that confirmed distinctions in class, breeding, and education. With a penchant for fast horses, handsome houses, and beautiful women, the Cavalier gentleman would forgive sins of the flesh if they were not blatant or excessive (Hubbell 5–6; Watson 4). Dignified and courteous at all times, he, from an idyllic country retreat, dedicated himself to public service and intended to build an ordered world based on slave labor. Like Augustine St. Clare of *Uncle Tom's Cabin*, though, he might question the morality of the slave system but would not divorce himself from it.

By contrast, the noble yeoman farmers of the Northern Neck of Virginia more closely resembled the Jeffersonian *aristoi*. Generally emerging from German or Scotch-Irish backgrounds, they held less conventional views on society and government, embracing a democratic spirit that nonetheless did not alter their adherence to Cavalier-like courtesy, politeness, and dignity. Often tradesmen who married into aristocratic families (as does Henry Colbert), these "half-breeds," as Jefferson called them in an 1815 letter (qtd. in Hubbell 7), differed from the Anglican planters of the Tidewater in their affiliation with Calvinist Protestant sects, their less ostentatious lifestyle, and a sociopolitical commitment to the parish rather than to the world. Like Owen Wister's Virginian, the Shenandoah gentleman was less pretentious and generally indifferently educated (Watson 25). His gentleman heritage was spiritual not genealogical (Watson 275), and unlike his Cavalier counterpart, a sense of tolerance and justice led him to reject the idea of slave labor.

In *Sapphira and the Slave Girl*, Cather draws upon these contrasts between the two types of southern gentlemen and places Henry Colbert squarely in the middle, and in a muddle. Married to a Tidewater aristocrat, he is bound by a code of honor to support and defend her and her standards, even though he does not see himself as assimilated into her social order. Like his modern counterparts in the works of Virginian writers William Styron and Garrett Epps, Henry struggles in a growingly chaotic world to "discard the limiting, false, and life-denying aspects of the aristocratic ethos while validating the positive and affirmative aspects" (Watson 275). Cather had written previously about the gentleman's dilemma in *The Song of the Lark* (1915) and *The Professor's House* (1925). As in the case of Henry Colbert, she writes of her gentlemen with compassion and understanding. Dr. Archie and Professor St. Peter also find themselves in nonintimate marriages and attracted to a vibrant young person. They retreat to the office or attic room to read, hoping to find in their books a guide for reconciling their own sense of morality with the world's.

In writing *Sapphira*, then, Cather does not undermine the stereotype of the southern gentleman in the person of Henry Colbert. Rather, she presents, as James Woodress notes, "a carefully drawn and sympathetic character" (*Willa Cather* 487) who suffers because he tacitly accepts both his role as the community's "moral consciousness" (Skaggs, *World Broke in Two* 173) and his socially prescribed position as the gentleman husband of a Tidewater aristocrat. The result is a character who is confused about who he is and who he might become, but he is neither morally inert nor static, as Joseph Urgo asserts (94, 96). Henry Colbert's problems stem from a sense of displacement, together with his aspiration to do all that is expected of him as "Master Colbert." Cather pointedly compares Henry's background to his wife's, noting that his lack of a southern accent makes him suspect at Back Creek and Timber Ridge while Sapphira's differing speech pattern is considered her inherent right as "a woman and an heiress."[2] From his arrival at Back Creek, Henry Colbert is both personally aware and made publicly aware of his outsider status. He stands among them but not of them. His powerful, solid figure and occupation place him among his yeoman neighbors, but his gentlemanly deportment, "reflective, almost dreamy" eyes (4), and penchant for cleanliness set him apart. Whereas Sapphira never projects "the air of a countrywoman come to town" (28–29), Henry Colbert cannot escape the aura of being a plain man, even though he resides in a planter's house.

In the opening chapters, Cather draws heavily upon the distinction between the Cavalier and yeoman gentleman as she had learned it and places Henry Colbert in the latter group. His "line" is non-English; his father, a tradesman; his religion, dissenting, non-Anglican. While he shares a Loudoun County origin with his wife, Henry "had never been so much as asked into the [Dodderidge] parlor" before his engagement (25). Just as he stands apart from the Dodderidge class, so does he stand apart from his own brothers. They ride with the fox-hunting set, are "shrewd judges of horses" (23), and are unapologetic for their licentiousness. Cather thus makes clear that the southern gentleman of her novel is neither exclusively lordly Cavalier nor Jeffersonian natural aristocrat. Exiled from his place of origin and divorced from social affiliation with any single group, Henry Colbert becomes a man caught in-between, struggling to maintain a gentleman's admirable values without bowing to the Cavalier's accompanying moral weaknesses.

His relationship with the slave girl, Nancy, exemplifies his efforts to reconcile these disparities. The young girl's purity and simple enjoyment of life, her attentiveness to his preference for order and cleanliness, and her eagerness to please (67) fall within his romanticized vision of womanhood. In the Cavalier tradition, he is bound to defend her honor—she, the submissive and obedient one, and he, the "master." His adamant and uncharacteristic objection to selling Nancy is, therefore, predictable. He is bound

by the chivalric code that one part of him would embrace. As long as he has
had thrust upon him slave ownership, something that he reminds Sapphira
was held against them in Back Creek (8), he, like a true gentleman, is bound
to defend and care for his charges. Following what he believes would be
a learned gentleman's approach to the problem of slave-owner relations, he
turns to the Bible. What he seeks is mercy, God's forgiveness for his involvement in a system that he instinctually feels is wrong but with which
he will not interfere because of his commitment to his wife. In equating
Nancy with Mercy from *The Pilgrim's Progress*, he thus reconciles the issue.
By treating the dear "child," as he calls her, with mercy and respect, he
follows the New Testament injunction "Blessed are the merciful, for they
shall obtain mercy."

Reviewers of the novel have heaped criticism on Henry Colbert and
his creator for the apparent equivocal stance both assume when Nancy's
safety is threatened and escape becomes her only alternative. But to claim
that Colbert's inaction implies an acceptance of slavery and undercuts the
novel's "chief significant action" of Nancy's escape (Randall 365) is to dis-
regard what Cather recognized as a real dilemma for a gentleman in Colbert's circumstances. His response to Martin Colbert's threats to Nancy is
not that of a "feminized bystander," as Elizabeth Jane Harrison claims (69),
but is the probable reaction for a man caught between two sets of expectations. Like Jim Burden, he is disturbed to find his idealized woman sexually
desirable to others, especially since his own blood-relative would seduce
and subdue her. Colbert curses the inherited impulses that he has so long
suppressed in his efforts to be the "gentleman of the manor." In Martin he
sees what he might have been and could become, and he hates the image:
"Wrath flamed up in him as he paced the floor; against his nephew and the
father who begot him, against all his brothers and the Colbert blood. . . .
there must have been bad blood in the Colberts back on the other side of
the water, and it had come to light in his three brothers and their sons. He
knew the family inheritance well enough. He had his share of it" (191–92).

What further disturbs him is that considering black women as sexual
objects available for their owners' pleasures was endorsed by the class into
which he had married and to which he owed another kind of allegiance. His
marriage vows, which he kept "as he would keep any other contract" (192),
also included the presumption that he would endorse his wife's right to
direct even the sexual lives of her slaves, as she had in marrying Till to the
"capon man." The yeoman gentleman, committed to respect for the individual, regardless of race, finds himself yoked to the Cavalier, whose respect for the individual is inextricably bound to race. While readers might
judge Henry Colbert harshly for not taking a stand and coming to Nancy's
defense, his failure to act is, as Jenny Pulsipher argues, "a matter of principle rather than of weakness or cowardice" (94). He cannot do what he

would do without breach of contract; by not overtly acting, he maintains a gentleman's integrity. He finds it "dreary business to be responsible for other folks' lives" (205), yet the role of gentleman demands such responsibility.

Richard Giannone correctly asserts that Henry Colbert is torn between a love of human freedom and love for his wife (32), which, one might add, requires adherence to the agreement that binds them, along with all its concomitant obligations. While Henry recognizes his "legal right to manumit any of his wife's negroes" and actually proposes manumission to Sampson, he admits that such an act would be "an outrage to [Sapphira's] feelings" (108). If Henry Colbert fears anything, it is not Sapphira's disapproval but the loss of her love. He is consistently sensitive to his wife's feelings, even "unquestioningly" changing his miller's garb for shirt and black suit when he sees Sapphira in her velvet gown (159). Cather writes that the miller had "always been proud" of his wife, even when he didn't understand her (268–69).

Critics often focus on the relationships between Colbert and Sapphira as an inverse master/mistress relationship (Harrison 69), pointing to his comment, "You're the master here, and I'm the miller. And that's how I like it to be" (50). But, the comment does not relegate Henry to passivity under his wife's rule. In the same parlor scene he politely offers the tea biscuits to Sapphira, delights in her clever masquerade of adding a jot of rum to his tea, and chides her for facetiously calling him "Master." Sapphira later defers to Henry for approval of her proposed trip to Winchester, a ploy the reader knows masks her plan to avenge herself upon Nancy. Henry, however, has neither the temperament for nor is trained to "nose out" deceit, and he accepts his wife's inquiry as sincere. While Sapphira is indulgent of and even amused by her husband, she expects him to respond to her as a gentleman would, denying only the most unreasonable requests. Sapphira's delight at her husband's unexpected and strong objection to Bluebell's acting as interim housekeeper for the miller's room is more a reaction to Henry's violation of gentlemanly decorum than evidence of her indulgence of an "inferior." "It was a treat to hear her husband break out like this," Cather writes (52).

Henry Colbert concludes that we are all, in some way, in bonds (110), and he is himself bound as an honorable husband who loves his wife in spite of their ideological differences. He cannot endorse Rachel's plan to help Nancy escape, as he tells his daughter, because he refuses to "be a party to make away with your mother's property" (227). This is a question of honor with Colbert, not a question of justice. While he is ashamed to show "irresolution" before his daughter (227), Colbert rationalizes that his own hesitancy to become involved in the plot coincides with his belief that "nobody is altogether free" (228). Even with "authority as head of his family"

(257), Henry Colbert's choices are limited by the standards of the southern gentleman.

Just as Henry feels bound to a certain code of behavior, based on his marriage to Sapphira and the place he must assume in their small world, he empathetically comes to realize his wife's bondage. In trying to fathom the meaning of Jezebel's life and death, he remembers the passage from Hebrews 13:3: "Remember them in bonds as bound with them." But as Giannone points out (42), the verse continues: ". . . and them which suffer adversity, as being yourselves also in the body." Henry Colbert is a literalist, and for him this passage takes on new meaning when Sapphira's physical suffering becomes acute. His once perceived gentlemanly obligation and affection for his wife evolve into identification with her: "He seemed in a moment to feel sharply so many things he had grown used to and taken for granted; her long illness, with all its discomforts, and the intrepid courage with which she had faced the inevitable" (267). The resultant Pietà scene is not a concession to Sapphira's power or evidence of Henry's weakness. Sapphira does not in that instant become a mammy to her husband, as Elizabeth Jane Harrison contends (77). Rather, Henry's tears are shed in pity for Sapphira's suffering and in compassionate love for another human being. Lavon Mattes Jobes's argument that Henry had married for security and that each got out of the marriage what each wanted (77) is also undercut by this scene. Sapphira approaches her death with the same composure that Henry had endorsed as proper for a gentleman. To him, she is a "gentlewoman" who is "mistress of the situation and of herself" (268). Immediately after Sapphira's death, though, Colbert frees her slaves. He never abandons his democratic yeoman ideals and realizes that the social codes to which he felt bound are insignificant before the bonds that make all persons human and mortal.

Contrary to Randall's claim that "in this book more than in any other the conflict between value systems destroys [Cather's] vision of reality and makes a hash of her art" (366), that very conflict makes Henry Colbert and his dilemma "real" and not a part of the southern literary convention of "a dream-like past in which realism is not demanded" (Gross 119). In showing Henry Colbert's struggle to act rightly while remaining true to the ideals of a gentleman, Cather created one of her most sympathetic characters. The miller's obligation not to undermine the aristocratic values espoused by his wife places him in the tenuous position of a gentleman whose sense of justice is threatened by adhering to a required code of conduct. Still, Henry Colbert is an honorable man who does, finally, admire Sapphira. He does not capitulate to her ethical ideas, as Randall suggests (365), but he comes to understand that she, like he, is bound to something. The "moral wandering" (Giannone 33) that constitutes the majority of Henry Colbert's "actions" in this novel is not reason to condemn him as weak or pathetic. Striving to live as a gentleman should, he finds the order of his world disrupted by slavery, "breaking in two," as such, and conventional sources that should offer solutions prove unsatisfactory. In Henry Colbert, Willa Cather thus presents an admirable gentleman who attempts to find meaning in an increasingly complex society while maintaining his personal dignity, his compassion, and his honor.

Notes

1. See Gwin, *Black and White Women;* and Romines, *"Sapphira and the Slave Girl"* 155–62.

2. Willa Cather, *Sapphira and the Slave Girl* (1940; New York: Knopf, 1968), 5. All further citations are to this edition, with permission of the publisher, Alfred A. Knopf, Inc., a Division of Random House, Inc.

White Dirt

The Surreal Racial Landscapes of Willa Cather's South

PATRICIA YAEGER

I want to begin by exploring two very different landscapes—each associated with femininity. Virginia Woolf records the first in *A Room of One's Own*. After discovering the power and rapture of women's writing, Woolf turns to the writing of men; she celebrates the virility of the masculine "I." But behind this virility Woolf imagines a treelike woman, a creature perpetually lost behind the force field of men's "I"-emblazoning fictions:

> After reading a chapter or two a shadow seemed to lie across the page. It was a straight dark bar, a shadow shaped something like the letter "I." One began dodging this way and that to catch a glimpse of the landscape behind it. Whether that was indeed a tree or a woman walking I was not quite sure. . . . One began to be tired of "I." Not but what this "I" was a most respectable "I." . . . But—here I turned a page or two, looking for something or other—the worst of it is that in the shadow of the letter "I" all is shapeless as mist. Is that a tree? No, it is a woman. But . . . she has not a bone in her body. (99–100)

Woolf's cartilaginous woman recalls Nancy, the black heroine of Cather's *Sapphira and the Slave Girl*: "Mrs. Blake sat watching Nancy's slender, nimble hands, so flexible that one would say there were no hard bones in them at all: they seemed compressible, like a child's" (18). What does it mean to introduce Nancy as someone so gelatinous, so flexible, that she contracts every time we see her, conforming to every available landscape until the very end of the novel? What does it mean to invent a black female character who first appears in Cather's novel as a woman without any bones?

Over against this land- and bodyscape of female abjection, I want to set another panorama: Ellen Moers's soaring affirmation of Cather's landscapes of female ecstasy.

> The whole Panther Cañon section of the novel [*The Song of the Lark*] is concerned with female self-assertion in terms of landscape; and the dedication to female landscape carries with it here the fullest possible tally of spiritual, historical, national, and artistic associations. . . . [T]hat certain lands have been good for women is clear—open lands, harsh and upswelling, high-lying and undulating, . . . cut with ravines

and declivities and twisting lanes. At the very least, the brilliant landscape writing that women have devoted to open country should give
pause to the next critic who wants to pronounce all literary women
housebound, and the next psychologist with a theory about "inner
space." (258, 262)

In *The Song of the Lark*'s Thea Kronborg we discover a character who ful-
fills Moers's desire to locate the female sublime geographically, as Thea's
voice and psyche become a locale. Before her trip to Panther Canyon, the
singer's strength has the flexibility of simile. Her beautiful voice "played
in and about and around and over them, like a goldfish darting among
creek minnows, like a yellow butterfly soaring above a swarm of dark ones"
(57–58). But within the stony heat of the cliff-dwellers' promontories, the
weightlessness of these similes drifts away, and Thea becomes the thing
itself: "[H]er power to think seemed converted into a power of sustained
sensation. She could become a mere receptacle of heat, or become a colour,
like the bright lizards that darted about on the hot stones outside her door;
or she could become a continuous repetition of sound, like the cicadas"
(259). Thea has absorbed the power of the landscapes she has inhabited;
she becomes a woman whose voice can create space. As she sings the part
of Elsa in *Lohengrin*, Dr. Archie is frightened and uplifted by her power:
"Archie did not know when his buckfever passed, but presently he found
that he was sitting quietly in a darkened house, not listening to, but dreaming upon, a river of silver sound" (349).

Thinking historically about Cather's preoccupations with place, literary
critics have begun to produce powerful work linking Cather's spatial imagination with the histories of migration and ethnicity in America. My thesis
will not address this epic space. While Walter Benn Michaels and Joseph
Urgo explore Cather's gigantism—her migratory urgency, her continental
drifts—I want, instead, to explore the rifts in her fiction, the ways in which
Cather's image-saturated landscapes become the central source for establishing her characters' complexities: their racially layered psyches.

I will first turn to object relations, to the ways in which Cather's white
characters are defined by an uncanny ability to interject or absorb the
places and objects around them. But I also want to contrast this construction of the white psyche *as* landscape with Cather's object-poor portraits of
black characters. In *Playing in the Dark: Whiteness and the Literary Imagination*, Toni Morrison describes a handful of white texts that struggle unsuccessfully to rearticulate race, even as they succumb to racist convention.
Although she argues that *Sapphira and the Slave Girl* is deliriously retro-
grade in its portrait of slave women, she adds that by trying to find aesthetic
forms equal to the story of slave-owning women's dependency upon and
abuse of African American "possessions," Cather both fails and succeeds;
she pushes her narrative toward a hitherto unrecognized breaking point.

In contrast to her portrait of Cather, Morrison describes a series of can-onized white male writers who struggle very little against "the parasitical nature of white freedom." At "the end of literary journeys into the forbid-den space of blackness," these white male canonical authors portray their heroes as "the inheritors of the blood of African Kings" as they dance over fields of "frozen whiteness." Snow becomes "the wasteland of un-meaning, unfathomable whiteness" in Poe; in Bellow's *Henderson the Rain King*, it becomes the sign of "a new white man in a new found land: 'leap-ing, pounding, and tingling over the pure white lining of the gray Arctic silence'" as Henderson carries "an Africanist child in his arms, the soul of the Black King in his baggage." In fictions by Melville, Faulkner, Hem-ingway, Poe, and Bellow, blackness is "evil and protective[,] . . . fearful and desirable—all the self-contradictory features of the self," while whiteness is simply "unfathomable" (57–58).

That "certain lands" have been good for white men seems clear. But I will argue that images of frozen whiteness speak very differently in fic-tions by white southern women, and that Cather's struggle with race gains a new dimension of disappointment and complexity when we place her fic-tion in the company of southern women writers. Here whiteness becomes a burden; the white characters invented by Katherine Anne Porter, Eudora Welty, and Carson McCullers have a schizophrenic perspective on their own skins. Throughout southern women's fiction we find weird images of whiteness: part bodies, fragments of face paint or skin, texts where images of pallor spill out of the atmosphere like ghosts going to the wrong wed-ding. The bifurcated, dissolving white bodies we find in Cather's last novel, compounded by *Sapphira*'s flour-ridden landscape, complicate Toni Mor-rison's theorems about white writing.

In the world of canonical males, Morrison finds landscapes in which "whiteness, alone, is mute, meaningless, unfathomable, pointless, frozen, veiled, curtained, dreaded, senseless, implacable" (*Playing* 59). But in the landscapes imagined by Cather and her white southern female contempo-raries, whiteness is both senseless and too mobile; it erupts with an excess of meaning and becomes *terrifyingly dynamic, vulnerable, agitated, tortured, vertiginous.* Or, it is *partial, fragmented, an intensive source of labor, a site of confusion that gums up the works.* In other words, white skin becomes a source of pollution; it enters the text with the unwashed power of defilement. Whiteness becomes something extraneous, inassimilable, or unclean: the scattered, disassimilated body a form of white dirt.

To understand this departure from canonical color codes, we need to pay more attention to the imbroglio of space and character in Cather's fiction, since Cather invents a fascinating technique for imbricating place and char-acter in her fiction. Unlike her modernist contemporaries Stein and Woolf, Cather would seem to use place straightforwardly, creating spatial relations between objects and subjects as a technique of psychic realism. Her spatial images increase her fiction's "reality effect," providing a sense that these are real people who live in real time and space who have converted the rumble of spatiality into "real" inner and outer lives. But the linguistic textures of Cather's realism border on surrealism—an evocation of the magic of matter, of the surrealists' discovery that found objects can release "the marvelous precipitate of desire" (Beardsley 36). That is, each character's spatial totemism becomes a way to release the uncanny—to create an effect of the marvelous that resists the oppressive harangue of the very reality principle the novels work so hard to support. We have already seen two examples. In the first, Thea's beautiful voice "played in and about and around and over them, like a goldfish darting among creek minnows, like a yellow butterfly soaring above a swarm of dark ones." Here the vocative becomes weirdly spatial; as voice "plays," it becomes a goldfish, a butterfly—a yellow foreground that depends, for its visibility, on the power of a darker background. As Cather's drifty metaphors go to work, subjectivity becomes thick with the density of the object-world: "She could become a mere receptacle of heat, or become a colour, like the bright lizards that darted about on the hot stones outside her door, or she could become a continuous repetition of sound, like the cicadas." This "receptacle of heat" turns abstract and particular in the miniature bodies of lizards and the gorgeous monotony of natural sound. These prose passages become crowded and hypnotic, suggesting that a character's quasi-magical relation to place can erupt at any moment to displace the verbal thinness of similitude with a hypermodernist quality of fantasmatic thickness and opacity.

In the midst of this concurrent sense of reality and unreality, what is important is just how often and how consistently Cather's sense of character is conveyed *spatially*. For Bakhtin, "the human being in the novel is first, foremost and always a speaking human being," for novels require "speaking persons bringing with them their own unique ideological discourse, their own language" (332). But for Cather, the human being in the novel is, first and foremost, a *spatial* human being. In *The Professor's House*, not only does St. Peter adore the garden where he works off his discontent, not only is he defined from the beginning by his relation to houses—his refusal to move, or his inability to use the official study as he retreats to his "dark den"— but his élan and convincingness as a character are also determined by the liquid space of Lake Michigan, "the inland sea of his childhood. . . . The sun rose out of it, the day began there; it was like an open door that nobody could shut. . . . it was the first thing one saw in the morning . . . and it ran through the days like the weather, not a thing thought about, but a part of consciousness itself" (20). This delicious inability to extricate self from setting, this sense of absorption by a landscape, is a central fact for many of Cather's white characters, making them dense symbolic sites for examining the labor of introjection—the act of taking in all or part of an object to make it a part of one's self.

Introjection works by a curious process of identification: we soak up objects and images from the settings we inhabit because these objects can become the gateway to desires that are otherwise inaccessible. That is, introjection is not about physical acts of collecting; it is not an object-greediness that feeds the self's material imperialism. Instead, Cather records her characters' psychic greediness. "The psyche is in a constant process of acquisition, involving the active expansion of our potential to open onto our own emerging desires and feelings as well as the external world" (Rand 100). The objects that we seek or repudiate offer a rebus for symbolizing impossible-to-articulate longings. As Maria Torok points out, when we seek to simulate or appropriate the objects, people, and prospects around us, what is sought is not so much possession *of* the object but possession *for* the object, a path for "including the Unconscious in the ego through objectal contacts" (Torok 113). Jameson puts this even more cogently in *Marxism and Form*:

> For Freud there is no such thing as an instinct or drive in its pure or physical state: all drives are mediated through images or fantasies. . . . so it is that some chance contact with an external object may 'remind' us of ourselves more profoundly than anything that takes place in the impoverished life of our conscious will. For unbeknownst to us, the objects around us lead lives of their own in our unconscious fantasies, where, vibrant with mana or taboo with symbolic fascination or repulsion, they stand as the words or hieroglyphs of the immense rebus of desire. (99)

Our desire for matter is more than a simple drive for survival, for excessive, greedy, willful, acquisitive swallowing. It is not a matter of gulping down the object-world, but of using objects to find a path into the hieroglyphic tangle of our own drives and desires. Thus the beginning of *The Song of the Lark* consists of a series of geographic sites—Mexican Town, the Germans' garden—that represent split-off aspects of a little girl's developing self. The child's task is to integrate these object-islands, these alienated or inaccessible aspects of her own being. Panther Canyon also occupies the novel as a singular site of integration and introjection: one combining a regressive sense of security, an archaic sense of being held by the object, with Thea's new capacity to absorb spatial power in order to enrich her vocal prowess and the designs of her desiring ego. These objects offer, then, a route into interior space that is more telling than the words that characters can speak; they offer a road to self-construction not always available in the rootedness of communicative syntax. Instead, real and imaginary objects can provide a map for reading the psyche and its hard-to-countenance longings.

If this seems abstruse, think of the ways in which both objects and spaces function in *The Professor's House* to create character boundaries and a sense of each character's qualities of inwardness or depth. For Tom Outland the mesa becomes a sublime cradle, a gigantic hieroglyph in which to shelter the immensity of his own desire. And what does he want? Both to be held and to be master, to be the rainbow-god of this floating world: "And the air, my God, what air!—Soft, tingling, gold, hot with an edge of chill on it, full of the smell of pinons—it was like breathing the sun, breathing the colour of the sky. Down there behind me was the plain, already streaked with shadow, violet and purple and burnt orange until it met the horizon." Breathing in the sun, Outland covers the landscape with his darkening body—absorbing the antiquity of the trees, mingling this ancientness with the sky's fluidity: "Before me was the flat mesa top, thinly sprinkled with old cedars that were not much taller than I, though their twisted trunks were almost as thick as my body. I struck off across it, my long black shadow going ahead" (217).

If my first proposition is that Cather builds desiring, sympathetic, complex characters (that is, characters with several different levels or zones of internal being) out of the object-detritus of the landscapes around them, my second proposition is that this complex relation to objects and landscapes is *not* available to her black characters. In *Sapphira* the landscapes that people inhabit are described more intricately than the psyches or personae of the black characters themselves. The space Cather invents within this novel is complex, inviting, and nuanced, if lacking in the panoramic grandeur of her novels of the West or Midwest. But unlike Cather's other settings, the sense of place that she invents around her black characters rarely supplements our sense of who they are. In the case of another novelist, this inertness of space in relation to character might not matter. But in Cather's novels one encounters a constant humming, an "endless melody," or "inexhaustible murmur" that is spatial (Jameson, *Marxism* 97). Her most fascinating characters inhabit an intimate, inarticulate, introjective relation to setting. For example, the professor accumulates a sense of depth that resonates beyond the commodity forms that surround him because he carries within himself the sensuous details of his oceanic childhood: "When the ice chunks came in of a winter morning, crumbly and white, throwing off gold and rose-coloured reflections from a copper-coloured sun behind the grey clouds, he didn't observe the detail or know what it was that made him happy; but now, forty years later, he could recall all its aspects perfectly. They had made pictures in him when he was unwilling and unconscious, when his eyes were merely openwide" (21). Cather bestows upon St. Peter an outside history and an inner holding environment in which, almost paradoxically, the key to his internal character is conveyed by the complex ways in which he has interiorized the outward spaces of his early life.[1] Similarly, in *My Mortal Enemy*, Mrs. Henshawe's devouring soul is defined spatially. At the end of the novel the narrator finds her dead, at the edge of a cliff, "wrapped in her blankets, leaning against the cedar trunk, facing the sea. . . . There was every reason to believe she had lived to see the dawn. While we watched beside her . . . I told Oswald what she had said to me about longing to behold the morning break over the sea, and it comforted him" (81).

The most primary or archaic spatial characteristic of Cather's fiction, then, lies in her ability to create complex landscapes that offer object-driven opportunities for character development and readerly seduction. So why does this playfulness cease when Cather invents her black characters—leaving them flat, unnuanced, and place-bereft? While Cather's white characters have an ability to appropriate objects and landscapes to create rich inner lives, her black characters have a curiously inert relationship to space, suggesting not only an arrested spatiality, but an arrested inventiveness on Cather's part: one that leads to a sense of these characters' listless subjectivities. Accompanying this flattening out of black characters, we will discover a third attribute of space in Cather's fiction—a kind of racial surrealism. What is most bizarre about *Sapphira*'s landscape is its agitated, tortured surfaces of whiteness: its portrayal of the shattered white body as something inassimilable, unsayable, and yet continually rearticulated by a mute and mutating white South.

If seascapes and cliffscapes migrate *inward* in Cather's novels, offering sites for defining and redefining the complexities of her white characters, why do we encounter in *Sapphira* a series of landscapes that cannot be introjected—that remain inert or outward, that fail to become part of her characters' object-world? Cather's black characters are not imagined as introjective beings (that is, she does not imagine for them an intricate relationship with the things and spaces around them), while her white characters are too busy consuming or disgorging the surrounding black characters (as well as the complex desires these black characters elicit) to engage in the place-based aspirations—the healthy annexation of unconscious into conscious life—that characters like Tom Outland or St. Peter or Thea Kronborg aspire to. Why?

To answer, I want to think about *Sapphira and the Slave Girl* as a southern novel, to examine its peculiar landscapes in more detail, and to chart the characteristics it shares with other modern texts by southern women writers. There are three arenas for tracing these similarities. First, we will examine the ways in which southern writing has been characterized by a peculiar relation to a shared space or place; second, the omnipresence in *Sapphira* and a series of cognate texts of the "southern" grotesque; and third, the importance of these texts of hidden or encrypted African American surrogate mothers. But before describing Cather's dialogue with her southern contemporaries, we need to note the spatial peculiarities of *Sapphira*'s landscapes and setting.

Why not begin with the "helter-skelter" world of the black cabins, a miniaturized space utterly unlike the landscapes of "earthbound ecstasy" that Moers finds in Cather's Great Plains novels (259)?[2] On the south side of these cabins Cather envisions gourd vines "which grew faster than any other creeper and bore flowers and fruits at the same time." The purpose of this plantscape is not decorative but appropriative; it is designed to incorporate bits and pieces of the big house, for the gourds are cut into bowls for holding "meal, butter, lard, gravy, or any tidbit that might be spirited away from the big kitchen to one of the cabins. . . . The gourd vessels were invisible to good manners" (21). Cather seems unable to glimpse the logic behind this legerdemain—a logic suggesting that black laborers' reappropriation of white wealth can be justified. In "Ruminations of Luke Johnson," a poem written ten years before *Sapphira*, Sterling Brown describes a black domestic whose empty basket is always full when she returns home from work:

> Well, tain't my business noway,
> An' I ain' near fo'gotten
> De lady what she wuks fo',
> An' how she got huh jack;
> De money dat *she* live on
> Come from niggers pickin' cotton,
> Ebbery dollar dat she squander
> Nearly bust a nigger's back. (36)

Brown argues that this black working woman's "theft" does not begin to redress what has been stolen from her. In contrast, Cather depicts a world in which African American penury simply insures the continual circulation of detachable objects of illicit desire: a landscape larded with unproductive detritus, with the uncared-for, with white throwaways, for the swept dirt yards outside these cabins are filled with workaday refuse. Beneath red calico dresses and overalls hung out to dry, "the ground . . . was littered with old brooms, spades and hoes, and the rag dolls and home-made toy wagons of the negro children. Except in a downpour of rain, the children were always playing there, in company with kittens, puppies, chickens, ducks that waddled up from the millpond, turkey gobblers which terrorized the little darkies and sometimes bit their naked black legs" (21–22). This is a landscape of pleasure that the narrator views with displeasure; for her it seems filled with part-objects and punitive objects. Till's room is also brimming with discards. Her chest contains the miller's old books, "the woolly green shawl he had worn as an overcoat, some of Miss Sapphy's lace caps and fichus, and odd bits of finery such as velvet slippers with buckles. Her chief treasure was a brooch, set in pale gold, and under the crystal was a lock of Mr. Henry's black hair and Miss Sapphy's brown hair, at the time of their marriage. . . . The miller himself had given it to her, she said" (291–93).

Each of these black settings contains stolen objects or throwaways from the big house, making the white environs of the big house the main reference point for Cather's portrait of African Americans' desires. And yet the white landscape is also filled with detritus: "The miller's furniture was whitewashed, so to speak, day by day, by the flour-dust which sifted down from overhead, and through every crack and crevice in the doors and walls. Each morning Till's Nancy swept and dusted the flour away" (47). This whiteness is unwanted but cannot be brushed off; it coagulates where it is least desired. "Colbert changed his old leather jacket for a black coat, brushed the flour-dust off his broad hat, and walked up through the cold spring drizzle which was making the grass green" (49). After complaining about Bluebell's housekeeping, "He said no more, but went out into the hall and took up his wide-brimmed hat—this morning white with two days' flour-dust" (64).

The environment Cather builds in this novel has the paradoxical qualities I mentioned earlier; it is at once realistic and surrealistic. The flour that sifts through the air creates a convincing reality effect for an episodic novel about a miller, and yet these flour particles are also charged with the uncanny—with a foreboding sense of whiteness as dirt. The air of the mill is filled with part-objects—with flour particles that everyone tries to brush away but no one can get rid of. In this weird atmospheric pallor, Cather creates an environment filled with digestible particles that fail to nourish, a space where food is detritus, where white, the most "valued" of colors, is regarded as dirt. An extraordinary space of dissociation is set up within Cather's novel, suggesting some failure—on an ontological level—to make sense of whiteness. As Leo Bersani suggests, an environment filled with a superfluity of detachable objects or part-objects produces archaic anxieties: "The self's integrity is threatened" by a series of separations: "by the infant's separation from its mother; the body's wholeness is destroyed by the actual or fantasized loss of feces or placenta or penis. The body no longer makes sense when something drops away from it" (59).

I'm suggesting that this flour floats through the air like so much dead skin, like the leavings of some decaying albino body. It creates an intriguing sense of disconnection, unanchored identity, fragmentation, and an "anguished preoccupation with the mobility of meaning"—a bizarre self-scattering (Bersani 59). *Why have we failed to recognize these persistent landscapes that are already in pieces, but cling to the body like a funky, disintegrating amnion?* For example, the miller is clean-shaven, "unusual in a man of his age and station," because "a miller's beard got powdered with flour-dust, and when the sweat ran down his face this flour got wet and left him with a beard full of dough" (4). In this world things seem to migrate, to coagulate, where they do not belong. This coagulation recurs in Sapphira's swollen white legs: "She regarded her feet and ankles with droll contempt while Till drew on the stockings and tied a ribbon garter below each of her wax-white, swollen knees" (32). Her body-parts become near-totemic objects vibrating with revulsion and fixation, as if the demonic aura of whiteness has dropped down on her body and immobilized it forever.

This whiteness—which is so very much there, and yet so "natural" a part of this environment that it is nearly invisible as a signifier, which is so essential to the realistic surface of the novel and yet so uncanny or obsessive as a symbolic site—becomes a haunting *signifier of what cannot be thought* or organized either in the nineteenth-century historyscape of the novel or in the landscape of the 1930s from which Cather herself is writing. These floating particles coalesce into an almost present *structure of feeling* that has not yet emerged as a *structure of thought*—a site of uncanny, inassimilable emotions, of an "epistemological disarray" that fails to organize the underanalyzed structures of race and racial oppression (Bersani 60).[3]

This environmental weirdness also resurfaces in the miller's obsessive peregrinations through his Bible, where, attempting to decipher the logic of slavery, he marks all the verses on captivity "with a large S" (110). We learn about Henry Colbert's hieratical bent at the end of book 3, but if we linger at the beginning of book 4, the *S*s haunting the margins of the miller's Bible suddenly coalesce into an eerie alphabet-landscape as Mrs. Blake foots her way around "the last loop of the Double S" on her way to Timber Ridge. These double *S*s are re-created typographically, in Cather's own text, marking the space before each numeral that denotes a chapter heading, suggesting that we should read each chapter as "Slavery 1," "Slavery 2," et cetera. The spatialization of these letters that stand in for "slavery" creates an odd transition, since these land- and chapterscapes rutted with *S*s seem almost too literal in their spatialization of the most fundamental conditions of the miller's world. And what follows seems at once too mimetic and too hyperbolic in its duplications of this world's sociology of color:

> In the deep ravine below the road a mountain stream rushed *coffee brown*, throwing up crystal rainbows where it gurgled over rock ledges. . . . from the *naked grey* wood the dogwood thrust its crooked forks starred with *white blossoms*—the flowers set in their own wild way along the rampant zigzag branches. Their unexpectedness, their singular *whiteness*, never loses its wonder, even to the dullest dweller in those hills. (115–16; emphasis added)

This dogwood is pronounced "the wildest thing and yet the most austere, the most unearthly" in the Virginia woodland (116). In such a deliberate prospectus of totemically reproduced whiteness, is it any wonder that there is nothing of value for Cather's African American characters to introject? This landscape reproduces the problem driving Cather's novel—that the black labor of slaves like Samson and Nancy continually produces the "unearthly" whiteness of the air-drifting flour as well as the ether of white capital that keeps them enslaved. When African Americans are so imbricated in the landscape, how can they participate in scenes of individuation that Cather chooses to invent for her most complex characters (that is, for those who are most personified or individualized in other novels)? Not only does the introjective potential of white characters, their capacity to absorb or master this environment, depend upon the object-producing labor of the black characters but, within Cather's fictional world, blacks could be said to lack an introjective potential *because they themselves are envisioned as objects;* they are defined *as* environment, as background or landscape. Think, for example, of the ways in which, as Nancy moves toward a more egalitarian or intersubjective relation with the miller, Sapphira tries to change her into a nonperson again by tearing Nancy away from the people she loves and setting her up as the object of seduction. Placed on a pallet outside Sapphira's own room, Nancy is both given object status and transposed into background, re-created as a veritable holding environment for her mistress. Calling out for Nancy in the middle of the night (and checking to make sure she isn't sharing a bed with Henry Colbert), Sapphira expresses her anxieties in terms of the disintegration of her own spatial security. Hearing Nancy's "sleepy, startled voice," Sapphira drops back in her chair and draws a breath: "It was over. Her shattered, treacherous house stood safe about her again. She was in her own room" (107).

These spatial anxieties extend to Sapphira's epistemic style, her ways of making sense of the world. In this environment where everything persists on the surface—the letter *S*, the drifting flour, the whiteness produced by black labor—Sapphira is only preoccupied with depth psychology, convinced that everything that matters happens *under* the surface: invisible, only decipherable, within a byzantine hermeneutics of suspicion. But around and against Sapphira, Cather's text keeps insisting that everything worth reading is instead on the surface, at the outermost layer of things—in the flour that keeps being shoved about, in the double *S* that marks every chapter heading. The novel's space-making signs seem almost too self-conscious, too premasticated or preinterpreted, and yet no one in the novel's world tries to read them.

In the final section of this essay I want to explore another venue for reading these troubled signs (these signifiers for what one might call "the unthought known" of Cather's text). For in fact, the novel's weird details also cast light on the symptoms or symbolic structures it shares with other novels by southern women writers. What is it about Cather's southern experience, or about her ideas of the South, that forces her into a different mode of fiction writing: one in which the relation between place and character becomes unexpectedly inert, lacking the dynamic interaction between place and person that appears elsewhere? What makes this mode of writing both so inert and so schizophrenic or labile, with objects drifting back and forth between black and white culture and body parts drifting through the air? To answer, we will need to think about *Sapphira* as a southern novel—as a text that is regionally biased and regionally based. How to begin?

We all know the truisms about southern writing. As Walker Percy intones, "the South [has] a tradition which is more oriented toward history, toward the family . . . [,] toward storytelling, and toward tragedy." Eudora Welty adds to these clichés: "We in the South have grown up being narrators. We have lived in a place—that's the word, Place—where storytelling is a way of life. . . . Our concept of Place isn't just history or philosophy; it's a sensory thing of sights and smells and seasons and earth and water and sky as well" (Prenshaw 93–95, 142–43).

Although I usually take great pleasure in debunking these truisms, for once I want to insist that the spaces depicted in southern women's writing *do* have a different aura; do, in fact, struggle with a peculiar set of southern problems (although not of the magical sort that Welty envisions); and I want to argue that these qualities have influenced Willa Cather's fiction. Welty's invocation of southern earth and water resonates with two proto-modernist stories from the 1890s: stories in which characters discover that, while they believe themselves to be "white," they are, in fact, socially defined as "black"; their whiteness is just a veneer. Both characters respond by committing suicide.

In Grace King's "The Little Convent Girl," a "white" woman meeting her black mother for the first time falls—or jumps—from the gangplank of a riverboat, her body merging with the undercurrent of the dark Mississippi. In Kate Chopin's "Désirée's Baby," a young woman who also believes herself to be white gives birth to a mixed-race baby and—rejected by her husband and peers—walks out with her child into the swamps, her body mingling with the mud at the edges of the bayou. Here the sensory qualities of earth and water that Welty celebrates take a particular turn. Both King and Chopin construct a landscape filled with white culture's throw-aways, with women who regard themselves as detritus and whose deaths create an ongoing landscape of melancholia, a place where racial abjection becomes a cultural site for the cycling and recycling of ungrieved grief.

In the period of writing that stretches from the New Deal through the civil rights movement and its aftermath, we find a series of southern fictions in which both black and white women are bent on excavating this landscape of melancholy, from Katherine Anne Porter's Miranda stories to Alice Walker's *Meridian*. In Walker's novel, the fetid corpse of a black child who has drowned in the drainage ditches left treacherously open by the whites' city services gets upgathered in Meridian's arms, carried to City Hall, and dropped on the mayor's desk. In bringing the mess of the margins to the center, Walker unearths the black women and children who have been buried in water or earth; she protests the landscapes of cruelty that surround her characters. Here the earth itself comes to represent lives and bodies that have been thrown away, stories that have never happened, foundations never plumbed. Place does become eerily important in southern fiction, but not in the breezy, auratic way that Welty describes. Instead, a series of women writers, including Welty herself, seem haunted by what mires the southern earth, by what has been buried or encrypted, by places that contain throwaway bodies that have been emptied of narration. Cather replicates these self-emptying stories in her tale of Tansy Dave, in the too-brief descriptions of the slave's dirt yards as refuse piles, in the coffee-brown streams that produce such whitely floriferous joy, in the death of Till's mother, in Jezebel's burial in the slaves' single-named, segregated plot.

We find more melancholic places in the echolalias of whiteness and floating white signifiers that not only haunt Cather's *Sapphira* but preoccupy other white southern women writers. In Welty's *Delta Wedding* the cotton wagons were filled with "white and were loaded with white, like cloud wagons. All along, the Negroes would lift up and smile glaringly and pump their arms," while the throb of the cotton compress vibrates incessantly through the objects that define the capaciousness of the big house: a reminder of the commodity resourcefulness whites have garnered while employing oppressively cheap black labor. The house itself fills up with cotton lint on ceilings and lampshades, "like a present from the fairies, that made Vi'let moan" (8, 37). Uncanny, anxious signifiers of whiteness repeat themselves in Carson McCullers's *Member of the Wedding* and Ellen Douglas's *Can't Quit You Baby* where Tweet, the white protagonist's maid, can only be heard (registered, humanized, half-understood) by her employer in the flurry of a Northeastern snowstorm.

This sense of southern place as an overscripted, unreadable blizzard of whiteness produced by oppressed and encrypted black multitudes coalesces in the meditations on place that dominate Welty's writing of "Where Is the Voice Coming From?"—a story about the murder of Medgar Evers—written in the first person from the bone-chilling perspective of a hypothetical white hick who plans Evers's assassination and pulls the trigger. As Welty says: "I did write a story the night it happened. I was so upset about this and I thought: I live down here where this happened and I believe that I must know what a person like that felt like—this murderer. . . . I was wrong in the social level of the man accused—that's interesting, isn't it?—but I think I still knew what the man thought. I had lived with that kind of thing" (Prenshaw 182).

Here Welty describes a truly southern sense of place from the bizarre double-consciousness of a white southern liberal: To feel horrified for

Medgar Evers but to know the mindset, the place-set, the "where" of the man who killed him, and to be driven to narrate this event, not because storytelling is a southern way of life but because the author/narrator can identify with the white murderer. That is, she knows too well this unspoken landscape of recycled grief, of endless racial melancholia attached to stories of thrown-away bodies, of daily traumas so quotidian that they simply repeat themselves, that mire the earth, that produce and reproduce whiteness as a signifier, not a story.

What has seemed most anomalous about Cather's *Sapphira* in relation to her earlier oeuvre—its strangely striated and nonintrojectable landscape—seems utterly ordinary in the context of white southern women's writing, where characters are continually struggling to make sense of, to repudiate, and at the same time, to internalize a landscape made out of undervalued, impoverished black labor—a feat that is impossible without gagging—impossible, that is, without producing the grotesque. Thus a second characteristic that Cather shares with her southern compatriots is a preoccupation with the grotesque, connecting her fiction with dozens of images for social deformity in stories by Welty, McCullers, O'Connor, and Walker. Cather matches them, blow for blow, in the bodies of each of her characters. Sapphira has dropsy; Nancy, a body without any bones (a body that is also indented at the beginning of the story by the blows of Sapphira's hairbrush); Martin Colbert has a weirdly blue tooth. In fact, the farther south the characters go, the more grotesque they become, as Michael Blake and his son contract yellow fever in New Orleans and begin to vomit black blood.

Third, and finally, like her precursors King and Chopin, Cather angles her text in the direction of hidden or encrypted black mothers. To understand this dimension of southern fiction, recall that in *A Room of One's Own* Woolf explains that we must write back through our mothers if we are women. But the question this raises for southern women is—which mothers? Many white southerners were raised by black women, while many black southerners lost the constancy of their mothers to underpaid work in white homes. Alice Walker pays homage to Zora Neale Hurston in *In Search of Our Mothers' Gardens*, but also to Flannery O'Connor. Chopin and King each posit, at the ends of "Désirée's Baby" and "The Little Convent Girl," a black mother who is writing or holding a plot-shifting letter. What is the status, in white women's fiction, of African American women's speech or writing?

This question surfaces in the stories of female suicide in "The Little Convent Girl" and "Désirée's Baby" that we examined earlier. In each story, the existence of a nurturant black mother is hidden by its white author until the story's end. In each story the mother is associated with writing, with the possession of a crucial, revelatory letter. In each instance the letter deflects the angle of the reader's racial gaze; it changes the ways we think about surfaces, about what is so obvious about race that it is hidden in plain sight. Similarly, in *Sapphira*, Till's intimate relation with the little girl narrator is withheld until the novel's end. She too holds the letter, in the sense that Till is named as the source of Cather's family stories. Till, Cather intimates, is also "tell," the source of hidden or disavowed verbal riches, of stories to be wrung, or tilled, from the unquiet southern earth.

What does all this add up to? Cather and her later white southern compatriots are writing fiction from a rich and troubled racial field. Their fictions rehearse and often recapitulate 1) a traumatically unjust environment of black detritus and white melancholia, 2) a field of grotesque bodies so unsupported by their environment that they seem at once misshapen and overwhelming, and 3) a world secretly mediated by hidden, disavowed, enslaved (and/or mercenary) black mothers who hold the letter, but whose figures of speech are marginalized or devalued. Each of these sites represent *arrested systems of race and gender knowledge* that southern women writers, white and black, deplore, reproduce, but also try from the 1930s to the 1990s, to disencode.

And yet, among these writers Cather is oddly exceptional. She seems less troubled than, say, Eudora Welty, Carson McCullers, or Katherine Anne Porter about the racial limits of her chosen symbols. In Carson McCullers's *Member of the Wedding*, when Frankie dispenses with her black caretaker, Berenice, whiteness suggests the transformation of African American selves into African American others and Frankie's new shallowness: frost silvers "the brown grass and the roofs of neighbors' houses, and even the thinned leaves of the rusty arbor" (151). The escapades of "Miss Snowdie Mac-Lain," a white albino, provide a snappish critique of the South's protected femmes when Snowdie tries, in Welty's *Golden Apples*, to live in a shower of whiteness—"and once they dressed Snowdie all in white, you know she was whiter than your dreams" (6). Finally, in Ellen Douglas's *Can't Quit You Baby*, Cornelia begins to talk to an imaginary Tweet—for the first time—amid the shattered skies of a New York snow storm: "I'm cold. The wind is blowing. This crosstown wind . . . And I have to watch my step every minute or I'll fall down. Listen. Cornelia put her foot on a slanting, icy mound, slipped, recovered her balance" (193). As Tweet begins to speak and Cornelia to listen, what she hears are Tweet's hallucinatory stories about the heaviness of southern things:

> Wait, Cornelia says, This is heavy. Too heavy. . . . .
>
> You think you know heavy? You hadn't drug a cotton sack twelve or fourteen hours a day, have you? Carried a load of somebody else's wash on your head. Carried two buckets of water from the cistern? That's heavy.

Whatever this is, it's heavy, too, Cornelia says.

If it's wash, carry it home, wash it and iron it. Get you a red wagon and a basket and carry it back. Hold on, that's the message. Keep your hand on the plow, hold on. If it's water, drink with it, wash with it, cook with it. If it's a cotton sack, hmmm. . . . My advice, if it's a cotton sack, go get you a better job. (196)

These texts point to an underanalyzed, underthought, and unexplored whiteness that tries, with middling success, to emerge as story, as theme. But Cather's white flight is shiftier; her flour-light people are both flatter and harder to grasp. Morrison suggests that Cather fails to control her themes in this novel—just as she fails to give full psyches to her black characters—because the material she confronts is so overwhelming. But what else perturbs her writing in this novel?

The dust jacket to the first edition of *Sapphira and the Slave Girl* contains a strange blurb written by Alfred Knopf, stating proudly that *Sapphira* caps off his first twenty-five years of publishing. He too focuses on landscape: "The setting is the beautiful Virginia countryside, and the narrative is peopled with unusual characters: the mountain people, grim disapproving 'Republicans,' and Sapphira's African slaves, who are, and doubtless were meant to be, the most interesting figures in the book. These colored folk are presented in an unusual way. They are attractive to the writer as individuals, and are presented by a sympathetic artist who is neither reformer nor sentimentalist." In today's world of literary criticism, this claim can only seem fabulous, that is, patently untrue. What's surprising isn't Knopf's hype but the basis of his claim. In the American literary marketplace that Knopf and Cather inhabited—a marketplace already saturated by the New Negro Renaissance—we find reams of individuated characters, from Clare Kendry and Irene Redfield in Nella Larsen's *Passing* to John and Lucy in *Jonah's Gourd Vine*. Cather's characters are anything but individuals; they seem stereotyped beyond belief.

I have argued that this lack of individuation springs from a leak in Cather's most characteristic mode of creativity; from her black characters' lack of a relationship to the landscape itself, "the beautiful Virginia countryside" Knopf praises with such minor eloquence. But I also want to point to the horror implicit in Knopf's honorifics. That these characters represent for him, in 1941, the acme of black individualism in a world so complexly populated by people of color is nothing short of absurd.

In citing Knopf's praise for this volume, I also want to insist that, in Cather's hands, the southern codes I have enumerated (the flirtation with scattered whiteness, with grotesque bodies, and with hidden or occluded black mothers) turn squalidly discontinuous or surreal; if these tropes provide a crazy texture for her book (one that has proven pleasurable for the deconstructive mania of this critic), these rebarbative codes also cease to function communicatively, turning into textual crypts. In borrowing a southern vocabulary to express the complex racial fantasies of her own childhood, Cather's own aesthetic goes on overload (as Morrison suggests, four hundred years of silence are too much to undo in the brief span of a novel).

Finally, in tracing Cather's powerful incapacities I want to double back to the spatial conundrums of my beginning and suggest that Cather's peculiar brand of spatial hunger feeds the conditions of Till's and Nancy's lost complexity—a loss that becomes particularly clear at the novel's end. Cather's description of the house where these women have been consigned to second-class status (where they eat downstairs at the "second table" while the white family enjoys the hierarchical pleasures of the upstairs dining room) is accurate, in its historicity, for a novel describing the South of the 1880s. But a lack of protest about these distinctions looks much more complex and unsavory from the perspective of the New Deal world of the 1930s—the very world Cather is writing from. Rather than question the etiquette of white eating by ironizing the upstairs-downstairs world that her novel portrays (as McCullers does in *A Member of the Wedding* [1945] or Welty does in *Delta Wedding* [1946]), Cather suggests that the big house, with its byzantine codes of racial separation, is, quite simply, a site of plenitude, a space perfectly designed to take care of the visual and oral needs of a little white girl:

> We had three kitchen tables: one for kneading bread, another for making cakes and pastry, and a third with a zinc top, for dismembering fowls and rabbits and stuffing turkeys. The tall cupboards stored sugar and spices and groceries; our farm wagons brought supplies out from Winchester in large quantities. Behind the doors of a very special corner cupboard stood all the jars of brandied fruit, and glass jars of ginger and orange peel soaking in whisky. Canned vegetables, and the preserved fruits not put down in alcohol, were kept in a very cold cellar; a stream ran through it, actually! (287)

Here is a little Cather landscape in miniature—a site ready for introjection, for forging the most intimate and appetitive connections with all those "objects" that define this delicious setting. To recognize Till and Nancy as angry, anxious, introjective, desiring subjects in their own right is to risk the disintegration—the spoiling—of this little girl's early holding environment and might also deflate the romance with place that drives Cather's most tumultuous fictions. Is it easier, then, for the author to follow Sapphira's lead and to maintain these women as a backdrop or a landscape: as milieu, ambience, or environment? Cather re-creates Till and Nancy not as psyches but as a weirdly floating field: a site for the little girl to take in, unchallenged, as her own private site of ungrieved grief, her own object-world of arrested pleasures, of remembered but never-to-be-excavated melancholy. At the novel's end, Nancy and Till still hover behind the "straight, dark bar" of Cather's own "I," even as they emerge in their gorgeous linguisticality as a newly gendered and racialized source of stories for that early "I." In using these African American women as "assets" for her fiction, Cather suggests the spatial layout of this Virginia society, but she remains caught in its insistence that black characters must always be converted into an atmosphere or environment. Contemplating these black subjects who always turn into space (rather than being allowed to introject or absorb it), we can barely see through, and we can never see into, the polluting whiteness that covers Cather's black characters like a fitful cloud of unthought knowledge.

Notes

1. Here as elsewhere in Cather, we experience a sense of being held by the object. The landscape becomes an enveloping, self-inviting, self-transforming object, the "unthought known"—omnipresent to sentient being, but not constellated in such a way that it is available to consciousness. For a more detailed reading of these terms, see Bollas.

2. With respect to these great western landscapes of ecstasy, it is worth noting that the landscapes the black characters inhabit in *Sapphira* always partake of the miniature. This is odd in a fictional world, where, as Moers says: "The greatest of [Cather's] landscapes are those inspired by the land she knew best, the Nebraska prairies . . . in which the setting itself evokes a sense of physical dissolution on a limitless, undulating, high-lying plain under a limitless sky; of a solitary, primordial land antecedent to, perhaps hostile to human life" (259). Why can't Cather imagine this capaciousness for her black characters? In the West, as well, they are limited to environment, to the "niggerhead cactuses" that dot the desert in *Song of the Lark*, to the ambient story of the blind piano player in *My Ántonia*.

3. This might also be a sign of the miller's ex-centricity, since it is associated with him, not Sapphira. In their diametrically opposed bodies, Cather seems to be searching for diverse locations for recognizing the shattering of intersubjectivity that the system of slavery purveys—the white body floating in the air, in bits and pieces, but not at all cognizant of its own disarray. In the miller's world there is too much mobility; flour operates, symbolically, like so much dead skin, falling off in bits and fragments that have to be brushed away, but recur—like an exponentially expanding virus—and cannot be disavowed. Sapphira, in contrast, has no mobility at all but, as Toni Morrison argues, experiences utter dependence on those she disavows.

PART

4

Cather and
(Other) Southern Writers

The Interlocking Works of
Willa Cather and Ellen Glasgow

MERRILL MAGUIRE SKAGGS

Bernice Slote taught us to acknowledge the years of gestation that precede the birth of a mature Willa Cather fiction.[1] *Sapphira and the Slave Girl*, Cather's last novel and bow to three generations of maternal ancestry, by Slote's rule, gestated longest both biographically and psychologically.[2] But Cather's hours of labor spent actually writing, as opposed to the years she carried her developing fictions in her head, often seem surprisingly short. She often wrote "at the white heat" when a triggering event set a plan or plot going. Cather claimed that reading an obituary triggered the writing of *A Lost Lady* (Woodress, *Willa Cather* 340), and Edith Lewis claimed that a first sight of Norman Quebec triggered *Shadows on the Rock* (Lewis 151). In fact, the whole prefatory chapter to *My Ántonia* dramatizes how one moment can trigger a subsequently written fiction distilling years of thought. I believe the spark setting off *Sapphira* was this passage Cather found in a new novel, Ellen Glasgow's 1935 *Vein of Iron*:

> "A puny breed," was the way her grandmother would have dismissed the whole post-war generation. Though the old woman was safely dead, Ada could hear her strong snort of disgust: "The Evil One Himself cannot stomach a puny breed."
>
> Why was it, she found herself thinking abruptly, that her grandmother, more than her own mother, seemed to live on in her mind and nerves, awaking whenever a bell rang from the past? And the stranger part was that the place Grandmother had filled on earth appeared to grow larger and more empty. A terrible old woman in some ways—yet immortal. "The empty hiccough of lust," she had once said in horror. (6:272–73)

This passage contains many of the basic ingredients Cather would measure into *Sapphira and the Slave Girl:* the terrible old grandmother, her cynical recognition of reflexive lust, her unforgettable—even immortal—place and presence, the strong family blood that contemptuously dismisses the puny, postwar breed, and a personal will to power not unfamiliar with the Devil himself. Even the bell that rings from the past and brings back such memories tinkles also in Cather's last novel to signal that the action is starting: Sapphira rings her bell to signal for old Washington to wheel her away from the breakfast table, after the novel's opening dialogue, so that she can lay her plans.

The thirty-year literary rivalry between Willa Cather and Ellen Glasgow, signs of which are compressed in *Sapphira*'s opening scenes, produced several splendid fictions. At points its players—two subtle southern women writers—seemed audacious enough for the Evil One to relax and leave the ladies to each other. Like the Scotswoman whose lifetime of domestic arguments over whose tool cut best left her pantomiming scissors as her husband watched her drown, Willa Cather sank to novelistic silence in 1940, while sending a summarizing rebuttal to Ellen Glasgow. Glasgow then wrote that last novel that finally won her a Pulitzer, like Cather's, and died, perhaps feeling squared up, two years before Cather.

The biographical facts about Cather and Glasgow suggest remarkably parallel lives. Both were born in Virginia in 1873, and both claimed to be younger than that.[3] Both had problematic relationships with their mothers as they grew up, though Cather's mother was strong to fight and Glasgow's was weak to pity. While Cather's mother broke the world in two by moving the family to Nebraska in Cather's ninth year, Glasgow's mother tore the world apart when Ellen was ten, by having a nervous breakdown and then dying. Both girls were precocious, self-motivating learners and both began writing early. Cather had published seven stories by the time she graduated from college in 1895, and Glasgow completed her first novel that same year (Wolff, "Artist's Palette" 10; Godbold 34), though it was not published until 1897. Both young women were eager to win public acclaim and both had to become aware of the other, sooner rather than later, from their competing literary reputations. In 1913 both published novels within a few weeks of each other, and both novels were included in the *New York Times*'s "Hundred Best Books of the Year," inviting comparison. Both writers were eventually compared to each other in the press.[4] Both felt themselves intimately linked to Virginia, and early on both wrote fictions set in that state. Before they died they had each claimed that birthright literary territory for about forty-five years.

Cynthia Griffin Wolff has organized several important first facts that are key to this study. Cather's first "Virginia" story was "The Elopement of Allen Poole," which she published in 1893, when Glasgow was futilely trying to reach print; this was followed by "The Profile" in 1904, the year Glasgow's novel *The Deliverance*, about Virginia Reconstruction, became the second-best-seller of the nation (Godbold 70). "The Profile" is noteworthy because it describes a scarred female named Virginia, a key name here. This Virginia forcefully denies her own handicaps, and eventually scars the artist who lives with her, as well as everything that artist loves best. Wolff, following Sharon O'Brien, speculates that the character of Virginia can symbolize Cather's mother, Mary Virginia, but adds, "To be sure, this is also a [state of] 'Virginia' story, . . . not even primarily in its spectral evocation of Virginia Boak Cather, but rather in the horrific violence of the painter-hero's origins" ("Artist's Palette" 12).

Ellen Glasgow too was aware of the ways in which the state of Virginia could mutilate an artist. She also wished to use a *lady* named Virginia as its symbol. As Glasgow explained of the lady years later, "fantastic as her image appears nowadays, the pattern of the lady had embodied for centuries the thwarted human longing for the beautiful and the good" (*Certain Measure* 96). And Glasgow depicted in her *heroine* Virginia, in her *novel* named *Virginia*, a woman who was "Beautiful, sheltered and devoted to her children and husband, but . . . unable to cope with her husband's career as a modern playwright or his attraction for women who were more intellectually alive" (Godbold 98). And that vigorous and vital artist husband whom Virginia's dowdy conventionality drives into the arms of a talented actress, one might add, bears a passing resemblance to the protagonist of Cather's first novel, Bartley Alexander.

Both Cather and Glasgow saw *Virginia* as a loaded and dangerously resonating word. For both it meant a place, a state of mind, and a name for mothers. One could call their Virginia a "mother state." Both associated the word with ambivalence, misfortune, pain, and home. And both knew such forces could create or could cripple an artist. Each was inclined to guard and be guarded about the characters this state produced. Each, in short, was inclined to defend her personal territory, this Virginia. Further, although Glasgow claimed the title *Virginia* in 1913, her biographer says that during the time she wrote this novel in 1912, it was clear that "Willa Cather and Edith Wharton were giving her almost insurmountable competition" (Godbold 98). Her reaction to this competition became an entertaining party piece in the years to follow. As Marcelle Thiebaux describes it, "Glasgow cleverness and vivacity could edge into sharpness. Her precisely enunciated, aristocratic voice grew metallic. She would beam out her brilliant smile while saying 'things that were as disturbing as they were true.' Her 'shrewishness,' wrote Cabell, in discussing her successful contemporaries was 'a never-failing well-spring of diverting malice; her remarks about Willa Cather were as unforgettable as they were unrepeatable'" (27).

At this point a quick synopsis will show where we're going. Our plot officially begins in the year 1913 when both Cather and Glasgow publish novels almost back to back. Cather's, set in Nebraska, is *O Pioneers!* Glasgow's, about a real southern lady, is *Virginia*, a title that did not fail to catch Cather's eye. As Bernice Slote puts it, Cather "wanted to be a Virginia lady like her mother" (xiii–iv). And Cather seems to have read the Glasgow novel with preternaturally focused attention,[5] for details presented first by Glasgow in *Virginia* appear in most fictions Cather wrote after 1913, three of which will be examined here. Besides its preemptive title, however, Glasgow's novel got better reviews than Cather's did.[6] Cather's initial response to *Virginia* may therefore have been a sweeping impulse to show Glasgow that she could do the job better while still disguising her own personal connection to this far-too-explosive Virginia subject. In any case, the appetite for making these corrections strengthened in her as she grew older; she eventually incorporated Glasgow's *Virginia* into her work as often as she did Virgil's *Aeneid* or Shakespeare's dramas.

So Cather, like Whitman, was simmering, simmering when reading Lyra Garber Anderson's obituary brought her to a boil. The result, as Patricia Lee Yongue has wonderfully demonstrated, is a novel about an aristocratic lady, *A Lost Lady.* Since only the South has a regional mythology embracing such a type, however, one of the title's dozen possible interpretations may be a pun: the lady is lost because she's set down in Nebraska, when she "belongs" in Virginia. Niel Herbert thinks, "how strange that she should be here at all, a woman like her among common people!" (21). He adds from his Nebraska point of view, "at the first moment he had recognized her as belonging to a different world than he had ever known" (22).

When we add that the lost lady is named Marian, by an author who plays subtly on mariolatries developed to adore the Divine Mother, as Susan Rosowski has shown us (184–87), we indeed have a pun to be reckoned with here. This Marian or Virgin-ian lady, like Willa's mother, Mary Virginia Boak, is the real article—found in Nebraska because she was first "lost" in Virginian Glasgow's defective portrayals ten years earlier. We will return to this *Virginia* connection shortly. Meanwhile, our plot continues.

Two years after *A Lost Lady,* Ellen Glasgow answered Cather in kind. If Willa Cather could take Glasgow's 1913 Virginia lady and set her down in Nebraska, Glasgow could take Cather's 1913 Nebraska pioneer Alexandra Bergson and set her down in the Cather country of western Virginia, in *Barren Ground* (1925).[7] Glasgow did so, to resounding acclaim.[8] And her feat in this novel seems audacious, to speak in understatement. If one casts a Catherian eye on the following summary of Glasgow's literary triumph, it serves also for *O Pioneers!*

Barren Ground is the story of Dorinda Oakley, an attractive and hard-working young woman who starts her life in a place emitting an air of discouragement and failure. She alone keeps her eyes on the road ahead, from the first sentence, as snow falls over the scene. As the novel opens in a country store located near a train station, Dorinda looks before her at that flat horizon that often features a red tinge in the wild grass. Sometimes this land seems to quiver and swell. But in the first moments, having registered the woodstove roaring like a furnace behind her and the dull farmers who are the store's customers, Dorinda glimpses a weak young man who seems fond of her. She certainly longs for more than her weak father, housebound mother, and two unimaginative brothers can offer her. After an interlude away from home in which she fortuitously ends a compromising condition but gains up-to-date information about agricultural innovations, she returns from this Great Divide in her life to Old Farm, the family homestead, to reclaim the land from barrenness and broomsedge. She learns to love the spirit of the land, which is personified in the novel, as she dreams of a large rescuer who comes and carries her away. Initially the land seems like a sullen animal that won't produce. But working slavishly as well as shrewdly, for she recognizes the promise in new-fangled crops like alfalfa, she slowly becomes not only her own boss but also an economic power in her state. As a stalwart citizen of independence and financial resources, she can afford to marry a man weaker than herself if she wants to, and she does. While her life must build itself around such misfortunes as her younger brother's "temperamental wildness" (32) and illegal actions, she overcomes even the crudenesses built into her family by men who are "big, humble, slow-witted" (32), eat like animals, display mean dispositions, and move "like giant insects" about their farm work (85). At the end Dorinda has earned everything she wants and can account herself a self-made success.

Slower-moving Cather didn't parody *Barren Ground* until six years later, when she made her ground colder, harder, and vastly more difficult to cultivate and removed herself as far as possible from the scene of the crime, in *Shadows on the Rock*.[9] And Glasgow, who professed to have loved *Shadows* (Glasgow, *Letters* 285), in turn appropriated or paraphrased passages from it and at least ten more Cather works, four years later still, in *Vein of Iron*.[10] What probably triggered Glasgow's deliberate sweep through Cather's works at this point, however, was "Old Mrs. Harris." I don't think Glasgow could possibly have missed the allusions to *Virginia* in that story. Soon thereafter, Cather was reading *Vein of Iron* attentively enough to have garnered ample details for three novels[11] when she turned the page and tripped over the passage with which this essay began. As Wolff might say, she had found her form, her frame, her vessel, her Taormina jar.

I believe *Sapphira and the Slave Girl* is as dense and inexhaustible as any other Cather masterpiece. Perhaps in the next millennium we readers will grow sophisticated enough to measure its volume. We'll easily decode the semaphore signal that the name *Sapphira* sends out: this is a drop-dead lie, a lie about fiction,[12] or a fiction about lying.[13] From Glasgow's perspective, however, it is Cather's one-volume social history of Virginia,[14] addressed to the self-acknowledged social historian of Virginia, Ellen Glasgow.[15] Central to this dialogue between Glasgow and Cather are their differing presentations of a southern lady. One finds in Glasgow's *Virginia* the remark, "I believe the whole trouble with her is that she isn't a Southern lady" (218). Now obviously, an ironist like Ellen Glasgow wrote ironically here: she once famously declared that "the South needs blood and irony." She may herself have been inclined to irony because she herself was occasionally charged with unladylike behavior. We can assume both Glasgow and Cather had some ambivalence toward stereotyped southern ladies— what intelligent southern female has ever lacked it? The important question, then, is how each writer worked out her ambivalences, expressed her ironies, and repossessed this type.

In Glasgow's novel, the name *Virginia* ironically suggests a Virgin Queen: for Virginia Pendleton, first adored and then married, is soon neglected, left untouched and emotionally abandoned. Cather's name *Marian*, just as ironically, suggests the Virgin Mother; for Marian Forrester, a daughter of Aphrodite, is happily neither Virgin nor Mother. Both writers, then, name their central female protagonists in irony. But that is all those heroines share.

The contrast between the two characters is instructive. While Glasgow's Virginia reveals a "natural tendency to undervalue the physical pleasures of life" (305), Cather's audacious Marian lives for dancing in Denver. While Glasgow's Virginia lady grows old, dull, and boring, Cather's Marian lingers in Niel's mind as the best thing of his youth. In fact, "in the eyes of the admiring middle-aged men who visited . . . , whatever Mrs. Forrester chose to do was "lady-like" because she did it" (5). While Glasgow's Virginia assumes "All women must expect to have children when they marry" (221), Cather's Marian remains childless and dependent, one who herself needs to be taken care of. While endless letters home pad accounts of Jinny's early married life, Cather lets us off with one of Marian's impeccably addressed envelopes. While younger folk speed by Glasgow's Virginia without noticing her, Marian Forrester's young men gather around her and her table whenever they get the chance, for they all know "Mrs. Forrester was a very special kind of person" (9). While Glasgow's Virginia learns "that in the case of a man, it is easier to inspire love than it is to hold his attention" (453), Marian holds her two husbands' and Niel's attention even beyond her grave.[16] Virginia lives to adore and Marian lives to be adored. Virginia is steadfast and Marian is flirtatious. Virginia upholds the old verities and Marian survives repeated falls to dance again. While Glasgow's southern woman tries to "paralyze her reasoning faculties" (22), Cather's impecunious lady schemes to finance a new start. Virginia's talented young lover protests *for* her when he says, "I've always had a tremendous sympathy for women because they have to market and housekeep. I wonder if they don't revolt some time?" (71). Cather's rule-breaking lady increases her sex appeal as she both housekeeps and appears dishabille, waving a cooking spoon at arriving male guests. While Glasgow's Jinny says, "I'm sure no man wants his wife to be conspicuous" (213), Cather's Captain Forrester wants a showy wife to preside over his dream house.

There are certainly similarities between these rivalrous fictions. Both novels start in what Glasgow calls "an age when the purely feminine was in

fashion" (100), which age Cather says was "certainly the idea of Mrs. Forrester's generation" (62). Both novels feature strong and powerful men,
now bankers, who made their money "commercializing the railroad" (*Virginia* 106; *Lost Lady* 3). Both explicitly center on recognized "belles" who,
"alas, grew older" (*Lost Lady* 5; *Virginia* 110). Both question the proper use
of time: in Glasgow's town, "the only use Dinwiddle made of time was to
kill it" (31), while Marian Forrester wonders how her husband can "like to
see time visibly devoured" at his sundial (62). But the last comparison I'll
mention here tells both tales: Glasgow's Virginia "could endure but she
could not battle" (480); Cather's Marian could "give one . . . the sense of
tempered steel, a blade that could fence with anyone and never break"
(56). We *could* say that Glasgow's Virginia endures while Cather's Marian
prevails.

If *A Lost Lady* denies that real ladies need to protect children and propriety, however, "Old Mrs. Harris" focuses on the southern lady as mother.
Again, it is details from *Virginia* that seem especially to demand Cather's
corrections. For example, Virginia's mother, Glasgow's Mrs. Pendleton,
repeats in the voice of Old Mrs. Harris, "spare Virginia" (54). Like Old
Mrs. Harris, Mrs. Pendleton believes that "to have trained her daughter
to a useful occupation would have been the last dregs of humiliation"
(54). The Glasgow daughter, thus untrained, produces children as her most
important reason for being and quickly becomes a family workhorse and
drudge. Revisionist Cather obviously suggests that even *starting* at Glasgow's premise, one does not end with Glasgow's conclusion: Cather's indulged daughter becomes imperious Victoria, not doormat Virginia; and
furthermore, whatever the size of her family, Victoria makes the best
mother by holding fast to her selfishness and thereby remaining a non-
martyr. "More and more I am learning," Glasgow's Virginia asserts, "that
if we love unselfishly enough, everything will work out for good to us"
(232). In justice, both authors seem to roll their eyes at that one. Mr. Rosen
even reminds his too-critical wife in "Old Mrs. Harris" that self-sacrificing
Rosen relatives don't have the same kind of pleasant children Victoria rears
in the Templeton, not Pendleton, family.

In Glasgow's *Virginia*, the South "lives out this . . . sacrifice of generation
to generation" (54). Cather is not willing to write off either that older generation or its sacrifices. She obviously admires Mrs. Harris most when she
keeps going "after every step cost something" (136). Glasgow's Mrs. Pendleton embraces an idealism which achieves an "absolute triumph over the
actuality" (65), and lives "by inventing a world of exquisite fiction around
her" (67). Conversely, Old Mrs. Harris can look any terrible actuality in
the eye—from the fatal distemper of her favorite cat to her own final moment of consciousness. Her leonine courage does not flinch in crisis.

In *Virginia* Glasgow satirizes the young heroine who asks, "Love is the only thing that really matters, isn't it mother?" (202). Cather seems to dislike Glasgow's satire about young daughters as much as her acerbic irony about old ladies. So Cather's Vickie belies all Glasgow Virginia's virtues: She doesn't want to become "a perfect wife," she doesn't "fall into waiting as a way of life," and she doesn't think it "the immemorial attitude of women" (*Virginia* 204). And though Glasgovian Virginia's (or Jinny's) youngest daughter Jenny, a Bryn Mawr student, can remind us of Catherian Victoria's daughter Vickie in her zest for education, we don't admire Jenny for her inconsiderate good works. We like Vickie, in spite of her youthful egotism.

"The obligation to think independently was . . . incomprehensible to Virginia" (431), we read in Glasgow. It is, of course, a comfortable habit with all three of Cather's symbolic women. Glasgow's Virginia "was satisfied with the crumbs of life, and yet they were denied her" (462). Not so, Vickie, Victoria, or Old Mrs. Harris. All three would object to the words "crumbs" or "denied." But Cather's corrective urge is perhaps most detectable when we read this Glasgovian passage from *Virginia:* "For a minute, while she was dressing, Virginia thought . . . of how hard life had been to her mother, of how pretty she must have been in her youth. What she did not think of was that her mother, like herself, was but one of the endless procession of women who pass perpetually from the sphere of pleasure into the sphere of service. It was as impossible for her to picture her mother as a girl of twenty as it was for her to imagine herself ever becoming a woman of fifty" (55). Transformed utterly, this passage becomes one of the greatest finales in Cather's or anyone else's fiction:

> Victoria and Vickie had still to go on, to follow the long road that leads through things unguessed at and unforeseeable. When they are old, they will come closer and closer to Grandma Harris. They will think a great deal about her, and remember things they never noticed; and their lot will be more or less like hers. They will regret that they heeded her so little; but they, too, will look into the eager, unseeing eyes of young people and feel themselves alone. They will say to themselves: "I was heartless, because I was young and strong and wanted things so much. But now I know." ("Old Mrs. Harris" 190)

Vein of Iron contributed as many details to *Sapphira* as Glasgow's novel *Virginia* did. Because space is limited, however, I'll focus here on Cather's last attempt to set *Virginia* straight. Sporadically, Glasgow threw into *Virginia* some Southern Gothic details about race. Cather decided these details were to be her southern novel's main subject.[17] In Glasgow's *Virginia* the "great man" of Dinwiddle is Cyrus Treadwell. Treadwell is a cruel husband and stingy father who once seduced a fifteen-year-old black child employed by his wife, fathered her mulatto son, and then refused to acknowledge or help either. That servant is Mandy, one name through which Cather conveys her thoughts about race: there are two Mandys in *Sapphira*. One is Mandy Ringer, the illiterate mountain woman who is heroic for staying interested in everything, but pathetic for having two daughters who are "fooled." The Ringer family lives in disgrace. Cather's second Mandy is the slave Mr. Cartmell offers to buy for his overworked daughter, Mrs. Bywaters. That slave represents quality work and genuine household help. Neither father nor daughter can finally justify owning a slave, but they both know that only a black servant is really worth having. No white mountain girl like Mandy Ringer's daughters could be trusted to do the work right.

Glasgow's Mandy is "a dark glistening creature, with ox-like eyes," and "an expression of animal submission and acquiescence" conveying "a primitive racial attitude toward life" (*Virginia* 87). That Glasgovian Mandy emits an "acrid odour" (172) and conveys "an expression which was half-scornful, half-inviting, yet so little personal that it might have been worn by one of her treetop ancestors while he looked down from his sheltering boughs on a superior species of the jungle" (172–73).

Cather splits Glasgow's Mandy in two halves, one white, one black. The device seems to say, in my Virginia such sad creatures exist, but they are more likely to be free white mountaineers, not black servants. The white mountaineers often struggle unsuccessfully to pull free of their shackles, as Casper Flight struggles until rescued by Mrs. Blake. But Mrs. Blake herself has willingly known bondage, in the years when she "slaved herself" to cook gourmet meals for her Congressman husband and his extravagant guests. In Cather's Virginia, free daughters can be fooled and are; slave daughters can remain chaste and do.[18] *Ladies* are females who convey upper-class self-possession, formal manners, and fine deportment. There are two clear examples here, both named in the title. The name "Saphira" appeared first in Glasgow's *Barren Ground* to indicate a milker described as "a big black woman" (296). Nancy, conversely, is Cather's former slave girl who returns from Canada looking, dressing, talking, and acting like a lady, and who is economically superior to those whites she visits. Ladies may lie, of course, as both white Sapphira and black Nancy do. But narrators or authors can lie as well. Willa Cather signals us repeatedly that she may be doing just that as she slips in and out of dialect, misquotes Benjamin Franklin and the Bible, and calls attention to her deliberate distortion of actual names. Cather concludes her presentation of ladies by suggesting that sometimes it's the ex-slaves who preserve the most aristocratic standards: "'She oughtn't never to a' come out here,' Till often said to me. 'She wasn't raised that way. Mrs. Matchem, down at the old place, never got over it that Miss Sapphy didn't buy in Chestnut Hill an' live like a lady, 'stead a' leavin' it to run down under the Bushwells, an' herself comin' out here where no-body was anybody much'" (*Sapphira* 295). And when the novel proper is over, Cather adds an italicized paragraph in which she stresses her delib-erate changes of actual names.

"What's in a name?" we ask, remembering that in Ole Virginie *Wash-ington* and *Jefferson* are names for founding fathers and also for slaves, that is, for opposite castes.

Well, I've always thought the names of the *real people* I'm actually talking about here are funny, a youthful Cather voice seems to remark from the text, suggestively.

"Funnier than Keyser or Fairhead or Bywaters or Sapphira?" we ask incredulously.

After that, the rest is silence. Till that memory bell rings in our heads. We remember that from her title onward, Cather has obliquely been talk-ing about liars and fictions, and for that matter, writers of fictions like herself and Ellen Glasgow. Lies, as well as writers' fictions, are built with names. With her last, italicized reminder that names can lie, while they can also seem funny, we realize that Cather ends her fiction pointing out that she's thinking of Virginia names, social histories, social historians, and lies; and she's also chuckling.

Notes

1. "Of great significance, I think, are the correspondences between the first things Willa Cather wrote and some of the last. . . . For Willa Cather it was an absolute, lifetime vision. . . . In the process of absorption, what is plainly on the surface and directly stated in the early writing is gradually taken into the substance of new work until it can no longer be easily identified" (Slote 90–92).

2. Woodress records a reference to Cather's long-held idea for a Virginia novel in a letter that Blanche Knopf wrote Cather in 1931 (*Willa Cather* 481).

3. Willa Cather's tombstone still claims an 1876 birthdate. Ellen Glasgow, after reading Cather's *Youth and the Bright Medusa* in 1920, wrote to Hugh Walpole, "I wish I hadn't begun as early as I did because I might be able to keep my interest better. Miss Cather—who has written a fine book of short stories recently—is still one of 'the younger writers,' though she is older than I am" (Glasgow, *Letters* 67).

4. The first book-length study of Glasgow mentions "Carl Van Doren's hint to try a spare plot of the difficult but rewarding length of *Ethan Frome*, *Miss Lula Bett* or *A Lost Lady*" ("Barren Ground," *New Republic* 42 [29 Apr. 1925]: 271; cited in McDowell 5). Woodress adds that Glasgow and Cather were both attacked as conservatives by bright young Marxists in the 1930s (*Willa Cather* 469).

5. Perhaps she read *repetitiously* also. Woodress describes Cather's reading three times the first two volumes of Thomas Mann's biblical tetralogy *Joseph and His Brothers* (*Willa Cather* 472). If she loved Mann's books enough to return to them, she seems to have loved hating the novel *Virginia* as much. One can scarcely find there a detail she does *not* eventually use. For

example, details from *Virginia* later pop up in *One of Ours* and *The Professor's House*. Glasgow's fundamentalist Academy for Young Ladies, which required of teachers "neither preparation of mind nor considerable outlay of money" (*Virginia* 11), becomes Claude's detested Baptist college in *One of Ours*. But in both educational institutions, the teachers have "courage that feared nothing except opinions" (*Virginia* 12). Glasgow's seamstress Miss Willy Whitlow is in occupation and importance to the households of the town a very clear prototype for Augusta in *Professor's House*. Glasgow also reappropriated details from *Professor's House* to use in the life of her great American philosopher John Fincastle. Cather surely noticed them, showcased in *Vein of Iron*.

6. In its celebratory centennial edition of 1997, the *New York Times* quoted with amusement its own misfired review of *O Pioneers!*, from 14 Sept. 1913: "Possibly some might call it a feminist novel, for the two heroines are stronger, cleverer and better balanced than their husbands and brothers—but we are sure Miss Cather had nothing so inartistic in mind." Later that year, the *Times*'s "Hundred Best Books of the Year" said of *Virginia*, "From the time of the appearance of her first book, 'The Descendant,' Ellen Glasgow has been recognized as one of the most capable of the present-day American novelists. . . . So one is not disappointed in finding her latest book the most mature and significant, as well as the broadest in sympathy and the most skillful in treatment of all her product. . . . The book is a noteworthy and significant study of our own times, done with an art that in its neatness and fineness is more like that of Jane Austen than is usual in modern writers" (30 Nov. 1913; 665).

7. As early as 1960, Frederick McDowell noted the resemblance between the asceticism of the two heroines—Alexandra Bergson and Dorinda Oakley—as well as between their failure fathers (149, 151).

8. Judith Wittenberg presented an extremely helpful summary of the widespread standing ovations for *Barren Ground* in a paper entitled "The Critical Fortunes of *Barren Ground*" (presented at the annual meeting of the Modern Language Association, Chicago, 28 Dec. 1977). But even the tepidly qualified review in the *New York Times* appeals today by announcing, "Southern romance is dead; Ellen Glasgow has murdered it" (H. T. Brock, "Southern Romance Is Dead," *New York Times Book Review*, 12 April 1925, sec. 3, p. 2; quoted in Scura 246).

The most important review for shaping Glasgow's subsequent sense of what she had accomplished, however, was James Branch Cabell's, in *The Nation*. It begins, "This is the best of many excellent books by Ellen Glasgow." He noted "the startling approach to completeness, presented by these books as a whole, of Ellen Glasgow's portrayal of all social and economic Virginia since the War Between the States" and the startling announcement, upon the dust jacket of this new book, that "with 'Barren Ground' realism at last crosses the Potomac" (521).

9. *Shadows* parodies *Barren Ground* when Cather takes Glasgow's title literally and thus requires her characters to live on a barren rock in a climate which is cold and dark most of the year. Cather's settlers can't even rely on pastures overrun with broomsedge, but have only the gods they've brought with them to help make life happen. But they answer Glasgow's and Dorinda's question, How do you make a land worth living in?

10. For example, from *O Pioneers!*: John, like Carl Linstrum, "could not push his own way; could not even . . . sell dry goods" (*Vein* 40); more obviously, the consummation scene repeats that of Emil and Marie (*Vein* 182). And from *The Professor's House*: the scholar "had been happy enough for a lifetime working on his [five-volume] book" (*Vein* 42); he sleeps on a sofa in his library (155); he had been happy as a student but found he *must* marry (43); a German Catholic equivalent of Appelhoff appears (262); a ten-year-old youthful self is heroine Ada's "shadowy companion" (61).

11. Lewis said, "She could have written two or three Sapphiras out of her material; and in fact she did write, in her first draft, twice as much as she used" (Woodress, *Willa Cather* 481). Among those small and large details, which appear first in *Vein of Iron* and then reappear in

Sapphira, are the themes of exile to or from the mountains (see Laura Winters's book *Willa Cather: Landscape and Exile*) in both books, as well as the central theme of being "fooled." For example, Ada is fooled in *Vein of Iron*, while both Mrs. Ringer's daughters have been fooled in *Sapphira*, and Sapphira herself cannot bear being "befooled" (106); the foolery of extramarital sex is central to both novels. Mrs. Ringer, in fact, occasions a quantity of these transferred details. Her motto is "I can bear anything" (120), an exhibit of Glasgow's "vein of iron."

In both novels, however, it is women who endure tenaciously, with or without veins of iron. Sapphira too shows a vein of iron in "the intrepid courage with which she faced the inevitable" (267). She is described accurately by Glasgow's line, "even in her old age she had not lost a certain legendary glamour" (*Vein* 45).

12. Cather wrote Viola Roseboro' that not very much of this novel *was* fiction (Woodress, *Willa Cather* 481).

13. See Acts 5 : 1–10, the story of that lying couple who drop dead, Ananias and Sapphira.

14. After her first draft, Cather halved her manuscript, because, as she explained, "after all she was not writing a history of Virginia Manners and customs before the Civil War. The parts she omitted, she claimed, weighed exactly six pounds" (Woodress, *Willa Cather* 481). The point this passage helps make is that at some point she *had* considered the book a social history, though she realized eventually that it would have to be much more, which it is.

15. In reviewing *Barren Ground*, James Branch Cabell called that novel the best of Glasgow's works and then declared her works, taken all together, a "portrayal of all social and economic Virginia since the War Between the States" ("The Last Cry of Romance," *The Nation* 120 [6 May 1925]: 521–22). Thereafter both Glasgow and Cabell accepted and promulgated her role and title as the social historian of Virginia.

16. The attention a reader is *meant* to give to questions about the nature and end of ladies is emphasized by Ophelia's lines from *Hamlet* that provide the epigraph to *A Lost Lady*:

> ". . . Come my coach!
> Good night, ladies; good night, sweet ladies,
> Good night, good night."

17. I have already described *Sapphira* as a reversal of expected Southern Gothic details about race relations. See Skaggs, "Willa Cather's Experimental Southern Novel."

18. The matter of Martin Colbert's wooden tooth, however, invalidates Mrs. Ringer's excuse that her daughters would not be in disgrace if they had a strong man to stand up for them. The Blue Ridge girl Martin "fooled" has two strong brothers who beat him up and knock his tooth out. Yet after he is beaten unconscious, she is still pregnant and he is still looking for sex.

"Aeneas at Washington" and
The Professor's House

Cather and the Southern Agrarians

ELSA NETTELS

In a highly favorable review of *Death Comes for the Archbishop* that appeared in the Nashville *Tennessean* on 25 September 1927, the poet and critic Donald Davidson noted that "Miss Cather was born in Virginia" and then lamented that "as a southerner I must grieve that the west has gained her while the south lost her."

As her letters and fiction show, the connections between Cather and the South were strong and enduring. She did not lose the South, and Davidson could have argued that the South did not lose her. Indeed, he might have observed important parallels and affinities between Cather and the group of southern writers he represented, the Fugitive-Agrarians—those poets, novelists, historians, and literary critics bound by ties of friendship formed during their association at Vanderbilt University after the First World War.

We recall the names of the best-known of the Agrarians—Allen Tate, John Crowe Ransom, Robert Penn Warren, Andrew Lytle, Donald Davidson, all of whom were educated at Vanderbilt and returned to teach there. Most of them, born near the turn of the century, belonged to the generation after Cather's. Ransom, the oldest, was fifteen years younger than Cather. But by 1930 they had published some of their best-known poems, including Ransom's "Blue Girls" and "Bells for John Whiteside's Daughter," Tate's "The Mediterranean" and "Ode to the Confederate Dead," and Warren's "Original Sin." They had set forth their aesthetic principles in *The Fugitive*, the journal of poetry that they published at Vanderbilt for four years, from 1922 to 1925. In 1930, three years after Davidson reviewed *Death Comes for the Archbishop*, Ransom, Davidson, Tate, Warren, Lytle, and seven others published their manifesto *I'll Take My Stand*, in which they launched their attack on modern commercial society. Their primary purpose was to assert the superiority of the culture of the agrarian South to what Ransom termed "the industrial gospel" (x), which they claimed had sacrificed individual genius to the commercial profits of standardization and had made money the goal of enterprise and the measure of success.[1]

Cather's affinity with the Southern Agrarians is most apparent not in her novel of Virginia, *Sapphira and the Slave Girl*, but in *The Professor's House*, in the lecture given by the protagonist, Godfrey St. Peter—like the

Southern Agrarians, a writer and teacher at a liberal arts university. In response to a student's question, St. Peter sets forth his fundamental belief: that art and religion, not science, have given human life its greatest value and importance, that the rituals and ceremonies performed in medieval cathedrals, far more than experiments conducted in modern laboratories, gave people "a feeling of dignity and purpose."[2] Science has not solved "the real problems" of life, he asserts, but has merely "given us a lot of ingenious toys" (62) in place of the religious faith that once made life "a rich thing," "a gorgeous drama with God, glittering angels on one side and the shadows of evil coming and going on the other" (63). He might have added that the fortunes made by the mass production of the "ingenious toys" breed spite and greed and jealousy that cleave families and destroy friendships. As the first part of the novel makes clear, St. Peter's hostility is directed at the effects of technology, not at the spirit of scientific inquiry exemplified by his beloved student and comrade, Tom Outland, whose discovery of the principle of the "bulkheaded vacuum" not only "revolutioniz[ed] aviation" (35) but corrupted almost all the relationships within St. Peter's family.[3]

Like St. Peter, the Southern Agrarians set science in opposition to art and religion, asserted the enduring value of ceremony and ritual as a source of meaning and happiness, and dwelt on the impoverishment of human life by the advances of modern science. Here is Donald Davidson, writing in a review in 1929 of the advantages enjoyed by "the great writers of the past [who] never felt the full impact of scientific teaching as we have felt it. They always had something to fall back on: Fate, the Gods, Divine Providence, a Moral Order, or at least some belief in the divinity or nobility of Man." Modern writers, he argued, had lost the sense of "Evil" as a reality and thus the power to write tragedy (*Spyglass* 95). (His reviews indicate that he did not include Cather in this indictment.) If St. Peter had been speaking of modern literature, he might have said something very similar.

Cather's novel again anticipates the manifesto of the Southern Agrarians when St. Peter reflects on his futile efforts to keep the state legislature from making "a trade school of the university." As he deplores what he considers the "vulgarizing" of a liberal arts education by allowing credit for "courses in book-keeping, experimental farming, domestic science, dressmaking" (135), so the historian John Gould Fletcher, writing on education in *I'll Take My Stand*, deplored the contamination of the liberal arts by allowing into the curriculum "courses in technical training, applied science, and business administration" (119). Unlike Fletcher, who openly declared his desire "to form an intellectual *élite*" (121), St. Peter does not say that some people are essentially inferior, mentally incapable of gaining from the study of history and the classics. But his powers of discrimination and judgment are no less highly developed: he pronounces Tom Outland's the "one re-markable mind" he has encountered "in a lifetime of teaching" (56).

One should not assume that St. Peter's ideas are necessarily Cather's ideas, but her fiction and essays indicate her basic sympathy with St. Peter's tastes and point of view, if not always with his behavior and actions. St. Peter shares Cather's fascination with heroic figures of history and legend, her love of French culture, her discriminating taste in food and wines, and her preference for restraint over excess. As Merrill Skaggs has noted, St. Peter's judgment that "too much is certainly worse than too little—of any-thing" (*Professor's House* 150) recalls Cather's ideal of the *novel démeublé* and her dictum that "the higher processes of art are all processes of simplifica-tion" (*Stories* 836).[4] As Cather valued the "qualities of good Latin prose: economy, elegance, and exactness" (*Stories* 832), so St. Peter (who reads Lucretius with Tom Outland) admires the "austerity" of Tom's diary and prefers its plainness to the "florid style" of Louie Marsellus (*Professor's House* 260, 42).

St. Peter's wholesale attack on science, however, reflects his own disillu-sionment with technology, with the effects of commercial success on family and friends; his lecture does not express the complexity of Cather's view of science. Her mistrust of "our whole scheme of life and progress and profit" (*Collected Short Fiction* 46), from which the destruction and death in "The Singer Tower" and *Alexander's Bridge* are inseparable, must be balanced by her youthful ideal of success: to be "a great anatomist or a brilliant natural-ist" (Rosowski, *Place of Literature* 9), by her lively interest in the discoveries in archaeology and anthropology, and by her devoted study of biology and botany, which trained her powers of observation and precise description.[5] But St. Peter's preoccupation with the corrosive materialism bred by tech-nology conveys the revulsion against commercialism that informs all Cath-er's novels of the middle west, from *O Pioneers!* to *Lucy Gayheart*. The bur-den of Cather's lecture in Omaha in October 1921—that technology, the enemy of art and religion, has created a race of Americans who live and die by machines (Brown and Edel 226)—anticipates St. Peter's lecture and es-tablishes the affinity of both author and character to the Southern Agrari-ans, who repeatedly contrasted the harmony of an idealized pastoral world to the alienation and rootlessness of modern industrial society.

In important ways, of course, Cather and her protagonist St. Peter differ from the Southern Agrarians. Unlike Ransom, Tate, Davidson, and the others, St. Peter seems compelled to feel himself isolated, without allies. Nor can one imagine Cather joining with other writers, as the Fugitive-Agrarians did, to promote a political agenda. Davidson noted approvingly that she was "quite dissociated from cults and propaganda" (*Tennessean*, 14 Nov. 1926). Unlike the Agrarians, she did not celebrate the plantation sys-tem of the antebellum South; she was not an apologist for slavery or the

Confederacy; she did not dwell on the supposed evils of Reconstruction or assert the superiority of southern culture and institutions over those of New England and New York.

Cather was not a reactionary. As Joseph Urgo has demonstrated, the characters of her fiction, including those in the novels set in the past, prosper only as they go forward and look to the future, not seek to re-create the world of the past (94–95). But like the Agrarians, she sought to keep alive a taproot to the past, to remember the "old centers and origins" (Davidson, *Spyglass* 5) of modern cultures. She had sympathy for the kind of provincialism Davidson defined, that which rejects "mass-thinking" and mindless conformity, which "begins its reasoning, not with the new, but with the old and established things, wherever they are the marks of a native character and tradition that seem to have contributed something valuable and interesting to life" (*Spyglass* 5). The author of *Shadows on the Rock*, who said that "a new society begins with the salad dressing more than with the destruction of Indian villages" (*Stories* 966), believed as Davidson did that culture "can, and ought to be, a matter of pots and pans, of tables, chairs, and quilts, of cooking and sewing and carpentering, and numerous other things which our mechanical age tends to despise and cheapen" (*Spyglass* 182–83).

Not surprisingly, critics hostile to Cather in the late 1920s and 1930s were hostile to the Southern Agrarians and for similar reasons. For instance, Granville Hicks, who criticized Cather as an escapist who evaded contemporary problems and sought in the past "a refuge" from "the central issues of the present" (225–26), likewise dismissed Ransom, Tate, and Davidson as futile quixotics who ignored "economic and political realities" (282) in their retreat to the past. Maxwell Geismar admired *O Pioneers!* and *My Ántonia* but felt as a weakness in them the impulse to "escape into a more heroic or idyllic past" (186)—the same impulse that he criticized in the Agrarians, who "retreating from the gross clamor of society in general, entrenched themselves securely in the classics" (357).

In her 1936 essay "Escapism," in which Cather rebuts her critics, she refers to the "literary radicals," the "iconoclasts and tomb-breakers" who "made a career of destroying the past" (*Stories* 972, 971). Whether or not she felt any kinship with the Agrarians who sought to recover and preserve the past, or an idealized vision of the past, is a question not answered by her biographers. Her published works contain no references to the Agrarians.

Evidence that the Agrarians were aware of Willa Cather, however, is easily found in their letters, reviews, and essays. Ransom, in a letter to Allen Tate (17 Sept. 1936), suggested the founding of an American Academy of Letters and included Cather in his list of twenty-five writers "who seem most eligible" (*Selected Letters* 218). (The other women were Edith Wharton, Ellen Glasgow, and Marianne Moore.) Allen Tate and John Peale

Bishop chose Cather's story "The Sculptor's Funeral" for their anthology *American Harvest* (1942) and identified her in the biographical note as "the dean of American women novelists" (543). Sometimes recognition came in the expression of masculine bias against women writers, in which the Agrarians were certainly not deficient. Davidson credited Cather and Elinor Wylie with "finesse and clear serenity" that Dreiser and Sinclair Lewis lacked, but he believed that the novels of the men had more "substance": "they get down to strata that the women seldom reach" (*Spyglass* 74). But Davidson lavished praise on the three novels of Cather that he reviewed for the Nashville *Tennessean*. He judged *My Ántonia* "one of the finest novels . . . written by an American in this century" (19 Sept. 1926). He appreciated the economy of *My Mortal Enemy*, in which Cather conveyed "the complete drama of two lives" by "selecting quietly a handful of moments, chaste and casual as jewels in a dark casket" (14 Nov. 1926). His entire sympathy with the ideal of the *novel démeublé* is again evident in his praise of *Death Comes for the Archbishop*, distinguished by its economy and its "insight and dignity . . . at once aloof and intimate, a feeling for the deepest sources of life" (25 Sept. 1927).

Had Davidson wished to claim Cather as a fellow southerner, he could well have considered the influence upon her fiction of her lifelong reading of the classics, particularly the poetry of Vergil. This part of her heritage is arguably the most clearly identifiable as distinctly southern. Of course, southerners were not the only Americans to venerate the classics. Colonists in New England as well as the South regarded knowledge of the Greek and Latin authors as "the mark of a gentleman," and classical texts as the foundation of a "gentleman's library" (Wright 130, 115–16). But for several reasons, the classical tradition of the English colonists had its most pervasive, enduring life in the South. The absence in the antebellum South of urban centers like Boston and New York and Philadelphia; the isolation of southerners in an agricultural society that fostered resistance to change; the continued predominance after the Civil War of the private academy over the public school; the attractiveness of ancient Rome as a model, where slavery coexisted with Stoic ideals of honor and virtue—all these conditions worked to perpetuate the classical traditions of Renaissance England, which English colonists tried to sustain in the New World by employing English tutors and sending their sons to English universities. By 1884 Harvard University had abolished Greek and Latin as requirements for the bachelor's degree. Vanderbilt University remained "a stronghold of classical culture" through the First World War, retaining its Latin and Greek requirement until 1919 (Cowan 6, 33).[6]

In *I'll Take My Stand*, the historian Frank Owsley made agriculture the link connecting Romans and southerners: both peoples were "lovers of the soil" (71). More generally, the Southern Agrarians saw the classics as part of a heritage that northern industrialism had destroyed but that southern agrarianism had preserved, by cherishing the values of the early republics —Roman and American. Donald Davidson took deep satisfaction in the idea of the South as unique, the only American society that had not destroyed its roots, a society that had "long cultivated a historical consciousness" signifying "a close connection with the eighteenth-century European America that is elsewhere forgotten" (*I'll Take My Stand* 53).

How much of the culture of this eighteenth-century America survived in the consciousness of a child growing up in Virginia in the 1870s is hard to say. We do know that Cather's family library in Winchester included translations of the Latin poets and historians, that her exposure to the classics began in early childhood when her grandmother Boak read to her stories of the Greek gods and heroes in *Peter Parley's Universal History*. Cather makes the love of the classics part of a southern heritage in two novels: in *My Ántonia*, where Vergil is the only author the Virginian Jim Burden is seen reading in high school and at the university; and in *A Lost Lady*, where Niel Herbert reads the *Heroides* in a copy of Ovid's complete works in the "Bonn Classics," which his uncle acquired while studying at the University of Virginia (44).[7]

Critics have associated a number of Cather's characters with Vergil's Aeneas: Alexandra Bergson, Ántonia Shimerda, Claude Wheeler, Father Latour.[8] But the character whom Cather most fully identified with Aeneas is Tom Outland, who on his first appearance in *The Professor's House* proves his mastery of Latin by reciting to St. Peter the first fifty lines of book 2 of the *Aeneid*, beginning with Aeneas's words of lamentation to Dido: *Infandum, regina, jubes renovare dolorem* (108). Thus Cather establishes the analogy between Tom Outland, who enters St. Peter's garden seeking his aid, and Aeneas, who gains temporary refuge in Carthage, at the court of Dido, where he tells of the defeat and destruction of Troy.

In evoking the devastation of Troy, Cather recalls that part of the *Aeneid* most poignant to the Agrarians: the destruction of Aeneas's homeland, which they associated with the ruin and defeat of the Old South.[9] The association is most pervasive in the poetry of Allen Tate, who repeatedly juxtaposes modern civilization and the heroic world of Aeneas to define what contemporary society has lost. Whether the speaker of the poem is Aeneas transposed to a modern city (as in "Aeneas at Washington" and "Aeneas at New York") or an unnamed contemporary figure seeking a spiritual homeland in the ancient world (as in "The Mediterranean" and "Ode to the Confederate Dead"), for the speaker, salvation in the modern world lies only in repossession of a lost heritage.[10]

In the works of Cather and Tate, the *Aeneid* most fully informs "Tom

Outland's Story" and "Aeneas at Washington" (1933)[11]—texts that illustrate Cather's affinities with and fundamental differences from the Southern Agrarians. In both poem and novel, the speaker, imbued with Aeneas's
sense of a heroic past, confronts in Washington the corruptions of the modern city and dwells upon his sense of isolation and alienation amid people
consumed by their struggle for wealth and power. In neither poem nor
novel does the speaker imagine reform or even express hope for change.

At the end of his narration in book 2 of *The Professor's House*, Tom Outland recalls his journey from the Mesa to Washington, where he hoped to
persuade the director of the Smithsonian to send archaeologists to the
Mesa to complete the work of excavation begun by Tom and Roddy Blake.
Soon he learns that money rules actions in official Washington: he can gain
access to the director only by buying his secretary an expensive lunch; instead of funding an expedition to the Mesa, the director and his staff will
seek lavish expense accounts and lucrative appointments at an exposition in
Paris. Tom not only fails in his mission but becomes increasingly depressed
in the city by the sight of "hundreds of little black-coated men pouring out
of white buildings" (235), slaves of the bureaucracy, all struggling to make
more money, to secure invitations and make connections, all living beyond
their means in order to keep up appearances. "They seemed to me like
people in slavery, who ought to be free" (232). Measuring worth by money,
the Bixbys, from whom Tom rents a room, speculate about the salaries
and promotions of co-workers, as preoccupied with material possessions as
St. Peter's family.

In Tate's poem, the speaker Aeneas remembers himself as he stood on
the shores of the Potomac, where "the great Dome lit the water," fusing in
one symbol the cities of ancient Rome and Washington. He reveals the
soulless materialism of the modern city indirectly, by dwelling upon all that
has been lost of his heroic past. "Far from home at nightfall," he recalls the
fall of Troy and his own conduct in battle and defeat.

> In that extremity I bore me well,
> A true gentleman, valorous in arms,
> Disinterested and honourable.

In the destruction of his city he sees the collapse of social order.

> That was a time when civilization
> Run by the few fell to the many, and
> Crashed to the shout of men, the clang of arms.

His arduous journey to the "uncitied littorals" where he was destined to
found a new state has ended in the modern capital, where the "vigor
of prophecy" has lapsed in "fixed triumphs" of leaders ruled by appetite.

Like heroic virtue, the fruitful land exists only in memory. He imagines "the glowing fields of Troy," reminiscent of the poet's native Kentucky, filled with

> hemp ripening
> And tawny corn, the thickening Blue Grass
> All lying rich forever in the green sun.

Thus Aeneas realizes the magnitude of his loss, not only of his homeland but of the ideal city he would found:

> The city my blood had built I knew no more
> While the screech-owl whistled his new delight
> Consecutively dark.
> Struck in the wet mire
> Four thousand leagues from the ninth buried city
> I thought of Troy, what we had built her for.

In Tate's poem, it is not difficult to read the lament of the southerner who mourns a lost homeland devastated by war, like Troy, and sees in the defeat of the Confederacy the passing of the "true gentleman, valorous in arms." Tate's speaker dwells not upon the destiny of Aeneas to found a new state but upon the defeated city recoverable only in memory. "Struck in the mire," he cannot go forward, but moves ever deeper into the past, beyond defeat in war to the founding of his city.

Like the lost world of Troy evoked by Tate's speaker, the Pueblo ruins discovered by Cather's Tom Outland signify an agrarian society, according to Guy Reynolds, "the organic, agrarian community beloved of American pastoral idealists from Jefferson through to the Fugitives" (140). But unlike Tate's speaker, Tom Outland moves forward to a transforming vision of the past that "brought with it great happiness" (249). He suffers the anguish of loss when he returns from Washington to the Mesa and learns that Roddy Blake has sold all the Indian artifacts to a German dealer for four thousand dollars. But the loss of the material objects enables Tom to gain what is more precious than pottery and turquoise. Alone on the Mesa, he is not, like Tate's speaker, "far from home," but he comes at last into possession of his spiritual home. On the Mesa, where he reads and memorizes long passages of the *Aeneid*, he gains his heritage, which inspires in him the "filial piety" (249) memorialized in the poetry of Vergil. Every morning, he recalls, "I wakened with the feeling that I had found everything, instead of having lost everything" (250). He looks to the future, not the past, and does not return for the diary he had hidden before going to Washington. "It would have been going backward. I didn't want to go back and unravel things step by step" (250).

Of all Cather's characters, St. Peter in some ways most resembles the speaker of "Aeneas at Washington." Tate's figure portrays himself as an old man, his life of action long over, his ambition dead.

> I see all things apart, the towers that men
> Contrive I too contrived long, long ago.
> Now I demand little. The singular passion
> Abides its object and consumes desire
> In the circling shadow of its appetite.

These could be the words of St. Peter, who looks back on his life as scholar, teacher, husband, and father as if it no longer belonged to him. "It seemed to him like the life of another person" (265). For him, as for Tate's Aeneas, the desire to strive, to build towers, seems dead, like the fire consumed by its ashes. As Aeneas recalls his youth "when the young eyes were slow, / Their flame steady beyond the firstling fire," so St. Peter recovers the reality of his solitary elemental childhood self, even as he dwells upon death, feeling himself "near the conclusion of his life" (266).

St. Peter's memories of Tom Outland—of their friendship, their conversations, their travels to the Southwest—are to him what memories of his homeland are to Tate's Aeneas—the most poignant and precious of life-giving images. But Tate's speaker remains transfixed by memory, which by itself can effect no spiritual change. St. Peter's refusal to leave his attic study, symbolic of his bitter resistance to change, nearly costs him his life when the gas from his rusty stove overpowers him. But the accident does what his will could not do—it frees him from the pain of futile longing for the irrecoverable. "His temporary release from consciousness seemed to have been beneficial. He had let something go—and it was gone: something very precious, that he could not consciously have relinquished, probably" (281). At the end, he is "outward bound" (280), prepared to live "with fortitude" if not with passion and delight, and the final words of the novel are "the future" (281).

Notes

The excerpt from "Aeneas at Washington" quoted in this essay is from *Collected Poems, 1919–1976* by Allen Tate. Copyright © 1977 by Allen Tate. Reprinted by permission of Farrar, Straus & Giroux, Inc.

1. The most detailed study of the Fugitive poets and their journal is Louise Cowan, *The Fugitive Group: A Literary History*. For analysis of the Agrarian Movement and the views of contributors to *I'll Take My Stand*, see Gray, 125–64, and Squires, *Allen Tate* 100–22.

2. Willa Cather, *The Professor's House* (Boston: Houghton Mifflin, 1938), 63. All further citations are to this edition.

3. The contradiction between St. Peter's denunciations of science in his lecture and his valuing of the scientific pursuits of his colleague Professor Crane and Tom Outland is noted by Harrell (193).

4. Skaggs, *After the World Broke in Two* 77–78. McDonald notes resemblances between St. Peter's attitudes and tastes and the "Southern aristocratic sensibilities" of Jim Burden (*My Ántonia*) and Niel Herbert (*A Lost Lady*) and sees all three characters as "exemplifying an ideology similar to Cather's, one that incorporates gentility, aesthetic values and tastes, and an admiration for idealized beauty and glorified conquest" (45). The case against identifying St. Peter with Cather is made by Harrell (185–203).

5. Rosowski demonstrates the importance of Cather's study of science to her literary achievement (*Place of Literature* 11–12). Reynolds documents Cather's enthusiasm for the scientific exhibits in the Carnegie Museum in Pittsburgh and emphasizes the distinction in her fiction between commercial success and the disinterested pursuit of knowledge (125 ff.).

6. See also Wright 13 ff., 112 ff.; Wyatt-Brown 92–96.

7. For Cather's reading and study of the classics, see McDonald 23–26; O'Brien, *Willa Cather* 80–81; Ryder 7–15; and Woodress, *Willa Cather* 53, 71–72.

8. For comparison of Cather's characters to Aeneas, see Murphy, "Cather's Archbishop" 146–50; Ryder 144, 194–97, 226–28, 262–63; Sutherland 125–26.

9. McDonald notes that Cather associates ancient Rome and the defeat of the Old South in three poems in *"April Twilights" and Other Poems:* "The Palatine," "The Gaul in the Capitol," and "A Likeness" (23).

10. For analysis of references to the *Aeneid* in Tate's poetry, see Dupree 141 ff.; Feder 175–79; Squires, *Allen Tate* 119–20.

11. Tate 68–69.

O'Connor's Vision and Cather's Fiction

JOHN J. MURPHY

While Willa Cather's career in fiction clearly curves toward religion, it seems as if religion in Cather is more a matter of culture than of truth, an enrichment of life on earth rather than a vision of life beyond. In order to complement this view, I would like to evaluate Cather against a writer who remained a southerner and left no doubt about the dead seriousness of her religious commitment. The importance of Flannery O'Connor as a fiction writer and theologian lies in providing readers with a different and frequently disturbing way of seeing. The idea of Christianity, the nature and economy of grace, and the definition of the grotesque within this economy are essential components that need to be studied (if not accepted as belief) in order for readers to begin to see with O'Connor's vision. After clarifying these components and briefly noting O'Connor's illustration of them, I will apply them to instances in Cather's fiction, concluding with suggestions on how to read *Sapphira and the Slave Girl* from O'Connor's perspective. Informing my comments on Cather's final novel is O'Connor's premise that there is something Christian in the southern way of seeing.

The late contemporary Jesuit theologian Karl Rahner defined the *idea* of Christianity as the ontological self-communication of God to humanity, the communication of absolute mystery (God) to a spiritual and personal being of transcendence (man—female and male). "The Christian message," writes Rahner, "is the result of a long development in the history of man and his spirit. A Christian interprets [this development] correctly as a history of salvation and of an ongoing revelation of God which has reached its climax in Christ" (117). Because the offering by God is of God's own being, what is communicated amounts to the (using Rahner's term) "divinization of humanity through the Holy Spirit, the bestowal of grace and vision" (118). "We have the obligation," claims Rahner, "to listen to [God's message in Christ's], and to agree with it or to reject it explicitly and responsibly" (117). "God's self-communication to man" is made to "a free being who exists with the possibility of an absolute 'yes' or 'no' to God" (118). The mystery of the acceptance process resides in its twofold nature: "the acceptance of God's self-communication must be based upon God's offer itself, and hence that acceptance of grace is . . . an event of grace itself" (118); that is, because our acceptance has its basis in a divine offer, the acceptance becomes divine, a moment of human transcendence.

The central drama in all O'Connor stories involves this process of the communication of the divine and owes to Thomas Aquinas's comparatively mechanical explanations of operating and cooperating grace, of how we are at once opened to grace and then assisted by grace to respond. Aquinas explains, "there is a double act in us. First there is the interior act of the will, and with regard to this act the will is a thing moved, and God is the mover. . . . And hence, inasmuch as God moves the human mind to this act, we speak of operating grace. But there is another, exterior act. . . . And because God assists us in this act, both by strengthening our will interiorly so as to attain to the act, and by granting outwardly the capacity of operating, it is with respect to this that we speak of co-operating grace" (Question 111, Article 2). Aquinas caps his argument with a quote from Augustine: "[God] operates that we may will; and when we will, [God] *co*-operates that we may perfect."

The human need for grace in the Christian mystery is compound. Grace is necessary first of all because humanity is human but ordained by God toward an end beyond itself, a supernatural (superhuman) destiny that requires the communication of divine life, the transfiguration of the human by the divine. The subsequent sinfulness of humanity because of the Fall complicates the process, in that grace is then needed not only to elevate humanity but to heal it. This human lapse explains the presence of grotesque characters and freaks in O'Connor's stories. O'Connor uses the freak hero, she says, "not simply [to show] us what we are, but what we have been and what we could become"; "when the freak can be sensed as a figure for our essential displacement [lapse] . . . he attains some depth in literature" (*Mystery* 118, 45). God's offer to elevate and heal the human freak is inextricably linked to Christ's sacrificial death and thus emphatically reflects what Rahner terms God's "universal salvific will," which destines "this fulfillment [elevation and healing] not only for some, but for all . . . , [and] which consists in the fully realized acceptance of . . . divine communication" (129).

These essential components of the Christian mystery are dramatized over and over again in O'Connor's stories. The call to transcend the sinful human condition is issued with increasing urgency to self-satisfied Ruby Turpin in "Revelation," to vindictive Mr. Fortune in "A View of the Woods," and to the vain and flighty grandmother in "A Good Man Is Hard to Find." O'Connor delineates the fallen state of each subject, depicts the insistence of God's salvific will, and analyzes the process of grace—the interaction of operating and cooperating grace and the wilful response (acceptance or rejection).

Ruby Turpin unmindfully boasts of her fallen state to her audience in the doctor's waiting room: "If it's one thing I am, . . . it's grateful. When I think who all I could have been besides myself [insert blacks and trash here] and what I got, a little of everything, and good disposition, besides, I just feel like shouting, 'Thank you, Jesus, for making everything the way it is!'" (*Works* 644). That "the way it is" is the way of sin startles Ruby when she is hit in the eye with a book titled *Human Development*; and subsequently, in her long struggle with grace, she recognizes herself as flawed, as one of those with "a little of everything and the God-given wit to use it right" at the very end of the purgatorial procession to Paradise, well behind "whole companies of white-trash . . . and bands of black niggers in white robes, and battalions of freaks and lunatics shouting and clapping and leaping like frogs" (654). O'Connor stays outside the interaction of operating and co-operating grace in this story, perhaps because that interaction is a mystery.

In "A View of the Woods," O'Connor draws closer to old Mr. Fortune, faced with the opportunity to fathom the eternal consequences of selling property to spite his son-in-law Pitts and block out the woods that O'Connor designated her Christ symbol (e.g., *Works* 1014). Puzzled that his nine-year-old look-alike granddaughter, Mary, opposes the sale, Fortune repeatedly gets up from an afternoon nap to contemplate the woods; however, each time he stifles revelation. In the last instance this is most emphatic: "He saw it, in his hallucination, as if someone were wounded behind the woods and the trees were bathed in blood. After a few minutes this unpleasant vision was broken by the presence of Pitts's pick-up truck grinding to a halt below the window. He returned to his bed and shut his eyes and against the closed lids hellish red trunks rose up in a black wood" (*Works* 538). But the "universal salvific will" is not this easily dismissed and violently forces itself on Fortune through granddaughter Mary, who attacks the old man and tries to force him to accept his connection to Pitts. The only way grace can be stifled is by dashing Mary's head against a rock until "his conquered image . . . [is] absolutely silent. . . . The eyes had rolled back down and were set in a fixed state that did not take him in" (545–46). Mr. Fortune is one of the damned, according to O'Connor (1015), emphatically damning himself by refusing God's self-communication.

Although we remain essentially outside the protagonist in O'Connor's most familiar story, "A Good Man Is Hard to Find," O'Connor herself has explained the meaning intended in her objective depiction of the grandmother's response to grace. That response, that "unexpected" yet "totally right" gesture that is "in character and beyond character," that is "on the anagogical level . . . which has to do with the Divine life and our participation in it" (*Mystery* 111), occurs when the grandmother's head clears and "she realizes . . . she is responsible for the man before her [The Misfit] and joined to him by ties of kinship which have their roots in the [Christian] mystery she merely has been prattling about so far. And at this point she does the right thing, she makes the right gesture" (111–12); she reaches out and touches the Misfit, identifying him as "one of my babies . . . one of my own children!" (*Works* 152).

Once defined, the theme of grace becomes apparent throughout Willa Cather's fiction, more emphatically from *The Professor's House* (1925) to the last completed story, "The Best Years" (published posthumously in 1948). The 1901 *Saturday Evening Post* story "Jack-a-Boy" not only anticipates this final work in using a child as a vehicle of grace but establishes Cather within an American tradition embracing O'Connor stories that feature children—like "A View of the Woods," "The Lame Shall Enter First," and "The Artificial Nigger"—and similar efforts by Hawthorne, with whom O'Connor claimed "more of a kinship . . . than with any other American" (*Works* 1157), like "The Gentle Boy," "Roger Malvin's Burial," "Ethan Brand," and others. These stories share the force of grace operating through children as an opportunity for community and rebirth. "Jack-a-Boy" concludes with a clarification of this theme as explicit as any in Hawthorne's fiction or O'Connor's commentaries on her own work. Responding to another character's wonder at the cohesive effect of the young boy as a revelation of beauty, Cather's narrator recalls "how the revelation of the greatest Revealer drew men together. How the fishermen left their nets, without questioning, to follow Him; and how Nicodemus . . . came to Him secretly by night, and Mary, of Magdala, . . . wiped his feet with her hair" (*Collected Short Fiction* 322).

The novels of Cather's post-Nebraska period—*The Professor's House* (1925), *My Mortal Enemy* (1926), *Death Comes for the Archbishop* (1927), *Shadows on the Rock* (1931), and *Sapphira and the Slave Girl* (1940)—develop the grace theme beyond its rather sentimental expression in the stories. Elsewhere I have discussed the final section of *The Professor's House* as a conversion story in process, one in which the rescue of the deeply depressed protagonist leads to new life: the professor is, as Cather writes, "not the same man" he was prior to this near-death experience (258). Although Cather refrains from defining the process as Christian conversion (Murphy, "Modernist Conversion" 71–72), her text is replete with suggestions of such: a devout Catholic maternal figure who rescues the professor, references to the Virgin Mary and medieval liturgy, Angelus bells, the Magnificat, etc. However, in her next novel, *My Mortal Enemy*, Cather abandons modernist reluctance to tell the complex story of an embittered woman's return, during her final illness, to the Catholicism she had renounced to pursue a youthful love that failed her in marriage. In *Death Comes for the Archbishop* Cather utilizes church history to dramatize the workings of grace that sustain the efforts of two missionaries to overcome adverse forces within and beyond themselves in order to reestablish the Lord's kingdom in the Southwest. I have chosen scenes from this novel and one from *My Mortal Enemy* as clear anticipations of O'Connor's dramas of grace.

The narrator of *My Mortal Enemy* takes Myra Henshawe to a headland

above the Pacific topped by a twisted cedar to relieve her from her dingy
rooms and tramping overhead neighbors during the final stages of her
physical and spiritual anguish. The tree and the intensity of the afternoon
sun generate a mysterious aura typical of O'Connor stories and transcend-
ing the unadorned realism of narrator Nellie's text: "From a distance I
could see her leaning against her tree and looking off to sea, as if she were
waiting for something. . . . The afternoon light . . . grew stronger and yel-
lower, and when I went back to Myra it was beating from the west on her
cliff as if thrown by a burning-glass" (60). A burning glass, which focuses
the sun's rays to set objects on fire, becomes in this context an obvious symbol of grace. Myra is affected: her smile becomes "soft," her face
"lovely." As in Ruby Turpin's case, the transformation is viewed from
the outside—we are distanced from the mystery of grace. "Light and silence . . . heal all one's wounds . . . but one, and that is healed by dark and
silence," Myra explains to Nellie, anticipating death's cure (60–61). This
healing involves both a sense of guilt and then hope for forgiveness as the
sun sets into the sea, a traditional crucifixion image (like the cedar). "I'd
love to see this place at dawn," Myra continues. "That is always such a
forgiving time. . . . it's as if all our sins were pardoned; as if the sky leaned
over the earth and kissed it and gave it absolution." The imagery here is
strategic in evaluating the force behind Myra's subsequent reconciliation to
the church, her taking the Sacrament, and her efforts (albeit harsh) to dis-
illusion her husband as to the reality of their relationship.

A scene in *Death Comes for the Archbishop*, in the last chapter of book 8,
illuminates the source of Bishop Latour's ability to deny himself and release
Father Vaillant to the Colorado mission. Through more than fifty pages of
this narrative the bishop has vacillated in his attempt to transcend his emotional need for his companion and satisfy Vaillant's compulsion to serve
their flock in remote areas of the territory. In an earlier scene Latour, after
a "sharp struggle" (208), snaps off a spray of tamarisk to emphasize his
release of Vaillant to the Arizona mission, a triumph immediately cele-
brated in doves dissolving into light around the Mexican servant Magda-
lena. Descending doves are traditional symbols of the Holy Spirit, whose
gifts, or "supernatural reflexes" (Hardon 230), include the fortitude or
courage necessary for Latour to overcome his human need. However, the
struggle is ongoing, as is the supernatural help, and Latour's subsequent
anxiety is temporarily relieved by the slave Sada in the Lady chapel of the
cathedral, where Cather clarifies the Virgin Mary's role as channel of divine grace and prepares us for full illumination of the source of the bishop's
strength. When the need for an administrator for the Colorado mission
arises, after Latour has lapsed and recalled his friend from Arizona, the
struggle to surrender Vaillant must be repeated. Cather distances us from
this struggle, telling us merely that the bishop "was shut in his study all

morning" (243), where he obviously responds to the grace, the fortitude channeled through the Virgin, necessary for his decision. But as he makes his way back from the hill where he parts from his Colorado-bound friend, Latour is dispirited, his solitude burdensome. When he returns to the rectory, however, he experiences a miracle of grace that explains the source of the strength necessary to overcome personal need once and for all: "The curtain of the arched doorway had scarcely fallen behind him when that feeling of personal loneliness was gone, and a sense of loss was replaced by a sense of restoration. . . . It was just this solitariness of love in which a priest's life could be like his Master's. It was not a solitude of atrophy, of negation, but of perpetual flowering. A life need not be cold, or devoid of grace in the worldly sense, if it were filled by Her who was all the graces; . . . Virgin-mother . . . and Queen of Heaven" (253–54). The distinction Cather makes between Latour's experience and "grace in the worldly sense" establishes her as one who readily would have understood the message O'Connor felt compelled to shout at a theologically indifferent world.

Let me now consider *Sapphira and the Slave Girl*, which lends itself to the O'Connor context because, like O'Connor's fiction, it is southern fiction without Catholic characters but drawing upon Catholic tradition. Cather had spent more than a decade working out Catholic themes prior to undertaking this novel, which she did not intend to be her last, for she was at work on another "Catholic" work, to be set in medieval Avignon, when she died. *Sapphira* draws on each of the novels discussed above and also on *Shadows on the Rock*, which views the world in the purgatorial terms of O'Connor stories and is populated like them with maimed and grotesque characters. This vision enhances the southern setting O'Connor recognized as haunted by the supernatural: " . . . in the South the general conception of man is still in the main, theological," she wrote. "I think it is safe to say that while the South is hardly Christ-centered, it is most certainly Christ-haunted. The Southerner, who isn't convinced of it, is very much afraid that he may have been formed in the image and likeness of God" (*Mystery* 44–45). Cather's main theme in *Sapphira* is the struggle with this "image and likeness"; it is human evolution from lower forms to ultimate divinization and subsumes racial issues. When old Jezebel is buried, Mr. Fairhead recalls her "long wanderings; how she had come from a heathen land where people worshipped idols and lived in bloody warfare, to become a devout Christian and an heir to all the Promises" (102). Alone that evening, Henry Colbert reflects on the ambiguity of slavery: "Jezebel's life . . . seemed a strange instance of predestination. For her, certainly, her capture had been a deliverance. Yet he hated the whole system of slavery" (108). That Jezebel came from "a fierce people" (91), looks on her deathbed like "a lean old grey monkey" (86), has a "cold grey claw" (89), and was called "the female gorilla" (93) by the mate she bit on the slaver is perhaps more

Christian than racist, or reflects the necessary political *in*correctness of the
Christian mystery of transcendence.

We are told early in the novel that the Mill House resembles Washington's Mount Vernon and is "all . . . orderly in front" (20); however, "behind
the house lay another world; a helter-skelter scattering." As Cather's story
progresses, that confusion comes to the fore, overtaking, as it does in Ruby
Turpin's world, a perfection that is merely illusion. The flawed reality of
the plantation and the province is reflected, rather, in "moonshiners and
sheep-stealers and fist-fighters who wore brass knuckles . . . , drank bad
whisky, and threw dice and told dirty stories" (233), among them one-eyed
Bill Hooker, who tries to stop the carriage carrying Nancy toward the Potomac; and in the pitiful figure of crazy, heartbroken Tansy Dave, a "scare-
crow man, bare-legged, his pants torn away to the knee, his shirt a dirty
rag" (204).

Disorder is also evident in the temperaments and relationships of the
major characters: Henry and Sapphira are an uneven match; Sapphira's
cruelty undermines her kindness; Henry is tainted by the Colbert blood;
Rachel is a zealot who deeply wounds her mother; Nancy lies, and Till
seems to favor position over mother love. The depressing reality is under-
scored, as in *Shadows on the Rock*, by images of illness, abnormality, and
death: the physically bloated Sapphira is carried about in a grotesque chair
made by a coffin maker, whose coffin-laden vehicle becomes the means of
deliverance; a diphtheria epidemic takes the lives of several schoolchildren,
including one of Rachel's daughters; Mandy Ringer's only son, Lawndis, is
a cripple, "a pore mock of a man" (129); Till's Jeff is a "capon man."

Instances of violent exploitation are hardly confined to Nancy's situation.
Martin Colbert's blue tooth is the result of his "fooling" a "pretty, home-
spun girl in the Blue Ridge" (163); both Mrs. Ringer's daughters had been
ruined by men who took advantage of Lawndis's inability to protect his
family; Casper Flight is tormented by resentful cousins who try to blame
him for their own thievery—indeed Cather suggests Christ's flagellation
as Casper, tied to a tree and stripped to the waist, is lashed with plaited
cowhide thongs. These instances mirror the overarching injustice of slavery, which little Rachel Colbert had recognized as wrong when she over-
heard a conversation between Postmistress Bywaters and her father in
which the word "owning" was used: "It was the owning that was wrong,
the relation itself, no matter how convenient or agreeable it might be for
master or servant. . . . It was the thing that made her unhappy at home, and
came between her and her mother. How she hated her mother's voice in
sarcastic reprimand to the servants" (137).

In spite of what is hateful in Sapphira, or perhaps because of it, she is the
one who unleashes the force of transcendence in sending for Martin Colbert, who plays the devil in this drama. As O'Connor observed, "the devil

accomplishes a good deal of groundwork that seems to be necessary before grace is effective" (*Mystery* 117). On the night of Jezebel's burial, between her invitation to Martin and his arrival, Sapphira has an experience that explains if not excuses her for her underhanded defensive measures. It occurs the same night Henry searches his Bible for guidance on slavery and rereads "Remember them [that are] in bonds[,] as bound with them" (Hebrews 13:3). The simultaneous scenes illustrate the condition of universal bondage Henry understands only superficially and applies locally: "were we not all in bonds? If Lizzie, the cook, was in bonds to Sapphira, was she not almost equally in bonds to Lizzie?" (110). The true mystery of bondage lies in Sapphira's situation. Sapphira tried to persuade her husband to spend the night with her, but he excused himself. Now she is haunted by an earlier conversation between Henry and Nancy that appeared intimate. She parts the curtains and sees lights burning in Henry's room in the mill. Hurt and remorseful, she remembers her father's last days and, now that she herself is an invalid, regrets her lack of tenderness toward her father. Her fortitude begins to break up; she struggles to the window, suspects that Nancy has left her pallet by the door and is with Henry. She wonders if anyone, even Till, can be trusted:

> The Mistress sat still, scarcely breathing, overcome by dread. The thought of being befooled, hoodwinked in any way, was unendurable to her. There were candles on her dressing-table, but she had no way to light them. Her throat was dry and seemed closed up. She felt afraid to call aloud, afraid to take a full breath. A faintness was coming over her. She put out her hand and resolutely rang her clapper bell.
> The chamber door opened, and someone staggered in.
> "Yes mam, yes mam! Whassa matter, Missy?"
> Nancy's sleepy, startled voice. Mrs. Colbert dropped back in her chair and drew a long, slow breath. It was over. Her shattered, treacherous house stood safe about her again. She was in her own room wakened out of a dream of disaster. (106–7)

But this night anticipates the ultimate shattering of Sapphira's house that follows Martin Colbert's arrival on the scene. While it is difficult to pin down Sapphira's exact purpose in having Martin at the Mill House, his intentions regarding Nancy are quite clear in the kiss he forces on her, his pursuit of her into the woods, the framing of his face with her legs. The interaction of Sapphira and Martin resembles that of devil and victim or of sinner and embodiment of sin, particularly in the cacophony of their laughter, hers alternately ladylike and scornful, his "on the edge of being vulgar—rather loose, caught-in-the-act" (164).

Together, these two transfer Sapphira's terror to Nancy, when, at Sapphira's door, the slave girl imagines Martin's stealthy footsteps approaching her: "It was a horrible feeling. . . . she wouldn't have the start of him. He would be there" (195). Nancy runs to Rachel: "He kin jist slip into my bed any night if I happens to fall asleep," she laments. "I got nobody to call to. I can't do nothin! . . . I tell you, I'd druther drown myself before he got at me than after!" (217). Rachel now acts on her convictions and does more about injustice than share the *New York Tribune* with the postmistress; she tries to shake her father out of his intellectual lethargy. Although she wins Henry's support, he will give it only backhandedly. The Martin Colbert episode deprives Henry of his idealization of Nancy as a figure out of Bunyan, but it fails to motivate him to direct action. Perhaps his moment of clear vision and transcendence comes years later, O'Connor fashion, when he hits his head on a rock in a fall from a haying wagon.

Rachel's and Sapphira's come earlier. When Rachel receives Sapphira's request to make no further visits to the Mill House, she is moved to sympathy for her mother and acknowledgment of her good qualities: "She unfolded the letter again, and as she looked at it, tears rose slowly to her eyes" (247). Rachel has second thoughts about what she has done and seems to appreciate the complexity of the human condition: "It's hard for a body to know what to do, sometimes. . . . Maybe I ought to have thought and waited." Sapphira's transcendence comes in two stages. When she is informed her granddaughters are ill, "she rose on her pillows and gave [Henry] a searching look" before sending for her doctor and instructing Till to go to Rachel to find out her needs. When little Betty dies of the diphtheria, Cather's description of Sapphira's response is telling: "the Mistress was thinking, turning things over in her mind. She had not seen Rachel since Nancy's disappearance, months ago. She was wondering how far she could count upon herself. At last, when she had quite made up her mind, she put her hand on her husband's drooping shoulder" (266), and she invites her daughter home.

Recall O'Connor's description of another grandmother, who, in extending her hand, achieves "a special kind of triumph. . . . both in character and beyond character . . . suggest[ing] both the world and eternity. [An] action or gesture . . . on the anagogical level, . . . the level which has to do with the Divine life and our participation in it. . . . a gesture which somehow made contact with mystery" (*Mystery* 111).

Playing in the Mother Country

Cather, Morrison, and the Return to Virginia

JANIS P. STOUT

In *Playing in the Dark: Whiteness and the Literary Imagination* (1990) Toni Morrison enunciates a provocative reassessment of the racial politics pervading American letters. Not only does Morrison point out, as have many other critics and scholars, the long-established and ongoing dominance of white-authored texts in the national literature of a society that is in fact composed of a rich variety of ethnicities and cultures, but she interrogates the even more vexed and vexing issue of the imaginative uses that blackness, or in her terms the "Africanist presence," has served *for white authors.* Among the major cases in point in Morrison's challenging polemic is Willa Cather's *Sapphira and the Slave Girl* (1940), a novel that Morrison says has been "virtually jettisoned from the body of American literature by critical consensus" (18). If so, the novel is now being resolutely hauled back on board.

The long and undue critical neglect of *Sapphira and the Slave Girl* has been, since Morrison wrote and even before, abundantly corrected. Except for that oversight, however, Morrison's argument is not only provocative but genuinely important, both with respect to the issues that she directly addresses (Cather's and other white writers' appropriation and manipulation of black experience for purposes of self- or group-enhancement) and with respect to a set of issues that she does not directly address. Her attention to *Sapphira* demonstrates that the set of concerns motivating Cather in this late work are resonant ones for Morrison as well. These concerns, which I see as central and shaping ones for both writers, are the ambiguities of the good mother/bad mother and the related, or even intertwined, ambiguities of South and North.

In *Sapphira and the Slave Girl*, Cather tells a story of pre– and post–Civil War Virginia, the state of her birth—a state from which, however, she was traumatically snatched away at the age of nine by her family's move to Nebraska. Leaving the verdant natural beauty of hilly northwestern Virginia, in the Back Creek area near Winchester—a landscape we might think of as an inland and southern version of F. Scott Fitzgerald's "fresh, green breast of the new world"—the family relocated to a landscape that Cather herself described as "lead-colored," an "iron country" (*O Pioneers!* 26, 169), and "a country as bare as sheet iron" (Bohlke 10). *Sapphira*, Cather's last published novel but the first in which she invoked a Virginia setting, is located in the community and countryside of her early childhood, and the epilogue is in fact set in a transparent representation of the house and farm where she lived during her first nine years. The act of writing the novel was for Cather an imaginative return home, a return to the mother-place.[1] Fitzgerald's image of the "green breast" is a pertinent one in more ways than simply the topographical. Moreover, the central action of the novel's plot line, to which Morrison reacts in *Playing in the Dark*, is also a return to the mother. Twenty-five years after her escape from Sapphira, the mistress who had developed an unreasoning hatred for her and had plotted to have her raped by a dissolute white man, the former slave girl, Nancy, returns for a reunion with the mother who had been unable but also sadly unwilling to protect her.[2] In the meantime the Civil War has intervened; Sapphira has forgiven the daughter, Rachel, who helped Nancy escape; and Till, Nancy's mother, has become the repository of family memory.

This rather bare plot serves as the structure through which Cather raises, though only partially addresses, a complex set of maternal and quasi-maternal problematics, seen in at least five relationships: Nancy's relation to her slave mother, Till; Till's relation to her mistress and owner, Sapphira, toward whom she feels an overriding loyalty as if to a mother; Till's relation to her actual mother, whose death by fire she witnessed; Rachel's relation to Sapphira, whom she has defied in arranging Nancy's escape; the child Willa's relation to the understanding mother who appears in the final pages of the novel; and the black mother and daughter's relation to the white mother and daughter, in whose home their reunion takes place and for whose benefit (Morrison insists) it is in some ways staged.[3] Yet another mother-daughter relation stands outside the text, though it is a very real problematic being addressed by it: the adult Willa Cather's actual relation to her own mother.

The question of Cather's relationship to her mother is one of the great issues in her biography. It seems to have been a tense relationship from early on. Not only was Cather's mother (portrayed as Victoria Templeton in the story "Old Mrs. Harris") judgmental, imperious, and severe in her punishment of her children but she was also beautiful, warm, and gracious, very much the southern lady. Her vision of a woman's life, however, was one that Cather insistently rebelled against and in fact escaped when she made her departure for the university and subsequently her career.[4] In "Old Mrs. Harris," where Cather's actual escape is traced in fictional form, the mother appears as a blocking figure or at best an uninterested spectator, while it is the grandmother, representing Cather's own Grandmother Boak, who takes the role of maternal advocacy and sacrifice. Even James Woodress, who insists that Willa Cather had a "happy relationship with both her parents," concedes that "relations with her mother were sometimes difficult" and the two "often clashed in her youth" ("Dutiful Daughter" 23, 30). That clash—indisputably an ambiguous one, entailing a very real closeness and a certainty that she was loved even as it entailed resistance and rebellion—set up a tension that would remain with Cather throughout her life. It would be exacerbated, in the years preceding her work on *Sapphira*, by her mother's illness and death. In the novel, then, Cather's mother is represented both by the bad mother, Sapphira, who becomes strangely good near the time of her death, and by the good mother who appears in the autobiographical closing scene. Cather herself appears both in Sapphira's resisting daughter, Rachel (based largely on Grandmother Boak), and in the child Willa, inserted in her own person into the fictional structure in the final scene of return and reconciliation in which mothers and daughters are posed in idyllic embrace and mutual care.

I have said that this novel is at once a return to the mother, in multiple ways, and a return to the mother-place, also in multiple ways, as the return is enacted by both author and character. That idea is reinforced by the fact that the name of the mother-place resonated in the name of Cather's mother, Mary Virginia. She was commonly called Jennie. In her fictional return to the mother-place, Cather was revisiting the place of the mother she had known in early childhood and also revisiting the ambiguities of her own relationship with her mother. That place, however, is itself ambiguous—a place, undeniably, of slavery[5] even as it was a place of beauty and, for the first child of a well-established and respected white family, a place of secure community. And the novel constructs it in both its characters; it celebrates the natural beauty of Virginia, but it also confronts the dark shadow of slavery—indeed, it confronts it in strikingly Gothic terms. The vision of home that the book conveys (in Sapphira's house, at any rate) is one in which home is a site of sickness, imprisonment, and sharply restricted possibility, for white as well as for black. Perhaps paradoxically, the novel resoundingly affirms both liberation by means of literal escape and joyful return to the home from which that escape was made. The house that is the scene of the concluding reunion has replaced the house where, twenty-five years earlier, Sapphira ruled in dropsical immobility over her enslaved chattel and her dominated husband, but Sapphira occupies the new one as well, in memories that emphasize not her sinister character but her achievement of a graceful death. Nancy's escape from Virginia, the South, is also an escape from her own unprotecting mother and from the vindictive white quasi-mother Sapphira. Her return to Virginia restores her emotional ties to her mother and to the place of origin where she had once reveled in the picking of flowers and cherries.[6] Mother and South are compounded; and both are caught in toils of ambiguity. Mother, home, and South are conceived both as that which is to be escaped or resisted and that to which one is to be restored in happiness and reconciliation.

It is probably easy for us to see that Virginia, the South, would represent for Cather a place of nostalgia, the good place lost. It is perhaps more difficult for us to see that it also represents for her, both historically and personally, through its association with her mother, the place of enslavement or personal restriction, the place to be escaped. With respect to Toni Morrison, these terms can surely be reversed: It is easy to see that she would regard the South as the place of evil and enslavement, the place to be escaped, and more difficult to see that Morrison would also think of the South with yearning or affection. But in fact the South is an ambiguous presence in Morrison's work as well—a place of nostalgia, a Sweet Home, as well as the site of an all-too-historically-rooted horror. And like Cather, Morrison associates this ambiguity with the figure of the mother, both fictionally and autobiographically.

The version of the South in Morrison's work that is probably the most familiar to her readers is the one that appears in *Beloved*, where the farm called Sweet Home is remembered by Paul D and Sethe as a place where men were accorded their manhood, where Sethe (like Nancy) could pick flowers and bring them into the house while she ironed for her mistress, where corn and sweet potatoes grew in abundance and a huge tree that provided noontime shade was a friend. For Sethe, it was the place of sexual delight; the consummation of her sadly unformalized marriage occurred on the fertile soil itself, in a dense cornfield. But the sweets of Sweet Home were delusive, just as the sweets of Cather's Virginia were crossed by the dark presence of slavery, jealousy, and malice. Morrison's Sweet Home was also a place of dehumanization and torture. Rather than *Beloved*, however, I want to propose parallels with the ambiguities of Cather's *Sapphira* in Morrison's more recent novel *Jazz*.

Houston A. Baker Jr. writes in *Blues, Ideology, and Afro-American Literature* (122) that the attitude felt toward the South by migrant blacks in the North is a "sharp dilemma." That dilemma is enunciated in *Jazz* in the story of Joe and Violet Trace, who leave Virginia during the period of the Great Migration, early in the twentieth century, and attempt to make a home for themselves in New York, first in the Tenderloin District and then (in a move that accurately parallels the history of black migration, as recounted by Anderson) in Harlem. Although the Harlem setting of their story is in many ways positive for them—it is a place of omnipresent music that sets their feet dancing—they maintain a troubled nostalgia for their life in the South. Joe recalls "fields and woods and secret lonely valleys"; Violet speaks of how they "ate good down home" (107, 81). The South they retain in memory is a maternalized landscape of dark hollows and abundant oral pleasure. But if that place "down home" was one of natural plenty, it was also a place of social deprivation. As the descendants of former slaves, they were denied the plenty that the South afforded, and instead were compelled to work inordinately for scant return and to suffer the effects of ancestral despair. As in *Beloved*, then, the Traces' memories of the South are both alluring and dark.

In the South, where Joe and Violet saw that the price paid to whites for their cotton was two dollars a bale more than the price paid to blacks, where black women sometimes earned ten cents a day for their work and black men a quarter, they had no hope of escaping grinding poverty. Like many others who left the South and migrated to the North during the Great Migration, Joe and Violet were impelled not only by economics but by terror: the very real threat of lynching, shockingly widespread in the South in the early decades of the century.

In a more individual sense, the darkness of their experience of the South is compounded, for both Joe and Violet, by the loss of the mother. Joe's mother, in the quasi parable of his strange parentage, was a woman who, like her name, Wild, ran wild in the woods, unclothed, uncommunicative, and who abandoned him soon after birth, dooming him to a lifetime of search for a nurturing maternal presence. Violet's mother killed herself in despair over her inability to provide even minimal support for her children, and Violet herself is left with a lifelong unwillingness, until it is too late, to take the risk of bearing children. Both Joe, raised as a foundling, and Violet, raised by her formerly enslaved grandmother, continually return in memory to their primal deprivation and its scene in the mother-place that was also Cather's mother-place, Virginia. Their past, centering on the loss of their mothers (loss of origins, the true past), haunts them long after they think they have put these old losses behind them by migrating. Violet carries away someone's baby for a few moments of holding, lies down in the street in disheartenment, buys herself a doll to sleep with. Joe renews his search for the mother in the form of a search for a young girl with whom he has had an affair and to whom he can sing his blues—who had herself been orphaned in the East St. Louis riots. As in *Beloved*, the past keeps coming back in different forms, like changes on core material in jazz.

In the North, though things are hard, the Traces can nevertheless find ways of making a place for themselves. They obtain decent housing and enjoy the life of the streets in a section shared with thousands of other African Americans. Yet they are pulled apart from each other, both by the weight of the unconfronted past and by the daily necessity of moving around the city on the separate routes by which they make their living— Violet dressing hair in people's homes because she isn't licensed and can't work in a shop, Joe working as a bellhop or selling cosmetics. At home, in the South, they had shared a small number of fixed places, the most important of which was the tree beside a cotton field where they met. They had roots and therefore a sense of home in that "very old place" (to borrow a phrase from Albert Murray) despite its very old hostilities.[7] In New York their separate movements both express their sense of separateness and of rootlessness and contribute to prolonging it.

Like Cather's *Sapphira*, Morrison's novel includes a fairy-tale-like story of return to the South, the interpolated but linked story of Golden Gray.

Rather than a quest for the mother, Golden Gray's return to the South—
the Sweet Home that is also his own place of deprivation, hardship, and
loss—is a quest for the father. Even so, it is elaborately linked with Morrison's theme of the loss of the mother and with Joe's search for his mother.
In the South, specifically in Virginia, Golden Gray confronts black maternity, in the form of the full-term pregnant Wild, who proceeds to give
birth to Joe in his presence. The generations are linked; past and present,
realism and fantasy, merge, much as they do in *Sapphira*.

The swirling stories of *Jazz* join country roads to city streets, join lost
mothers to found orphans who can share stories of the lost mother, join
memories of a sweeter home to the achievement of a home that will
sweeten the present. Throughout, the novel is structured by music, both in
the riffing itself and in the jazz-paced city where Joe and Violet find each
other again. The novel's structure becomes an elaborate set of changes signifying on the core material of maternal loss, displacement from the South
(home), search for home (mother), and, at the end, the achievement of
community. It concludes with the narrator him/herself—a narrator who
intrudes on the action of the novel with free comments, much as Cather
does in *Sapphira*—singing a sorrow song that becomes ecstatically lyrical,
constituting Joe and Violet and Felice as the nucleus of a sense of community that draws together the countless and varied newcomers and old-
timers of the big city—implicitly, the nucleus of the community that is
Harlem.[8]

I am emphasizing the musical aspect of the novel here because it provides
a link to the autobiographical resonance of *Jazz* and the return to the South
that I see as a striking parallel to the better-known autobiographical significance of *Sapphira*. Morrison has commented in a number of interviews on
the prevalence of music in her childhood home and in particular on her
mother's singing. What I want to propose is that the sweetness of the lingering memories of the South in *Jazz*, as well as in *Beloved* and others of
Morrison's works, is a linkage to the figure of the mother, just as the return
to the South is simultaneously a return to the mother for Cather. Place,
history, and the problematics of troubled maternity are, for both Cather
and Morrison, implicated in a single complex whole. Morrison has said
that her own mother "never once went back South to visit" after she migrated north to Ohio "because her experience of it had been so bad."
Nevertheless, Morrison continues, she "'talked about it as though it were
heaven, absolute heaven'" (Taylor-Guthrie 284)—or in other words, a
very Sweet Home.

It is ironic, perhaps, that after polemically exposing the shortcomings
of Cather's dual vision of the home place and the return home in *Sapphira*,
Morrison goes far toward replicating that vision here, in her mingled tribute both to the road of departure from the South, the place of the lost
mother, and to the solace of homing (in memory, in the imagination) and

reconciliation. Near the end of *Jazz*, as she hovers meditatively, in the person of the androgynous narrator, over the figures of Joe and Violet and their quasi daughter grouped in mutual need and mutual regeneration, she envisions a perfect place of refuge, a womblike hollow of the rock, out in the free, woodsy outdoors, "both snug and wide open. With a doorway never needing to be closed" (221). Morrison's felicitous place here, like Cather's in *Sapphira*, is a place in the mother-region, the South. Much as Cather turns back to Virginia, the name of the mother, so Morrison echoes the mother-talk she has recalled from her own childhood: "'she talked about it as though it were heaven, absolute heaven.'"

Notes

1. Cather made real-life returns to Virginia to visit in 1913 and in 1938.
2. Cather told critic Henry Seidel Canby that not only had the events described in the final section actually happened, but Nancy's reunion with her mother had provided the reminiscences that enabled her to write the book at all (4 Feb. 1941, Unpublished Letter). She responded to an admiring letter from Langston Hughes by assuring him that Nancy and the other black people in *Sapphira* were drawn directly from people she had been fond of as a child (15 Apr. 1941, Unpublished Letter). Following the stated time-setting of the novel at its opening, 1856, we can see that the return twenty-five years later would have occurred in 1881, which was the last full year Willa Cather spent in Virginia.
3. Cf. Stout, *Through the Window, Out the Door* 152, and more generally, 98–102 and 151–53.
4. Ann Romines writes that in *Sapphira* "autobiography, history, and fiction are inextricably interwoven" (*Home Plot* 174).
5. See Arnold, "'Of Human Bondage,'" for a reading of the novel in which the institution of slavery is seen as a metaphor for a variety of kinds of enslavement.
6. Nancy's reveling in the fruits and flowers of Back Creek, Virginia, was echoed in Cather's delight in the beauties of hills and woods during her return to Virginia in 1938 (Lewis 183). Lewis's recollections of her attention to the blossoming bushes and trees growing along the road up Timber Ridge are confirmed in Cather's own copy of Mathews's *Field Book of American Wild Flowers*, where she wrote "Virginia 1938" in the margin beside entries for calamus or sweet fig (16) and flowering dogwood (318) and "Timber Ridge, Virginia, 1938" beside the entry for pinxter flower or wild honeysuckle (336). Woodress mentions her long use of the Mathews *Field Book* in *Willa Cather: A Literary Life* (286). An extended celebration of the dogwood, the wild honeysuckle, and the flowering locust appears in the novel when Sapphira's daughter, Mrs. Blake, climbs Timber Ridge to see a family of hill folk (115–17).
7. Murray's virtuosic book *South to a Very Old Place* (1971) is one of the chief of those blues songs on which Morrison is virtuosically riffing in *Jazz*.
8. Another similarity between *Jazz* and *Sapphira* is that both are experimental novels. *Jazz* is of course commonly regarded as such—as is Morrison's work generally. *Sapphira* has until recent years been regarded as a nostalgic self-indulgence by a writer out of pace with the narrative experimentalism of her time, who might be described either as a rather old-fashioned realist or as an old-fashioned romantic. On the contrary, it is merely the most conspicuously experimental of her novels, all of which, except perhaps *Alexander's Bridge*, are in various ways experimental and innovative.

5

Epilogue

Leaving the South?

Dressing for the Part

[What's] The Matter with Clothes

CYNTHIA GRIFFIN WOLFF

Willa Cather turned fifteen on December 7, 1888, and shortly thereafter, she cut off her long hair, began to wear boy's jackets, and announced that henceforth she preferred to be called "William Cather, M.D.";[1] in 1893, after several years in college, she once again assumed feminine dress. These appear to have been odd, extravagant gestures, even for adolescence—and gestures that would have been particularly distasteful to a southern-born lady like her mother. And yet, surprisingly, Willa Cather's mother accepted the transformation in her daughter's appearance with equanimity. One wonders why. What is going on in the relationship between Willa Cather and her mother? Indeed, in a more general sense, what *is* the matter with clothes in the case of the young Willa Cather?

The year 1888 was an inauspicious time for any young woman to begin negotiating her passage into maturity. The characteristics of "femininity," that designated "normal" at that time—"dependence, submissiveness . . . [,] and passivity" (O'Brien, *Willa Cather* 98, quoting Dr. Kellogg)—are today understood as symptoms of pathology (and even at that time, were viewed as unacceptably inhibiting by a great many young women). Clothing was the most visible, pervasive, and painful signifier of this late-nineteenth-century construct of the "feminine": attire that society prescribed for all decent women—and attire that society increasingly used to separate "ladies" from less genteel women (like women who aspired to have a career). In fact, at this time in the women's movement, "fashion" had become one of society's most insidious techniques for countering women's increasing demand for greater freedom, a cudgel to keep them in their place—a punitive form of dress that prohibited vigorous, independent activity of any kind: merciless corsets tightening toward an "ideal waist" of sixteen inches, bustles, petticoats, trains, towering pompadours, and lavish hats. An ensemble that could weigh thirty pounds or more to clothe a body that had been contorted into caricature.

One might suppose that Willa Cather's isolated, rural situation protected her from the more extravagant follies of "femininity" thus defined. Yet by 1888, train tracks had crossed and recrossed the great plains; Red Cloud, Nebraska, with both a station and a roundhouse, was a railroad center; the train (eight stops a day [Woodress, *Willa Cather*, 44]) brought salesmen, mail, newspapers, catalogs, and ladies' magazines into the heart of the Midwest; and the value structures and semiotic systems of the cosmopolitan

world beyond inevitably came with them. Thus, by the age of fifteen Willa
Cather could hardly have escaped knowing the terms of her culture's elaboration of Victorian beauty; and as a brilliant, ambitious, and insightful
fifteen-year-old, she was preternaturally alive to their implications.

Moreover, the most influential presence in Cather's life was her own
mother, Virginia [Jennie] Boak Cather, a stunningly attractive, displaced
Virginia belle who dominated the house and vigorously enacted her own
complex version of turn-of-the-century "femininity." "Always meticulous
in appearance, never stepping out of her bedroom without first being perfectly groomed, Virginia Boak Cather allowed no one to see her until her
lovely hair had been pinned up." [2] Even in the obscurity of small-town life,
Jennie Cather respected society's rules for the display of feminine charms. [3]
Yet anyone could see that she openly ignored its rules regarding "feminine
passivity." She "was always the dominating figure in the family. . . . Mary
Virginia Boak was a handsome, imperious woman, with a strong will and
a strong nature . . . , and her personality made a deep impress . . . on her
children" (Lewis 6). Willa Cather's attitude toward this stern taskmaster
was mixed: as an adolescent, she resented the demands that Mother made
of her. However, she admired Mother's beauty (even though she would
not—could not—emulate it); and she admired the force of Jennie Cather's
character (which she could, and did, adopt for herself). By the time Willa
Cather had reached maturity, she had grown easy with the conflict. She
"always said she was more like her mother than like any other member of
the family," her friend, Edith Lewis, attests (7). Yet as an adolescent, still
striving to define her own, unique place, the aesthetic issues of "femininity" and Jennie Cather's strikingly mixed example of them were problematic for her daughter.

Given the strong-mindedness of the two females in question, it is not
surprising that, like her mother, Willa Cather was determined to negotiate
her own compromises with society's rules. Thus she adopted Mother's
strength, will, and determination; and she retained an essentially female
identity. However, she vigorously and flamboyantly renounced the "uniform" of late Victorian "femininity" that Mother had so faithfully hon-
ored—an elegant appearance and everything it signified.

Cather accomplished much of this goal with that one simple but brilliant
stroke when she cut her hair, donned mannish jackets, and introduced herself as William Cather, M.D. It was a stunning response to the immediate
dilemma of impending "young womanhood," and one in which Mother
took an amused interest, displaying a degree of tolerance that was considerably more flexible than some scholars have supposed.

Unmindful of the social implications of female fashion in the late 1880s
(and heedless of the inevitable and diverse forms of rebellion against it),
many scholars have seen Willa Cather's form of defiance as both unique

and idiosyncratic: thus they have been inclined to construe her behavior in sinister, relatively rigid and dogmatic terms. James Woodress writes: "She refused to be a girl, [and] adopted male values. . . . Her mother, who *no doubt* deplored the male masquerade, nevertheless let her develop in her own way. What effect this denial of her sex had on her psychological development, her sexual orientation, and her life as an artist is a matter of considerable interest" (*Willa Cather* 55–56; emphasis added). Even Sharon O'Brien, who has examined the girl's relationship with her mother at very great length, takes a mixed, but on the whole negative, view of Cather's season of make-believe:

> She was using the transformative power of costuming and performance to reject Red Cloud's confining definition of femininity and to construct an alternative self—powerful, heroic, male. . . . [Yet] to construct this alternate self she . . . was trapped by her contemporaries' polarization of gender traits and roles. . . . In accepting the prevailing definition of male and female identity, Cather was also accepting the culture's polarization of "masculine" and "feminine." Hence this was a period of fragmentation rather than integration. (*Willa Cather* 101–102, 110)

O'Brien is correct in commending the girl's defiant creativity and in asserting that Cather wished to embrace the many attributes of power. However, she is deeply misguided in concluding that Willa Cather was accepting the culture's polarized constructs of gender. In fact, Willa Cather was doing precisely the opposite: she was engaged in a kind of parody of society's dichotomous definitions of "masculine" and "feminine"—lampooning *polarity itself*. As Lesley Ferris has observed, "cross-dressing" is a form of performance,

> an exemplary source of the writerly text, a work that forces the reader/ spectator to see multiple meaning in the very act of reading itself, of listening, watching a performance. Unlike the stationary, handheld, literary text, a performance text operates in dimensions of real time and real space. Its primary mode of communication is not the spoken or written word; communication occurs through the use of the human body: its movement, gestural language, physicality, costume. One of the first readings we are taught in our lives is gender. Is it a man? Is it a woman? We are taught these as bedrock definitions, with no possibility for multiple meanings, no playful ambiguity. [In the case of cross-dressing], we are forced to concede to multiple meanings, to ambiguities of thought, feeling, categorization, to refuse closure. (8)

The adult Willa Cather was a complex woman: she had anxieties, phobias, and despondencies, but she also had passions, many sources of enjoyment, and a profound sense of mastery and accomplishment. During adolescence, the same richly dense intelligence was at work devising mutiny. And this matter of costume was a complex gesture: an act that both defied Jennie Cather's pattern for femininity and invited her collaboration in a elaborate escapade. Far from being a "symptom," Cather's personation was whimsy tinged with impudence—revolution suffused with play.

There were several sources for the explicit costume of Cather's *persona:* initially, she devised her apparel by rummaging through the family's memorabilia and donning parts of the Civil War uniform that had been worn by her mother's brother, a young Confederate hero who had been killed at the First Battle of Bull Run. In part, then, this ensemble was a tribute to Jennie Boak Cather; even more, it was an explicit alliance with mother on an issue that was sensitive within the family, for all of Mr. Cather's people had been Unionists. Indeed, since Mr. and Mrs. Cather argued regularly about the Civil War throughout their marriage, cordially but (on each side) firmly, this stage of the masquerade was freighted with meaning. While paying homage to Mother's valiant brother, it also alluded to the many legends of courageous Confederate *women* who had put on men's uniforms to fight for "the cause"—women whose stories had recently been rekindled by the sensational novel *The Woman in Battle* (1876).[4] This history and these legends, rife in the Virginia of Cather's childhood, suggest one reason for Jennie Cather's tolerance of her daughter's flamboyant behavior. Yet as the masquerade continued, the circle of play expanded, and for a time left explicit references to the Civil War behind. It became "play" in the most dramatic sense of the word: subsequently, most of Willa Cather's mannish costumes stepped directly off the contemporary stage. And Cather's indisputably broad-minded mother seems both to have understood her daughter's joke and to have continued as at least a passive conspirator.

In 1888, Red Cloud, Nebraska, was a very small town. At the age of fifteen, Willa Cather had neither independent means nor the myriad resources that a big city like New York might have offered. Thus while it is conceivable that Willa Cather could have begun the sartorial personation against her mother's opposition, it would have been all but impossible for her to have sustained it for as long as three or four years unless Mother had cooperated (at least tacitly). And the "play" did go on, apparently without maternal demur.[5]

Actually, Jennie Cather's acquiescent reaction may have been entirely predictable: she had always enjoyed theatricals; and there is reason to suppose that she had always been amused by her oldest and most precocious child's tendency toward self-dramatization. Willa Cather's own lifelong interest in the theater has been documented, and this fondness for the stage began even before she had ever seen professional players. The entire family had always entertained themselves by putting plays together and performing them. Willa herself started performing in public at a relatively early age. And the Red Cloud newspaper carries accounts of her histrionic efforts: Willa Cather (age eleven) enacting Hiawatha, longbow in hand, for example.

> Willa was not a child who cared for dressing up dolls. She would rather dress herself up and pretend. Her model and instructor in dramatic arts was Bess Seymore, a cousin who lived with the Cathers and who took the lead in the community plays. Usually rehearsals took place at the Cather home where Bess improvised costumes from Mrs. Cather's wardrobe, and where the large front room with adjacent hallway made an excellent stage. By the time Willa was thirteen, she was improvising and managing plays of her own. (Bennett 170–71)

Moreover, isolated as Red Cloud was, the Cathers, along with other theater-lovers, were not cut off from the world of contemporary theater. They could follow the plays, the actors, the fads, and the trends in magazines and newspapers. But most of all, by 1888 (the year that Cather began her own great experiment), the theater finally came to them. William Curtin, the editor of Willa Cather's theatrical reviews, observes: "The last three decades of the nineteenth century saw the emergence of theatre as a nation-wide institution in the United States. . . . By 1880 smaller towns along the road were being included in the bookings, and about fifty companies, complete with their own scenery and costumes, were on the road" (30).

Red Cloud built its own "Opera House" over the local hardware store in 1885. No more than a large room with folding chairs and a stage at one end, it nonetheless became the focus of political and artistic activity. Politicians spoke there, local dramas were staged there, and when professional actors came to town, they performed in the Opera House. For Willa Cather, by now active in local drama herself, these visits were like heaven. "Half a dozen times during each winter," Cather remembered, "a traveling stock company settled down at the local hotel and thrilled and entertained us for a week. . . . My chums and I always walked a good half mile to the depot . . . to see that train come in. . . . We found it delightful to watch a theatrical company alight, pace the platform while their baggage was being sorted. . . . If by any chance one of the show ladies carried a little dog with a blanket on, that simply doubled our pleasure."[6]

Inevitably, the players brought panoramic glimpses of New York and London with them; and because of a relatively new and quite lucrative business they were able to exploit the increasingly avid "fandom" of late-nineteenth-century audiences.

It had become a general custom to sell pictures of actors and actresses in theater lobbies before and after performances; and prints of the women, actresses, and soon "society beauties" as well were much more in demand than likenesses of the men. These celebrity photographs, duplicated hundreds of times and thus available for a relatively modest price, were wildly popular with theatergoers. In fact they were such a rage that in New York, London, Paris, and other centers of the drama, entire shops were devoted exclusively to the display and sale of these pictures, posters, and other stage memorabilia. In the case of a traveling company, impromptu booths could take the place of shops.

The peripheral aspects are intriguing. Sometimes adulation for stage players became very intense. For example, adolescent girls might, as a group or club, devote themselves to the admiration of a single actress (almost never an actor), and Julia Marlowe was a particular favorite during this period. These girls came to be known as "matinee ladies" because, whenever possible, a group of them would attend plays in the afternoon to watch "their" actress perform; and above all, they banded together to collect and trade memorabilia to put in scrapbooks—photos, playbills, and the like. To be sure, not all theatergoers were as passionate as these teenage fans; nonetheless, a great many people did collect such photographs, and those who didn't could look through a friend's picture album. People also learned to recognize these popular images from magazines and newspapers, or advertisements and posters. Even contemporary sheet music generally carried the image of a popular star. Thus by the mid-1880s, any recent stage fashion would soon become immediately familiar even to those living in smalltown America. As a vehicle for popular culture, the stage was perhaps similar to television today.[7]

In 1888, the latest theatrical craze (by then almost a decade old) was women who went on stage dressed as men, occasionally to play a heroine in disguise, but usually to play male roles. Some historians of the theater have suggested that the sedate burlesque of Lydia Thompson's "British Blondes" began the rage in the late 1860s and 1870s. However, by Cather's time, the origin had probably grown irrelevant, because, for whatever reason, in the early 1880s dispensing with skirts on stage had become more than merely respectable. It had become an all but indispensable component of success. Actresses who sought large audiences, actresses in pursuit of variety, actresses who wanted strong and challenging roles: all sought to find some way of performing in trousers or tights. This fad made it possible for women to renounce passivity and embrace roles of power, at least on stage. Even more important, far from renouncing the feminine, this attire both called attention to the female sex of its wearer, and opened the entire social construct of "the feminine" to experimentation, both on and off the stage.

Willa Cather was no giddy "fanatic"; however, both Cather and her mother loved the professional theater, as did most of the family; thus when

Willa Cather decided to present herself to the public as "William Cather, M.D.," both mother and daughter would have known that this presentation echoed the most recent, most impudent, and most tantalizing and daring theatrical vogue:[8] a vogue that had been emphatically endorsed by the great Bernhardt herself. Cather did not always admire Bernhardt's interpretation of the roles she played (Cather's reviews occasionally chided her for emotional extravagance). However, no one could deny the Divine Sarah's supremacy for several decades on the international stage; thus Cather wrote of her performance in *La Tosca:* "Of course the play is a play made largely of one part. It was written for that great Frenchwoman who dominates any single play as she has dominated the whole world of dramatic art for years" (*World and the Parish* 1:424).

Bernhardt was profoundly influential in enlarging the range of possibility for all actresses because it was she who so firmly established a female's "right" to perform in male attire. Her own first great triumph had been the role of an ardent minstrel-boy in Francois Coppee's play *Le Passant* (1869).[9] Subsequently, she played in any number of cross-dressing roles: *Pierrot* (with Rejane as Colombine); Pelleas (with Mrs. Patrick Campbell as Melisande); L'Aiglon (in Rostand's play of the same name); and the male-attired soldier-saint, *Jeanne d'Arc.* Later in her career (several years after Cather's sartorial experiment had been concluded), Bernhardt notoriously played *Hamlet.* Moreover, early in her career, this multitalented actress, who happened also to be a very gifted sculptor and painter, had photo-portraits taken while she worked in her studio. They display her elegantly attired in a casual (practical) suit of trousers and jacket; thus did art converge with life. These photos may seem entirely unexceptional today; however, during the 1870s they were almost as scandalous as the garb of the cigar-smoking George Sand—or as the "bloomer"- and "trouser"-clad females whose pictures peppered British and American magazines.[10]

Sarah Bernhardt's theatrical innovations were imitated almost immediately, even by actresses who were, by gifts and temperament, least suited to follow her example—Maude Adams, for example. Yet in America, the beautiful Julia Marlowe is perhaps most noteworthy. Marlowe performed in a wide range of plays either as a female wearing male attire (in *Twelfth Night,* for example) or playing a male role outright. Besides *Twelfth Night,* which she performed often, a sample would include *Chatterton* (see figure 17.1); *Robin Hood,* in which she played Alan o' Dale (see figure 17.2); and *L'Aiglon.*

While in Lincoln, Willa Cather reviewed this actress with some regularity; in dealing with Marlowe, Cather was consistently Spartan with praise and blunt with criticism. "Charming" is the word that flows contemptuously from her pen as she attacks another reviewer who is one of the actress's admirers. "[Quoting the other reviewer] 'She (Marlowe) is

17.1. Julia Marlowe in "Chatterton." The Harvard Theatre Collection, The Houghton Library, Fredric Woodbridge Wilson, Curator.

17.2. Julia Marlowe in "Robin Hood." The Harvard Theatre Collection, The Houghton Library, Fredric Woodbridge Wilson, Curator.

altogether piquant and charming'; the final word of doom to any great artist. One could not breathe that fatal word 'charming' anywhere near even
the *pictures* of Siddons, Modjeska, Rachel, or Bernhardt. In literature,
painting or acting charmingness means agreeable mediocrity" (*World and
the Parish* 1:49; emphasis added). Yet occasionally, Cather could allow the
reader to understand what other theatergoers might find to praise in Miss
Marlowe: "We are not often subjected to the influence of beauty pure and
simple, beauty of face, beauty of acting, beauty of form and movement."
But then, invariably, she let the meat-ax fall: "Miss Marlowe is the embodiment of beauty and good taste and good spirits, and she is very little
more. . . . I remember every attitude she struck in *Twelfth Night*, but I do
not remember any acting which gave anything of the undercurrent of passion in the play" (*World and the Parish* 1:36).

Julia Marlowe's decision to play male-dressing roles, despite the fact that
they were so inappropriate for her, suggests just how popular and widespread the cross-dressing trend had become. Marlowe's most consistently
successful role was as Juliet; and according to Cather, that is exactly where
she ought to have remained—in the role of the Shakespearean ingenue
(*World and the Parish* 1:36).[11] As Cather's acidulous commentary suggests,
Marlowe's many and compelling feminine charms, entirely conventional
charms that she was unwilling to relinquish even when wearing male camouflage, softened every cross-dressing role that she played. Worshippers at
the shrine of these charms, devotees of the kind of orthodox beauty that
Jennie Cather had embodied, remained staunch and loyal fans of Julia Marlowe. For these fans, male dress may have been little more than a legitimate
excuse to see a good deal more of Miss Marlowe than customary dress
would allow.

In the last analysis, Julia Marlowe's kind of masquerade was, perhaps,
merely prurient: it lacked wit, invention, subtlety, or vigor; even worse, it
disempowered the suggestive, ambiguous implications of the role-reversal.
Thus it is little wonder that Willa Cather deplored it, consistently prefer-
ring the harsh tensions that a great actress like Helen Modjeska could bring
to these roles.[12] The adolescent Willa Cather understood the fact that un-
conventional dress could act as force for social disruption. Ferris describes
its unique power as "one way of playing with liminality and its multiple
possibilities and extending that sense of the possible to the spectator/
reader; a way of play, that while often reinforcing the social mores and
status quo, carries with it the possibility for exposing that liminal moment,
that threshold of questioning, that slippery sense of a mutable self" (9).
Garber posits the more general hypothesis that introducing "the third"
always disrupts conventional binary systems—being neither "the one" nor
"the other": "The 'third' is a mode of articulation, a way of describing a
space of possibility" (11).

Thus throughout Willa Cather's season of play, the years beginning in 1888 and concluding in 1893, her masquerade/camouflage/costume neither reinforced the conventional notions of Victorian "femininity" that Jennie Cather had advocated (though it surely called attention to them) nor announced the daughter's desire to "become a boy" (though it surely announced her intention to engage in pursuits that hitherto had been reserved for males). In fact, one must not overlook the fact that although Cather affected a "shingled" haircut and mannish shirts and coats during this period, there is no evidence whatsoever that she was "trousered." Her charade was limited and relatively mild by the standards set elsewhere: it proclaimed her desire, as a woman, to search for something . . . "other" . . . something as yet undefined. Audacious and ambiguous: it was a clarion call—the prologue to change and a demand for some space of possibility.[13]

In one respect, the "status" of Bernhardt, Adams, Marlowe, Modjeska, and others like them was unambiguous: they were female actresses playing female characters who were disguised as males; or alternatively, female actresses who had elected to play male roles—often already well established male roles—and who played them "straight." The principal aim of these actresses was always to play the role. Disrupting the binary certainties of their audiences was a part of that role; however, the audiences watching them were allowed to understand the underlying facts of "gender" quite clearly. However, by 1888, another kind of cross-dressed female figure had begun to appear on stage, one whose agenda was rather different. These were the "Male Impersonators" like Hetty King, Bessie Bonehill, and the "Incomparable Vesta Tilley" (see figure 17.3). For these players, confusion was a principal aim, the humorous and seductive conflation of definitions and desires. And *this* form of cross-dressing charade was essentially different from the other in one crucial respect: sexual innuendo was everywhere apparent; in fact, sexual innuendo—titillation—was the point of the game.

Although they reigned for a relatively short period, from the early 1880s until the end of World War I, the male impersonators were immensely popular. Characteristically, while on stage they "assumed the values of the 'dominant' sex and undermined them, with satirical lyrics and a parody of male mannerisms" (Aston 247). Their masculine dress was impeccably realistic (often they presented themselves as dandies or in uniform as sailors or soldiers); frequently they sported a moustache and carried a cigarette or cigar; and during their performances, they sustained the seamless fiction of a masculine identity without ever, ever breaking "tone." Yet offstage, their lives were often quite the opposite, and widely advertised as such: sedate, self-consciously "proper," and unmistakably "feminine." Vesta Tilley, for example, "kept to her 'true sex' and even chose female dress for some of her publicity posters or illustrated song sheets. . . . She did not carry over

17.3. Vesta Tilley portraying "The Dandy," sheet music cover. The Harvard Theatre Collection, The Houghton Library, Fredric Woodbridge Wilson, Curator.

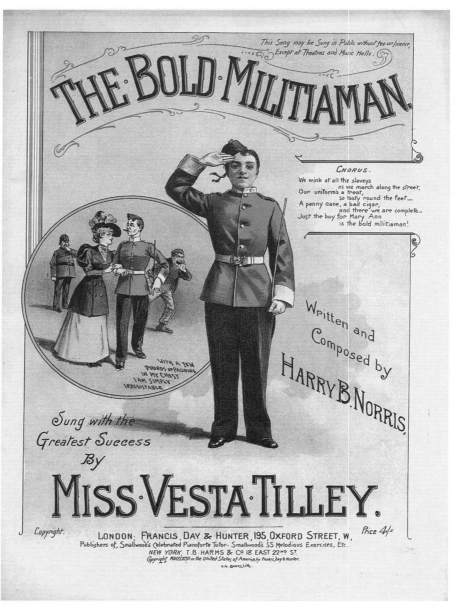

17.4. Vesta Tilley as "The Bold Militiaman," sheet music cover. The Harvard Theatre Collection, The Houghton Library, Fredric Woodbridge Wilson, Curator.

into her private life her performance of the 'high life' johnnies she imper-
sonated on stage" (see figure 17.4).[14]

Unlike Bernhardt, Marlowe, and Modjeska, these actresses made the disruption of binary gender categories their principal aims; and they did so by
conflating genders while on stage. Ambiguity and provocation in the widest
sense were the purpose of the presentation. Moreover, reviewers and play-
goers alike understood the nature of the performance they were watching.
Complexity and tantalizing uncertainty were the source of enjoyment, and
the audiences watching these "male impersonators" were encouraged to
feel equivocation with each lyric and every dance. "Miss Bonehill is slight
and a little tall [a reviewer wrote in 1890]. Her voice is clear, her face fresh,
and her short cut hair parted on the left side. She looks like a handsome
boy, and dances like a sprightly girl."[15] The songs these "man/women"
sang were often "love" songs, but humorous "love" songs—"love" songs
with a sting. Consider, for example, a Vesta Tilley favorite: "The Giddy
Little Isle of Man."

> Oh! the Isle of Man, where the Manx cats grow.
> Oh, the Isle of Man, where the good folks go.
> You can spend your holidays on a strictly moral plan.
> For everyone is single in the giddy little Isle of Man.

Yes, the "good" folks go to the Isle of Man; yes, they live on a "strictly
moral plan." And yes, Manx cats have no tails—and yes, the "Man" singing
has no "Male" equipment! Cather went to hear Vesta Tilley "with joyful
anticipations" in 1897. Yet her review of the performance makes it clear
that the singer had fallen short of expectations. Tilley's sin? She had not
been naughty enough![16]

It is little wonder that audiences loved these performers; for every conceivable interactive possibility was genially considered.

> So long as the boundaries are clear, aberrations of the "true sex" are
> licensed. In Tilley's case, the conventions and framework of the
> music-hall act permitted collective spectatorship of an image of sexual
> ambiguity. Essential to the pleasure of the experience was the distance
> in the proxemic relationship between solo artist and audience. . . . The
> sexual ambiguity of Tilley's act was such that spectators of both sexes
> could foreground her male or female "self," according to gender-
> based desires and expectations. (Aston 255–56)

Yet if these players derived their theatrical energies from the intense
and sustained ambiguity of their performances, the underlying message
(whether or not it was always intended by a particular player) was the call
for a radical revision of political realities. As Aston and others have
observed pointedly: this turn-of-the-century revolutionary masquerade

coincided precisely with the years of the Feminist Revolution. Every woman then knew—as every woman *still* knows—that the male costume always signifies "Power": thus the primary significance of "Woman-in-Male-Attire" is always "Woman with Power."

The most explicit implication of this broad context for Cather's rebellious interval of cross-dressing is that her experiment signified neither some "desire to be a boy" nor an affirmation of the binary code by which society had defined sexuality. Instead, it signified the demand for a "space of possibility," a vague and indefinable demand for the time to explore talents, roles, and the potential for power without being prematurely locked into the prison of late-nineteenth-century "femininity." Perhaps the only specific label that we can give her intention is to say that Willa Cather wanted "something" that in her culture was generally available only to men.

As an adolescent schoolgirl, Willa Cather was far from alone in this inchoate aspiration (although in the immediate vicinity of her home she found few understanding souls); she was even far from alone in the means she devised to protest her situation. One of the most familiar "types" that began to appear in the early 1880s was the "New Woman."

> The New Woman was athletic, wore masculine-style clothing, and showed little interest in appearing feminine and frilly. As early as 1881, one New York periodical lamented that "our young ladies . . . [have] taken to dressing so much like our young men that the sexes above the waist present an identical appearance." . . . She preferred the more interesting outlets of settlement house work or the new field of social work to the dullness of domestic duties. College-educated and ambitious, the New Woman frequently remained single in order to pursue her career ambitions in an era when few married women had careers. Presumably many New Women also failed to marry because they could not find males who would tolerate what seemed to them like over-masculinity in females. . . . [The New Woman] threatened the fixed norms of gender differences and intimated that femininity and masculinity might not be such opposite poles after all. (Inness 16)

The "New Woman" became a focus for intense controversy during the final two decades of the nineteenth century; and the popular press engaged in passionate discussions of the "New Woman's" mode of dress. *Punch* regularly featured cartoons of women wearing "bloomers," which were rendered as any one of a number of fantastically conceived sets of trousers. American periodicals elaborated the argument to cover such problematic issues as "women and education," or "women and work," and of course "men's distaste for the 'New Woman.'" Most of these chiding journals chose not to address the real issue: "that many feminists, while adopting male manners and clothes as an *outward* expression of philosophy, really sought for the less tangible rewards of independence and equal treatment" (Marks 178).

The most flagrant transgressors were college girls. During the 1880s and 1890s, eastern college women within the protected community of an all woman's school presented an increasingly "inappropriate" appearance. They began to cut their hair, dispense with corsets, discard skirts for trousers—even smoke![17] This behavior did not reach the heartland of Nebraska during Willa Cather's day; however, Cather's fellow rebels in the Seven Sisters would have understood the message of her garb immediately. Indeed, if only Willa Cather could have attended one of the great women's colleges, she would undoubtedly have had an easier time pursuing her atypical professional aspirations. As it was, she flailed.

She was, after all, barely fifteen when the masquerade began, and the broadly indeterminate nature of the her mission can be seen in the variety of costumes that she wore (although to some extent, "costume" must always have been a function of "available clothing," for her ensembles varied widely). A perhaps only tentative beginning: the male part in a family play—undertaken because she was big for her age or because no boys would join in the activity. Still, the germ of the idea may have begun here. Then the first real rebellion, Willa Cather in Uncle William's Confederate uniform: a powerful acknowledgement of her southern roots; a gesture inviting Mother's alliance; an expression of her potential for heroism; a recollection of those southern women whose wartime exploits had required them to wear a male uniform; not incidentally, an echo of many cross-dressed actresses; but perhaps most important, a male-encoded costume that established enough distance from her own gendered body so that she might have time and space to define "identity" more in terms of role than of rigidly confined social expectations.

Several of her early ensembles seem quite unexceptional, boyish, but neither bold nor tactless; however, others continued clearly to reference the stage (see figure 17.5). Willa Cather as Robin Hood, invoking a romantic world, but "romance" turned upside-down because a female had appropriated the active role (see figure 17.6). Most dramatic of all, Willa Cather and her friend Louise Pound stylishly turned out as "male impersonators"— Eton Boy (Pound) and Dandy (Cather)—readily recognizable as explicit replicas of Bessie Bonehill and/or Vesta Tilley, college girls setting out to titillate friends and family by confuting their comfortable binary categories: not merely a "third," but as many possibilities in life as intelligence and emotional vigor could discover (see figure 17.7).

If the merging of life and stage, male and female, had ceased when Cather shed the costumes of adolescent rebellion, we might read this period as no more than aberration—a curiously inventive way of getting

17.5. Willa Cather (as Chatterton?). By permission of the Nebraska State Historical Society.

17.6. Willa Cather as Allan-a-Dale in *Robin Hood*. By permission of the Nebraska State Historical Society.

attention and of protesting the limitations of "femininity." However, just as the story did not end when Willa Cather once again let her hair grow long, so her exploration of the liminal areas of power and gender continued. In their ambiguities and their renunciations of closure, Willa Cather's first imaginative acts for the public anticipated her art. Even more important, however, the playful innovations of her adolescent "passage" became strong, often silent forces within the great fictions to follow—intrinsic elements in her construction of the woman as hero.

It took Willa Cather a long time to grow into her talent—she was close

17.7. Louise Pound and Willa Cather as the Schoolboy and the Dandy. By permission of the Nebraska State Historical Society.

to forty when her first novel was published. The delay was not for want of diligence: she supported herself first as teacher and then as the distinguished editor of *McClure's Magazine*. Nor was it some symptom of writing block: she began to publish short stories in college and continued to produce a steady stream of them insofar as her other work permitted. No. Cather's long apprenticeship had much in common with her long adolescent rebellion: she was seeking the components for an authentic woman hero, someone whose life-narrative was not confined to the conventional marriage-plot.

As an unworldly fifteen-year-old girl, Willa Cather had reached into her southern past for a solution to what was then her merely personal problem. At length, as a mature artist confronting a series of much more general dilemmas, Cather would return—explicitly—both to that earliest moment of personation in her own life and to the southern heritage from which it had sprung. A heritage of strong, determined women. "His sister was a tall, strong girl, and she walked rapidly and resolutely, as if she knew exactly where she was going and what she was going to do next. She wore a man's long ulster not as if it were an affliction, but as if it were very comfortable and belonged to her; carried it like a young soldier" [from the opening paragraph of *O Pioneers!*]. This is our initial introduction to Alexandra Bergson of Nebraska; however, at this moment she bears an uncanny resemblance both to some courageous, post–Civil War southern girl and to the tentative, defiant fifteen-year-old Willa Cather.

Readers associate Willa Cather so strongly with Nebraska and the Great Plains that they often fail to notice how often she referenced her southern origins—lightly, but unmistakably—the legacy of a mother at least part of whose example Willa Cather could, gratefully, follow. For example, the artist in an early tale, "The Profile" (intended for inclusion in *The Troll Garden*), uses his skill to compensate for the pain of women, which he had understood at too early an age: "Dunlap had come from a country where women are hardly used. He had grown up on a farm in the remote mountains of West Virginia, and his mother had died of pneumonia contracted from taking her place at the washtub too soon after the birth of a child . . . and the suffering of the mountain women he had seen about him in his childhood had left him almost morbidly sensitive" (126). This memory recalls a post–Civil War South, full of misery and hard work; and Dunlap's inclination as an artist is to recoil from this anguish by rendering only that which is beautiful—a strategy that is doomed to failure. (Much later, Alexandra Bergson will demonstrate the more successful tactics of patience and fortitude).

Jim Burden, the narrator of *My Ántonia*, is another refugee from the latter-day South. He is inclined to recollect his family's forebears, the "old portraits [of distinguished men] I remembered in Virginia."[18] But if he remembers a safer, more illustrious time, he also remembers dangers— "wildcats and panthers in the Virginia mountains" (66). And when Jim hears the tale of Peter and Pavel (ferocious wolves pursuing the sleighs of a large wedding party and devouring the guests, even the bride and groom, one sleigh at a time)—it merges curiously with his memories of Virginia. "At night, before I went to sleep, I often found myself in a sledge drawn by three horses, dashing through a country that looked something like Nebraska and something like Virginia" (59).

The vivid connection in Jim's mind between the dangers of Virginia and the other dangers he encounters links him with the artist, Dunlap.

However, his rather lofty notions of ancestral portraits and the "Ladies" and "Gentlemen" of the South links him with another of Cather's great creations, Marian Forrester. Yet another displaced southerner, Marian Forrester in *A Lost Lady* is the embodiment of all that was appealing in that antique ideal of southern womanhood. One "could not imagine her in any dress or situation in which she would not be charming. . . . Where Mrs. Forrester was, dullness was impossible. . . . One could talk with her about the most trivial things, and go away with a high sense of elation."[19] But now, the woman who might have been merely a "lady" of a very special sort has become no more than a "lost" lady. Marian's brand of femininity requires a strong male attendant: it was not fashioned to survive alone; and the postlapsarian world that Marian inhabits is indifferent to the necessary accoutrements of her identity. The world for which she might be suited, perhaps some dreamlike "Old South," has vanished—if it ever existed at all.

A Lost Lady is one of the last major volleys in Willa Cather's long season of rebellion against the ideal of "femininity" that had threatened to engulf her as an adolescent. In the end, we can find a good deal of Virginia Cather in her daughter's work—the mother against whose dainty "refinements" Willa Cather rebelled so colorfully (but whose strength of character she both admired and emulated). And although it is true that Willa Cather elaborated her mutiny against society's mutilating norms for women by rebelling against her mother's example, it is also true that the independence Jennie Cather displayed—the strength of character and the ability to endure—are the very qualities that best define Cather's heroic characters.

Notes

1. The facts surrounding this infamous "haircut" suggest that something more than mere rebellion was at work. "When her brother Jim was born, her mother was too ill to comb Willa's long curly hair, and the girl went to the barber shop and had it cut short. . . . Margie Miner . . . appears in *My Ántonia* as 'Sally,' the wild one, and like tomboy 'Sally,' had short hair even before Willa had her own chopped off in 1888" (Bennett 178–79, 45).

One girl with a "crew cut" is, perhaps, rebellion; but two is a trend, or perhaps an epidemic. Indeed, the most logical explanation for both girls' short hair is an epidemic: most likely, an epidemic of lice, the bane of the frontier school. Moreover, mother's being "too tired to comb" her daughter's hair also makes much more sense if we postulate that Willa had contracted lice because the process of combing in this case is lengthy, tedious, and tiring even under the most benign circumstances. Finally, if one looks at Willa Cather's earliest "short-hair" pictures, the extreme shortness of the hair is very striking: Cather looks more like a new army recruit than some boy of her own age; and these military "crew cuts" are so short precisely because they are given to eliminate lice among inductees.

2. Bennett 29. Even after she moved to the prairie and even after more than seven pregnancies, Jennie Cather had maintained her splendid appearance.

3. There was one *intimate* area in which Jennie Cather demurred: having a beautiful, trim figure, she spurned corsets entirely. Like her oldest daughter, she responded to life vigorously and would not tolerate the limitation of "stays."

Willa followed Mother's example in this respect—not because her figure was beautiful and trim, but simply for the blissful emancipation that it gave. There are pictures indicating that occasionally (for "dress-up" occasions) Willa Cather did submit to corsets; but often she did not. As a result, she could move, could ride a bike to work, could go camping with her brothers even in midlife. In short, she had the freedom to do whatever she wanted!

4. See Mary Elizabeth Massey, *Bonnet Brigades* (New York: Knopf, 1966), 78 ff.; and Kay Larson's two essays: "Bonny Yank and Gun Reb," *Minerva* 8.1 (spring 1990): 33–48; and "Bonny Yank and Gun Reb Revisited," *Minerva* 10.2 (summer 1992): 35–61.

5. It is important to remember that every remaining picture of Willa Cather in the modified "cross-dressing" that she adopted is a *studio photograph*. Without these pictures, we would have little or no information about this phase of the author's life. Studio photographs of young people, being something of a formal record and a pricey one at that, are underwritten by *parents*, not by the adolescents, themselves. If Mr. and Mrs. Cather had thought of their daughter's behavior as shameful or markedly deviant, they would scarcely have preserved a visual record of it.

The situation changed only after Willa Cather arrived in Lincoln. And from this period, there are many fewer images—perhaps precisely because they were expensive to obtain.

6. Cather writing for *Omaha World-Herald*, 27 Oct. 1929. Reprinted by Bennett in *Nebraska History* (winter 1968).

7. Anyone familiar with the flood of theater criticism that Willa Cather wrote during her college years—and especially anyone who has remarked the extraordinarily knowledgeable and self-confident tone with which she wrote this criticism—will realize that she must have acquired a very comprehensive acquaintance with the stage even before she came to Lincoln. Willa Cather was always quite candid about her delight in and fascination with every actor, actress, and play that ever came to Red Cloud. Thus, given her avid interest, there were ample avenues of information.

8. It also explicitly asserted an intention to enter the profession of medicine, which had only recently been opened to women in America. Sarah Orne Jewett's novel, *A Country Doctor* (1884), had presented an appealing and heroic portrait of a young women, reared in rural circumstances, who resolves to become a doctor. Although the young woman undergoes a series of conflicts regarding the possibility of getting married, she finally concludes that for women, marriage is incompatible with a serious commitment to the medical profession. Like all of Jewett's work, the novel is beautifully written; moreover, the isolation and limitations of northern New England may have seemed very like those of "heartland" Nebraska to the young Willa Cather.

9. For an account of this triumph, see Arthus Gold and Robert Fizdale, *The Divine Sarah* (New York: Knopf, 1991), 71–73.

10. Bernhardt was an astonishingly talented artist; her work, paintings, but especially sculpture, appeared with regularity at the Paris *Salon;* Gold and Fizdale 129–136.

11. Julia Marlowe's "Juliet" is fondly recollected in "The Best Years."

12. Most likely Cather saw Modjeska in *As You Like It* in 1892.

13. Her various hobbies—dissecting frogs, for instance—served much the same purpose. She talked about them widely, not necessarily because she wanted to pursue this kind of activity professionally, but because this "shocking" behavior *signified* "that which had been forbidden to females." Hence bragging about it was perhaps even more important to her than engaging in the activities itself.

14. Since her husband was eventually knighted, she moved, in midlife, from the stage to a round of church fairs and charity teas (Aston 248).

15. Unsigned review in *The Era*, 18 Jan. 1890.

16. "At last Miss Vesta Tilley, London's Idol," appeared, "dressed as an Eton boy who is showing his aunt about the town. . . . Despite the fact that Miss Tilley wore masculine attire, I kept thinking I was at a church concert in Red Cloud, so proper and so stupid and so wholly without individuality was she. And yet her boys were all nice, bright, clever little chaps, who ought to stay on their own side of St. George's channel and take care of their illusions" (*World and the Parish* 395–96).

17. See Sherrie Inness. See also Patricia Campbell Warner, "The Gym Suit: Freedom at Last," *Dress in American Culture*, ed. Patricia A. Cunningham and Susan Voso Lab (Bowling Green: Bowling Green State University Popular Press, 1993); and Helen Lefkowitz Horowitz, *Alma Mater: Design and Experience in the Women's Colleges from Their Nineteenth-Century Beginnings to the 1930's* (Amherst: University of Massachusetts Press, 1993).

18. Willa Cather, *My Ántonia*, scholarly ed. (1918; Lincoln: U of Nebraska P, 1994), 23.

19. Willa Cather, *A Lost Lady* (New York: Grosset and Dunlap, 1925), 13, 70. To savor the full ambiguity of this "compliment," we must remember Cather's reviews of Julia Marlowe (written a quarter of a century earlier); "charming" was the rather empty attribute that "made up" for actual acting.

Works Cited

Albertini, Virgil. "Cather Syllabi: A Study." *Willa Cather Pioneer Memorial Newsletter and Review* 41 (summer–fall 1997): 50–51.

Ammons, Elizabeth. "Cather and the New Canon: 'The Old Beauty' and the Issue of Empire." *Cather Studies* 3 (1996): 256–66.

———. *Conflicting Stories: American Women Writers at the Turn into the Twentieth Century.* New York: Oxford UP, 1991.

Anderson, Jervis. *This Was Harlem: A Cultural Portrait, 1900–1950.* New York: Farrar, Straus & Giroux, 1981.

Aquinas, Thomas. "Of the Division of Grace" (question 111). *Summa Theologica.* Trans. Fathers of the English Dominicans. 5 vols. Westminster, Md.: Glencoe, 1981. 2: 1135–40.

Arnold, Marilyn. "Cather's Last Stand." *Research Studies* 43 (1975): 245–52.

———. "'Of Human Bondage': Cather's Subnarrative in *Sapphira and the Slave Girl.*" *Mississippi Quarterly* 40 (summer 1987): 323–38.

Aston, Elaine. "Male Impersonation in the Music Hall: The Case of Vesta Tilley." *New Theatre Quarterly* 4.15 (August 1988): 247–57.

Baker, Houston A., Jr. *Blues, Ideology, and Afro-American Literature: A Vernacular Theory.* Chicago: U of Chicago P, 1984.

Bakhtin, Mikhail. *The Dialogic Imagination: Four Essays.* Ed. Michael Holquist. Trans. Caryl Emerson and Michael Holquist. Austin: U of Texas P, 1981.

Baldwin, James. "A Talk to Teachers." *Multi-Cultural Literacy: Opening the American Mind.* Ed. Rick Simonson and Scott Walker. St. Paul, Minn.: Graywolf Press, 1988. 3–12.

Beardsley, John. *Gardens of Revelation: Environments by Visionary Artists.* New York: Abbeville P, 1995.

Bennett, Mildred R. *The World of Willa Cather.* 1951. Lincoln: U of Nebraska P, 1961.

Berlant, Lauren. "National Brands/National Body: *Imitation of Life.*" Ed. Hortense J. Spillers. New York: Routledge, 1991. 110–140.

Bersani, Leo. *Baudelaire and Freud.* Berkeley: U of California P, 1977.

Bhaba, Homi. "'Race,' Time and the Revision of Modernity." *Oxford Literary Review* 13 (1991): 193–219.

Birkerts, Sven. *The Gutenberg Elegies: The Fate of Reading in an Electronic Age.* New York: Fawcett Columbine, 1994.

Bloom, Edward A. and Lillian D. *Willa Cather's Gift of Sympathy.* Carbondale: Southern Illinois UP, 1962.

Bohlke, L. Brent, ed. *Willa Cather in Person.* Lincoln: U of Nebraska P, 1986.

Bollas, Christopher. *The Shadow of the Object: Psychoanalysis of the Unthought Known.* New York: Columbia UP, 1987.

Breeden, James O., ed. *Advice among Masters: The Ideal in Slave Management in the Old South.* Vol. 51. Westport, Conn.: Greenwood P, 1988.

Brown, E. K., and Leon Edel. *Willa Cather: A Critical Biography.* 1953. Lincoln: U of Nebraska P, 1987.

Brown, Sterling. *The Collected Poems of Sterling A. Brown.* Ed. Michael S. Harper. Evanston: Northwestern UP, 1980.

Buhle, Mari Jo. *Feminism and Its Discontents: A Century of Struggle with Psychoanalysis.* Cambridge: Harvard UP, 1998.

Bunyan, John. *The Pilgrim's Progress.* Ed. N. H. Keeble. Oxford: Oxford UP, 1984.

Burke, Kenneth. "Language as Action: Terministic Screens." *On Symbols and Society.* Ed. Joseph R. Gusfield. Chicago: U of Chicago P, 1989.

Butler, Judith. *Bodies That Matter: On the Discursive Limits of "Sex."* New York: Routledge, 1993.

———. "Variations on Sex and Gender: Beauvoir, Wittig, Foucault." *Feminism as Critique.* Eds. Seyla Benhabib and Drucilla Cornell. London and Minneapolis: Basil Blackwell, distr. by U of Minnesota P, 1987. 128–42.

Cabell, James Branch. "The Last Cry of Romance." *The Nation* 6 (May 1925): 521–22.

Cable, George Washington. *The Creoles of New Orleans.* Intro. Arlin Turner. New York: Garnett P, 1970.

———. "My Politics." *The Negro Question: A Selection of Writings on Civil Rights in the South.* Ed. Arlin Turner. New York: Doubleday, 1958.

Carlin, Deborah. *Cather, Canon, and the Politics of Reading.* Amherst: U of Massachusetts P, 1992.

Cash, Wilbur J. *The Mind of the South.* 1941. New York: Random House, 1969.

Cather, Willa. *Alexander's Bridge.* Boston: Houghton Mifflin, 1912.

———. *April Twilights.* 1903. Ed. Bernice Slote. Lincoln: U of Nebraska P, 1962.

———. *Collected Short Fiction, 1892–1912.* Ed. Virginia Faulkner. Lincoln: U of Nebraska P, 1970.

———. *Death Comes for the Archbishop.* 1927. New York: Vintage Books, 1990.

———. *The Kingdom of Art: Willa Cather's First Principles and Critical Statements, 1893–1896.* Ed. Bernice Slote. Lincoln: U of Nebraska P, 1966.

———. *A Lost Lady.* 1923. *The Later Novels of Willa Cather.* Ed. Sharon O'Brien. New York: Library of America, 1984.

———. *My Ántonia.* New York: Houghton Mifflin, 1918.

———. *My Mortal Enemy.* 1926. New York: Vintage Books, 1990.

———. "The Namesake." *Willa Cather: Stories, Poems, and Other Writings.* New York: Library of America, 1992.

———. *Not Under Forty.* 1936. Lincoln: U of Nebraska P, 1988.

———. "The Novel Démeublé." 1922. Rpt. in *Willa Cather on Writing.*

———. "Old Mrs. Harris." *Obscure Destinies.* 1932. New York: Vintage Books, 1974.

———. *One of Ours.* 1922. New York: Vintage Books, 1971.

———. *O Pioneers!* 1913. Scholarly edition. Lincoln: U of Nebraska P, 1992.

———. *The Professor's House.* 1925. New York: Vintage Books, 1990.

———. "The Profile." *Collected Short Fiction.* Ed. Virginia Faulkner. Lincoln: U of Nebraska P, 1965.

———. *Sapphira and the Slave Girl.* 1940. New York: Vintage Books, 1975.

———. *The Song of the Lark.* 1915. New York: Signet, 1991.

———. *Stories, Poems, and Other Writings.* New York: Library of America, 1992.

———. Unpublished Letter to Henry Seidel Canby. 4 Feb. 1941. Henry Seidel Canby Papers, Beinecke Library, Yale University.

———. Unpublished Letter to Langston Hughes. 15 Apr. 1941. Langston Hughes Papers, Beinecke Library, Yale University.

———. Willa Cather Collection, Pierpont Morgan Library, New York.

———. *Willa Cather on Writing: Critical Studies on Writing as an Art*. 1949. Ed. Stephen Tennant. Lincoln: U of Nebraska P, 1988.

———. *The World and the Parish: Willa Cather's Articles and Reviews, 1893–1902*. Ed. William M. Curtin. Lincoln: U of Nebraska P, 1970.

Chesnut, Mary. *The Private Mary Chesnut: The Unpublished Civil War Diaries*. Ed. C. Vann Woodward and Elisabeth Muhlenfeld. New York: Oxford UP, 1984.

Clayton, Bruce. *The Savage Ideal: Intolerance and Intellectual Leadership in the South, 1890–1972*. Baltimore: Johns Hopkins UP, 1972.

Clinton, Catherine. *The Plantation Mistress: Woman's World in the Old South*. New York: Pantheon Books, 1982.

———. "Southern Dishonor: Flesh, Blood, Race, and Bondage." *In Joy and Sorrow: Women, Family, and Marriage in the Victorian South*. Ed. Carol Bleser. New York: Oxford UP, 1991. 52–68.

Collins, Robert. *Essay on the Treatment and Management of Slaves*. Boston: Eastbrun's P, 1853.

Condit, C. Michele, and John L Lucaites. *Crafting Equality*. Chicago: U of Chicago P, 1993.

Congressional Quarterly's Guide to Congress. 3d ed. Washington D.C.: Congressional Quarterly, 1982.

Cowan, Louise. *The Fugitive Group: A Literary History*. Baton Rouge: Louisiana State UP, 1959.

Davidson, Donald. Nashville *Tennessean*. Reviews: 19 Sept. 1926 (*My Ántonia*); 14 Nov. 1926 (*My Mortal Enemy*); 25 Sept. 1927 (*Death Comes for the Archbishop*).

———. *The Spyglass: Views and Reviews, 1924–1930*. Ed. John Tyree Fain. Nashville: Vanderbilt UP, 1963.

Degler, Carl. "The Third American Revolution." *Conflict and Consensus*. Ed. Allen Davis and Harold Woodman. Lexington: D. C. Heath, 1992. 330–344.

DeKoven, Marianne. *Rich and Strange: Gender, History, Modernism*. Princeton: Princeton UP, 1991.

de Lauretis, Teresa. "Sexual Indifference and Lesbian Representation." *The Lesbian and Gay Studies Reader*. Ed. Henry Abelove, Michele Aina Barale, and David M. Halperin. New York: Routledge, 1993. 141–57.

Description of Property. Appliqué Album Quilt. Abram's Delight, Winchester, Va. 1993.

Douglas, Ellen. *Can't Quit You Baby*. New York: Penguin, 1988.

Dupree, Robert S. *Allen Tate and the Augustinian Imagination: A Study of the Poetry*. Baton Rouge: Louisiana State UP, 1983.

Egerton, John. *Speak Now against the Day: The Generation before the Civil Rights Movement in the South*. New York: Knopf, 1994.

Ely, Melvin Patrick. *The Adventures of Amos 'n' Andy: A Social History of an American Phenomenon*. New York: Free Press, 1991.

Emerson, Ralph Waldo. "The Transcendentalist." *The Portable Emerson*. Ed. Carl Bode, with Malcolm Cowley. New York: Penguin, 1982. 92–110.

Fabre, Genevieve. "African-American Commemorative Celebrations in the Nineteenth Century." *History and Memory in African-American Culture*. Ed. Genevieve Fabre and Robert O'Meally. New York: Oxford UP, 1994. 72–91.

Faulkner, William. *Absalom, Absalom!* 1936. New York: Random House, 1964.

———. "An Introduction to *The Sound and the Fury*." *Mississippi Quarterly* 26 (summer 1973): 410–15. Rpt. in *The Sound and the Fury*. Ed. David Minter. New York: Norton, 1987.

———. *The Mansion*. New York: Random House, 1957.

———. *The Sound and the Fury*. The corrected text. New York: Vintage Books, 1984.

Feder, Lillian. "Allen Tate's Use of Classical Literature." *Allen Tate and His Work: Critical Evaluations*. Ed. Radcliffe Squires. Minneapolis: U of Minnesota P, 1972. 172–92.

Fellman, Michael. "Sleeping with the Elephant: Reflections of an American-Canadian on Americanisation and Anti-Americanisation in Canada." *Saturday Night* 111.8 (October, 1996): 43–46.

Ferris, Lesley, ed. *Crossing the Stage*. London and New York: Routledge, 1993.

Fiedler, Leslie. *Waiting for the End*. 1966. New York: Stein and Day, 1972.

Foucault, Michel. *Discipline and Punish: The Birth of the Prison*. New York: Vintage Books, 1979.

Fox-Genovese, Elizabeth. *Within the Plantation Household: Black and White Women of the Old South*. Chapel Hill: U of North Carolina P, 1988.

Garber, Marjorie. *Vested Interests*. New York: Routledge, 1992.

Geismar, Maxwell. *The Last of the Provincials: 1915–1925*. Boston: Houghton Mifflin, 1947.

Giannone, Richard. "Willa Cather and the Unfinished Drama of Deliverance." *Prairie Schooner* 52 (1978): 25–46.

Glasgow, Ellen. *A Certain Measure*. New York: Harcourt, 1943.

———. *Barren Ground*. 1925. New York: Hill and Wang, 1957.

———. *Letters of Ellen Glasgow*. Ed. Blair Rouse. New York: Harcourt, 1958.

———. *Vein of Iron*. 1935. New York: Harbrace, 1963.

———. *Virginia*. 1913. Garden City: Doubleday, 1920.

Godbold, E. Stanly, Jr. *Ellen Glasgow and the Woman Within*. Baton Rouge: Louisiana State UP, 1972.

Gold, Arthur, and Robert Fizdale. *The Divine Sarah*. New York: Knopf, 1991.

Gray, Richard. *Writing the South: Ideas of an American Region*. Cambridge: Cambridge UP, 1986.

Greeley, Horace. *A History of the Struggle for Slavery Extension or Restriction in the United States from the Declaration of Independence to the Present Day*. New York: Dix, Edwards, and Company, 1856.

———. "Slavery at Home: Answer to an Invitation to Attend an Anti-Slavery Meeting." *Hints towards Reforms in Lectures, Addresses, and Other Writings*. New York: Harper, 1850.

Green, Constance McLaughlin. *The Secret City: A History of Race Relations in the Nation's Capital*. Princeton: Princeton UP, 1967.

Gross, Theodore L. *Thomas Nelson Page*. New York: Twayne, 1967.

Gwin, Minrose C. *Black and White Women of the Old South: The Peculiar Sisterhood in American Literature*. Knoxville: U of Tennessee P, 1985.

Hardon, John A. *Modern Catholic Dictionary*. Garden City, N.Y.: Doubleday, 1980.

Harrell, David. *From Mesa Verde to the Professor's House*. Albuquerque: U of New Mexico P, 1992.

Harris, Jonathan. *Federal Art and National Culture: The Politics of Identity in New Deal America*. Cambridge: Cambridge UP, 1995.

Harrison, Elizabeth Jane. *Female Pastoral: Women Writers Re-visioning the American South*. Knoxville: U of Tennessee P, 1991.

Haygood, Atticus G. *Our Brother in Black: His Freedom and His Future*. 1896. Miami: Mnemosyne Publishing Inc., 1969.

Hicks, Granville. *The Great Tradition: An Interpretation of American Literature since the Civil War*. Rev. ed. New York: Macmillan, 1935.

hooks, bell. *Yearning: Race, Gender, and Cultural Politics*. Boston: South End P, 1990.

Hubbell, Jay B. *The South in American Literature, 1670–1900*. Durham, N.C.: Duke UP, 1954.

Hunter, Jane. *The Gospel of Gentility: American Women Missionaries in Turn-of-the-Century China*. New Haven: Yale UP, 1984.

I'll Take My Stand: The South and the Agrarian Tradition, by Twelve Southerners. New York: Harper, 1930.

Inness, Sherrie. "Girls Will Be Boys and Boys Will Be Girls: Cross-Dressing in Popular Turn-of-the-Century College Fiction." *Journal of American Culture* 18.2 (summer 1995): 15–23.

Irving, Katrina. "Displacing Homosexuality: The Use of Ethnicity in Willa Cather's *My Ántonia*." *Modern Fiction Studies* 36.1 (1990): 91–102.

Jacobs, Harriet. *Incidents in the Life of a Slave Girl*. 1861. Ed. Henry Louis Gates Jr. New York: New American Library, 1987.

Jameson, Fredric. *Marxism and Form: Twentieth-Century Dialectical Theories of Literature*. Princeton: Princeton UP, 1971.

———. *The Political Unconscious: Narrative as a Socially Symbolic Act*. Ithaca: Cornell UP, 1981.

Jobes, Lavon Mattes. "Willa Cather's Last Novel." *University Review* 34 (1967): 77–80.

Kanneh, Katiatu. "Place, Time and the Black Body: Myth and Resistance." *Oxford Literary Review* 13 (1991): 140–63.

Kerns, Wilmer L. *Frederick County, Virginia: Settlement and Some First Families of Back Creek Valley, 1730–1830*. Baltimore, Md.: Gateway P, 1995.

Kluger, Richard, with Phyllis Kluger. *The Paper: The Life and Death of the* New York Herald Tribune. New York: Knopf, 1986.

Knopf, Alfred A. Blurb for *Sapphira and the Slave Girl*. New York: Knopf, 1940.

Larson, Kay. "Bonny Yank and Ginny Reb." *Minerva* 8.1 (spring 1990): 33–48.

———. "Bonny Yank and Ginny Reb Revisited." *Minerva* 10.2 (summer 1992): 35–61.

Levine, Lawrence. *The Unpredictable Past: Explorations in American Cultural History*. New York: Oxford UP, 1993.

Lewis, Edith. *Willa Cather Living: A Personal Record*. New York: Knopf, 1953; reprint, Lincoln: U of Nebraska P, 1976.

Lindemann, Marilee. *Willa Cather: Queering America*. New York: Columbia UP, 1999.

Lumpkin, Katharine Du Pre. *The Making of a Southerner*. 1947. Athens: U of Georgia P, 1981.

McCullers, Carson. *Member of the Wedding*. Boston: Houghton Mifflin, 1946.

McDonald, Joyce. *The Stuff of Our Forebears: Willa Cather's Southern Heritage*. Tuscaloosa: U of Alabama P, 1998.

McDowell, Frederick P.W. *Ellen Glasgow and the Ironic Art of Fiction*. Madison: U of Wisconsin P, 1960.

McElvaine, Robert. *The Great Depression*. New York: Times Books, 1984.

McLaughlin, Thomas. *Street Smarts and Critical Theory: Listening to the Vernacular*. Madison: U of Wisconsin P, 1996.

Madigan, Mark. "Willa Cather and Dorothy Canfield Fisher: Rift, Reconciliation, and *One of Ours*." *Cather Studies* 1 (1990): 115–29.

Marks, Patricia. *Bicycles, Bangs, and Bloomers: The New Woman in the Popular Press*. Lexington: UP of Kentucky, 1990.

Massey, Mary Elizabeth. *Bonnet Brigades*. New York: Knopf, 1966.

Mathews, F. Schuyler. *Field Book of American Wild Flowers* (1902), copy owned by Willa Cather. Harry Ransom Humanities Research Center, University of Texas.

May, Samuel. *The Fugitive Slave Law and Its Victims*. Revised and enlarged edition. Freeport, N.Y.: Books of Libraries P, 1970.

Mencken, H. L. "The Sahara of the Bozart." *Prejudices: Second Series*. New York: Knopf, 1920.

Michaels, Walter Benn. *Our America: Nativism, Modernism, and Pluralism*. Durham: Duke UP, 1995.

———. "The Vanishing American." *American Literary History* 2 (summer 1990): 220–41.

Middleton, Jo Ann. *Willa Cather's Modernism: A Study of Style and Technique*. Rutherford, N.J.: Fairleigh Dickinson UP, 1990.

Miller, Robert K. "Strains of Blood: Myra Driscoll and the Romance of the Celts." *Cather Studies* 2 (1993): 169–77.

Mobley, Marilyn Sanders. *Folk Roots and Mythic Wings in Sarah Orne Jewett and Toni Morrison: The Cultural Function of Narrative*. Baton Rouge: Louisiana State UP, 1991.

Moers, Ellen. *Literary Women*. Garden City, N.Y.: Doubleday, 1976. Moore, John L., ed. *Congressional Quarterly's Guide to U.S. Elections*. 3d ed. Washington, D.C.: Congressional Quarterly, 1994.

Morrison, Toni. *Beloved*. 1987. New York: NAL Penguin Plume, 1988.

———. *Jazz*. 1992. New York: Penguin, 1993.

———. *Playing in the Dark: Whiteness and the Literary Imagination*. Cambridge: Harvard UP, 1992.

Murphy, John J. "The Modernist Conversion of Willa Cather's Professor." *The*

Calvinist Roots of the Modern Era. Ed. Aliki Barnstone et al. Hanover, N.H.: UP of New England, 1997. 53–72.

———. "Willa Cather's Archbishop: A Western and Classical Perspective." *Western American Literature* 13 (summer 1978): 141–50.

Murray, Albert. *South to a Very Old Place.* New York: McGraw-Hill, 1971.

Newton, Esther. "The Mythic Mannish Lesbian: Radclyffe Hall and the New Woman." *Signs* 9.4 (1984): 557–75.

O'Brien, Sharon. "The Case against Willa Cather." *Reading in America.* Ed. Cathy Davidson. Baltimore: Johns Hopkins UP, 1989. 240–58.

———. *Willa Cather: The Emerging Voice.* New York: Oxford UP, 1987.

O'Connor, Flannery. *Collected Works.* Ed. Sally Fitzgerald. New York: Library of America, 1988.

———. *Mystery and Manners: Occasional Prose.* Ed. Sally and Robert Fitzgerald. New York: Farrar, 1969.

Oklahoma Heritage Quilts. Paducah, Ky.: American Quilters Society, 1990.

Olmstead, Frederick Law. *A Journey in the Seaboard Slave States in the Years 1853–1854 with Remarks on Their Economy.* 1856. New York: G. P. Putnam's Sons, 1904.

Painter, Nell Irvin. "Of *Lily,* Linda Brent, and Freud: A Non-Exceptionalist Approach to Race, Class, and Gender in the Slave South." *Georgia Historical Review* (spring 1992).

Parsons, Stanley B., William W. Beach, and Michael J. Dubin. *U.S. Congressional Districts and Data, 1843–1883.* Westport, Conn.: Greenwood P, 1986.

Parsons, Stanley B., William W. Beach, and Dan Hermann. *U.S. Congressional Districts and Data, 1788–1841.* Westport, Conn.: Greenwood P, 1978.

Peter Parley's Universal History on the Basis of Geography. New York: Ivison, Blakeman, Taylor, and Co., 1874.

Petrie, Paul R. "'Sulking Escapist' versus 'Radical Editor': Willa Cather, the Left Critics, and *Sapphira and the Slave Girl.*" *Southern Quarterly* 34.2 (1995): 27–37.

Prenshaw, Peggy, ed. *Conversations with Eudora Welty.* Jackson: UP of Mississippi, 1984.

Pulsipher, Jenny Hale. "Expatriation and Reconciliation: The Pilgrimage Tradition in *Sapphira and the Slave Girl.*" Willa Cather Issue, ed. John J. Murphy. *Literature and Belief* 8 (1988): 88–100.

Rahner, Karl. "Man as the Event of God's Free and Forgiving Self-Communication." *Foundations of Christian Faith.* Trans. William V. Dych. New York: Crossroad, 1989. 117–37.

Rand, Nicholas T. "New Perspectives in Metapsychology: Cryptic Mourning and Secret Love." Editor's note to *The Shell and the Kernel* by Nicolas Abraham and Maria Torok. Trans. Nicolas T. Rand. Chicago: U Chicago P, 1994.

Randall, John H., III. *The Landscape and the Looking Glass.* Boston: Houghton Mifflin, 1960.

Ransom, John Crowe. "Reconstructed but Unregenerate." *I'll Take My Stand . . . ,* by Twelve Southerners. 1930. Baton Rouge: Louisiana State UP, 1977.

———. *Selected Letters.* Ed. Thomas Daniel Young and George Core. Baton Rouge: Louisiana State UP, 1985.

Review (unsigned). *The Era*, 18 Jan. 1890. Fragment in Harvard Theatre Archives, Harvard University.

Reynolds, Guy. *Willa Cather in Context: Progress, Race, Empire*. London: Macmillan, 1996.

Roiphe, Katie. "Making the Incest Scene." *Harper's*. Nov. 1995. 65–71.

Romines, Ann. *The Home Plot: Women, Writing, and Domestic Ritual*. Amherst: U of Massachusetts P, 1992.

———. "*Sapphira and the Slave Girl:* The Daughter's Plot." *Willa Cather: Family, Community, and History*. Ed. John J. Murphy. Provo: Brigham Young University Humanities Center, 1990. 155–62.

Rosowski, Susan J. *The Place of Literature and the Cultural Phenomenon of Willa Cather*. Lincoln: U of Nebraska P, 1998.

———. *The Voyage Perilous: Willa Cather's Romanticism*. Lincoln: U of Nebraska P, 1986.

———. "Willa Cather's American Gothic: *Sapphira and the Slave Girl*." *Great Plains Quarterly* 4 (fall 1984): 220–30.

———. "Willa Cather's Subverted Endings and Gendered Time." *Cather Studies* 1 (1990): 68–88.

Ryder, Mary Ruth. *Willa Cather and Classical Myth: The Search for a New Parnassus*. Lewiston, N.Y.: Edwin Mellen P, 1990.

"Sapphira." ⟨http://www.ici.net/cust_pages/eddy/a01.txt⟩. April 1997.

Scura, Dorothy M., ed. *Glasgow: The Contemporary Reviews*. Cambridge: U of Cambridge P, 1992.

Sedgwick, Eve. "Across Gender, across Sexuality: Willa Cather and Others." *South Atlantic Quarterly* 88.1 (winter 1989): 53–72.

Sergeant, Elizabeth Shepley. *Willa Cather: A Memoir*. New York: J. B. Lippincott, 1953.

Simkins, Francis Butler, Spotswood Hunnicutt, and Sidman P. Poole. *Virginia: History, Government, Geography*. New York: Scribners, 1957.

Skaggs, Merrill Maguire. *After the World Broke in Two: The Later Novels of Willa Cather*. Charlottesville: UP of Virginia, 1990.

———. "Thefts and Conversation: Cather and Faulkner." *Cather Studies* 3 (1996): 115–36.

———. "Willa Cather's Experimental Southern Novel." *Mississippi Quarterly* 35.1 (1981–82): 3–14.

Slote, Bernice, ed. *The Kingdom of Art: Willa Cather's First Principles and Critical Statements, 1893–1896*. Lincoln: U of Nebraska P, 1966.

Smith, Lillian. "Buying a New World with Old Confederate Bills," "Addressed to Intelligent White Southerners." *South Today* 7.2 (autumn–winter 1942): 7–30, 34–42.

———. *Killers of the Dream*. New York: Norton, 1949.

———. *Now Is the Time*. New York: Dell, 1955.

Sollors, Werner. *Neither Black nor White yet Both*. New York: Oxford UP, 1997.

Spillers, Hortense. "Mama's Baby, Papa's Maybe: An American Grammar Book." *Within the Circle: An Anthology of African American Literary Criticism from the Harlem Renaissance to the Present*. Ed. Angelyn Mitchell. Durham, N.C.: Duke UP, 1994. 454–81.

Squires, Radcliffe. *Allen Tate*. New York: Pegasus, 1971.

———. "'The Permanent Obliquity of an In(ph)allibly Straight': In the Time of the Daughters and Fathers." *Changing Our Own Words*. Ed. Cheryl A. Wall. New Brunswick, N.J.: Rutgers UP, 1989. 127–49.

Stein, Gertrude. *Three Lives*. 1908. New York: Signet, 1985.

Stoddard, Henry Luther. *Horace Greeley: Printer, Editor, Crusader*. New York: G. P. Putnam's Sons, 1946.

Stouck, David. *Willa Cather's Imagination*. Lincoln: U of Nebraska P, 1975.

———. "Willa Cather's Last Four Books." *Novel: A Forum in Fiction* 21 (1973): 41–53.

Stout, Janis P. *Strategies of Reticence: Silence and Meaning in the Works of Jane Austen, Willa Cather, Katherine Anne Porter, and Joan Didion*. Charlottesville: UP of Virginia, 1990.

———. *Through the Window, Out the Door: Women's Narratives of Departure, from Austin and Cather to Tyler, Morrison, and Didion*. Birmingham: U of Alabama P, 1998.

Stowe, Harriet Beecher. *Uncle Tom's Cabin*. 1851–52. New York: Bantam, 1981.

Stowe, Steven M. *Intimacy and Power in the Old South: Ritual in the Lives of the Planters*. Baltimore: Johns Hopkins UP, 1987.

The Suppressed Book about Slavery. 1864. New York: Arno, 1968.

Susman, Warren. *Culture as History: The Transformation of American Culture in the Twentieth Century*. New York: Pantheon, 1984.

Sutherland, Donald. "Willa Cather: The Classic Voice." *Willa Cather: Modern Critical Views*. Ed. Harold Bloom. New York: Chelsea House, 1985. 123–43.

Swift, John N. "Narration and the Maternal 'Real' in *Sapphira and the Slave Girl*." *Legacy* 9.1 (1992): 23–24.

Tate, Allen. *Collected Poems, 1919–1976*. New York: Farrar, Straus & Giroux, 1977.

Tate, Allen, and John Peale Bishop, eds. *American Harvest: Twenty Years of Creative Writing in the United States*. New York: L. B. Fischer, 1942.

Taylor-Guthrie, Danielle, ed. *Conversations with Toni Morrison*. Jackson: UP of Mississippi, 1994.

Thiebaux, Marcelle. *Ellen Glasgow*. New York: Ungar, 1982.

Thomas, Brook. "Turner's 'Frontier Thesis' as a Narrative of Reconstruction." *Centuries's Ends, Narrative Means*. Stanford: Stanford UP, 1996. 117–37.

Torok, Maria. "The Illness of Mourning and the Fantasy of the Exquisite Corpse." *The Shell and the Kernel* by Nicolas Abraham and Maria Torok. Trans. Nicholas T. Rand. Chicago: U of Chicago P, 1994.

Trilling, Lionel. "Willa Cather." *Willa Cather and Her Critics*. Ed. James Schroeter. Ithaca: Cornell UP, 1967. 148–55.

Urgo, Joseph. *Willa Cather and the Myth of American Migration*. Urbana: U of Illinois P, 1995.

Van Doren, Carl. "Barren Ground." *New Republic*, 29 April 1925, 271.

Wasserman, Loretta. "Cather's Semitism." *Cather Studies* 2 (1993): 1–22.

Watson, Ritchie Devon, Jr. *The Cavalier in Virginia Fiction*. Baton Rouge: Louisiana UP, 1985.

Webster, Daniel. "The Constitution and the Union." *The Speeches and Orations of Daniel Webster*. Boston: Little, Brown, 1914. 600–25.

Welsch, Roger L., and Linda K. *Cather's Kitchens: Foodways in Literature and Life*. Lincoln: U of Nebraska P, 1987.

Welter, Barbara. "The Cult of True Womanhood." *American Quarterly* 18 (1966): 151–74.

Welty, Eudora. *Delta Wedding*. New York: Harcourt, Brace, Jovanovich, 1946.

———. *The Golden Apples*. New York: Harcourt, Brace, Jovanovich, 1947.

Whigham, Frank. "Sexual and Social Mobility in *The Duchess of Malfi*." *PMLA* 100 (1985): 167–86.

White, Deborah Grey. *Ar'n't I a Woman? Female Slaves in the Plantation South*. New York: Norton, 1985.

Williams, Harold A. *Baltimore Sun, 1837–1987*. Baltimore: Johns Hopkins UP, 1987.

Winters, Laura. *Willa Cather: Landscape and Exile*. Selinsgrove: Susquehanna UP, 1993.

Wittenberg, Judith. "The Critical Fortunes of Barren Ground." Paper presented at the annual meeting of the Modern Language Association. Chicago, 28 Dec. 1977.

Wolff, Cynthia Griffin. "Time and Memory in *Sapphira and the Slave Girl*: Sex, Abuse, History." *Cather Studies* 3 (1996): 212–37.

———. "The Artist's Palette: Early Cather." *Willa Cather Pioneer Memorial Newsletter* 40 (spring 1996): 1, 9–14.

Woodress, James. "A Dutiful Daughter and Her Parents." *Willa Cather: Family, Community, and History*. Ed. John J. Murphy. Provo: Brigham Young U Humanities Publications Center, 1990. 19–31.

———. *Willa Cather: A Literary Life*. Lincoln: U of Nebraska P, 1987.

———. "Willa Cather and History." *Arizona Quarterly* 34 (1978): 239, 253, 254.

Woolf, Virginia. *A Room of One's Own*. 1929. New York: Harcourt, Brace, Jovanovich, 1981.

Wright, Louis B. *The First Gentlemen of Virginia*. Charlottesville: UP of Virginia, 1940.

Wyatt-Brown, Bertram. *Southern Honor: Ethics and Behavior in the Old South*. New York: Oxford UP, 1982.

Yongue, Patricia Lee. "Willa Cather's Aristocrats." *Southern Humanities Review* 14 (1979): pt. 1, 43–56; pt. 2, 111–25.

Contributors

ROSEANNE VAILE CAMACHO taught for over a decade at Gordon School in East Providence, Rhode Island, devising an interdisciplinary humanities curriculum for middle-school students. She then returned to graduate studies in American Civilization at Brown University, completing her Ph.D. in 1991. Southern culture and women's writing are among her major scholarly interests. She currently teaches at the University of Louisville.

JUDITH FETTERLEY is Professor of English and Women's Studies at the University at Albany, State University of New York. She is the author of *The Resisting Reader: A Feminist Approach to American Fiction* (1978) and *Provisions: A Reader from 19th-Century American Women* (1985) as well as several articles on nineteenth- and twentieth-century American writers. She is a cofounder of the Rutgers University Press American Women Writers series, for which she edited a volume of the short fiction of Alice Cary, and she is coeditor of *American Women Regionalists, 1850–1910* (1992). She is currently working on a critical study of the writers included in this anthology, as well as a series of essays entitled "Reading the Unread: American Women Writers and the Politics of Recovery."

LISA MARCUS is Assistant Professor of English and Chair of the Women's Studies Program at Pacific Lutheran University, where she teaches courses in American ethnic literature and feminist studies. Her work on Pauline Hopkins has appeared in *Speaking the Other Self: American Women Writers* (Georgia, 1997), and she is a regular contributor to *The Women's Review of Books*. Her essay in this volume is part of a book project on American women's slavery narratives.

MARILYN MOBLEY MCKENZIE is Associate Professor of English and African American Studies at George Mason University in Fairfax, Virginia. She is the author of *Folk Roots and Mythic Wings in Sarah Orne Jewett and Toni Morrison: The Cultural Function of Narrative* and of numerous articles on black women writers, African American literature, and American culture. She is president of the Toni Morrison Society.

ROBERT K. MILLER is Professor of English at the University of St. Thomas in St. Paul, Minnesota. He edited *Great Short Works of Willa Cather* (1989) and has published articles in *Willa Cather: Family, Community, and History* (1990) and *Cather Studies* (1993). His current research focuses on Cather's consideration of virtue.

JOHN J. MURPHY, Professor of English at Brigham Young University, is the author of *My Ántonia: The Road Home* (1989) and of dozens of essays on Cather and other American writers, including the bibliographical essay "Fiction: 1900 to the 1930s" in *American Literary Scholarship* (1980–87). He is editor of *Critical Essays on Willa Cather* (1984), *Willa Cather: Family, Community, and History* (1990), and

Flannery O'Connor and the Christian Mystery (1997). He is volume editor of the University of Nebraska Press Scholarly Edition of *Death Comes for the Archbishop* (1999) and the Penguin *My Ántonia* (1994).

ELSA NETTELS retired from full-time teaching in 1997, after thirty years in the English Department at The College of William and Mary. Her publications include *James and Conrad* (Georgia, 1977; SAMLA Award for 1975), *Language, Race, and Social Class in Howells' America* (Kentucky, 1988), and *Language and Gender in American Fiction: Howells, James, Wharton, and Cather* (Macmillan, Virginia, 1997), as well as many articles in journals and essay collections. Her current project is a study of representations of readers in late-nineteenth- and early-twentieth-century American fiction.

SHELLEY NEWMAN completed her M.A. at Simon Fraser University; her thesis, "Purloined O: Reading Dominique Aury's (Pauline Réage) *Story of O* with Jacques Lacan," explored psychoanalytic notions of exceptionality in the woman-authored pornographic text. She is now a doctoral candidate at the University of British Columbia, studying psychoanalytic theory and American literature. Her dissertation will focus on women authors of the Great Depression.

TOMAS POLLARD is a Ph.D. candidate at Texas A&M University whose dissertation will focus on humorous treatments of World War II, including the Holocaust, in American literature and culture. His main fields of research are satire, war fiction, and twentieth-century American literature.

ANN ROMINES is Director of the Graduate Program in English and Professor of English at The George Washington University. She is author of *The Home Plot: Women, Writing and Domestic Ritual* (Massachusetts, 1992) and *Constructing the Little House: Gender, Culture, and Laura Ingalls Wilder* (Massachusetts, 1997; Children's Literature Association Award) and of many articles on American women's writing and cultures. She is volume editor of the University of Nebraska Press Scholarly Edition of *Sapphira and the Slave Girl* and was program director of the Seventh International Willa Cather Seminar, which generated this volume.

MARY R. RYDER is Professor of English and Director of Graduate Studies in English at South Dakota State University. Her book *Willa Cather and Classical Myth* (Mellen, 1990) earned the Mildred Bennett Award from Mellen Press for outstanding scholarship in Cather studies. She is the author of many essays on Cather and on other writers associated with American literary realism and naturalism.

MERRILL MAGUIRE SKAGGS, Professor of English at Drew University, is author of *The Folk of Southern Fiction* (Georgia, 1972), *After the World Broke in Two: The Later Novels of Willa Cather* (Virginia, 1990), and numerous articles and essays on Southern writers. She is coauthor of *The Mother Person* and editor of the forthcoming *Willa Cather's New York*.

JANIS P. STOUT is Professor of English at Texas A&M University, where she also serves as Dean of Faculties and Associate Provost. She is the author of three novels and five scholarly books, including *Strategies of Reticence: Silence and Meaning in the Works of Jane Austen, Willa Cather, Katherine Anne Porter, and Joan Didion* (Virginia, 1990), *Katherine Anne Porter: A Sense of the Times* (Virginia, 1995), and *Through the Window, Out the Door: Women's Narratives of Departure, from Austen and Cather to Tyler, Morrison, and Didion* (Alabama, 1998). Her newest book, *Willa Cather: The Writer and Her World*, is forthcoming from Virginia.

JOSEPH R. URGO is Professor and Chair of the Department of English at the University of Mississippi. He is the author of four books, *In the Age of Distraction* (Mississippi, 2000), *Willa Cather and the Myth of American Migration* (Illinois, 1995), *Novel Frames: Literature as Guide to Race, Sex, and History in American Culture* (Mississippi, 1991), and *Faulkner's Apocrypha: A Fable, Snopes, and the Spirit of Human Rebellion* (Mississippi, 1989), and of various essays on American literature and culture.

GAYLE WALD is Assistant Professor of English at The George Washington University. She is author of *Crossing the Line: Narratives of Racial Passing in Twentieth-Century Literature and Culture* (Duke, 2000) and of several essays on aspects of American and African American literature and culture.

CYNTHIA GRIFFIN WOLFF is Class of 1922 Professor of Literature and Writing at the Massachusetts Institute of Technology. She is the author of two biographies of American women writers, *A Feast of Words: The Triumph of Edith Wharton* (Oxford, 1978) and *Emily Dickinson* (Knopf, 1986), as well as numerous essays and chapters about American women writers. Now she is at work on a biography of Willa Cather.

PATRICIA YAEGER is Professor of English at the University of Michigan, Ann Arbor. She is the author of *Honey-Mad Women: Emancipatory Strategies in Women's Writing* (Columbia, 1986), *Dirt and Desire: Southern Women Writers, 1930–1990* (Chicago, 2000), and numerous essays. She is coeditor of *Nationalisms and Sexualities* (Routledge, 1992) and *Refiguring the Father: New Feminist Readings of Patriarchy* (Southern Illinois, 1989), and she is editor of *The Geography of Identity* (Michigan, 1996).

MAKO YOSHIKAWA is a Ph.D. candidate in English at the University of Michigan, Ann Arbor. She is the author of a novel, *One Hundred and One Ways* (Bantam, 1999), and is Adjunct Assistant Professor of Creative Writing at Columbia University. She is currently the Schuyler Fellow of Creative Writing at the Bunting Institute of Harvard University and is at work on a second novel and on a project that investigates the taboos of incest in twentieth-century American literature.

Index